A Miracle, A Universe

Lawrence Weschler has been a staff writer at the *New Yorker* magazine since 1981, his work ranging widely among political and cultural themes. A two-time winner of the George Polk Award (and variously, as well, of the Mary Hemingway Prize of the Overseas Press Club, the Sidney Hillman Foundation Award, the James Aronson Award for public conscience journalism, and a Guggenheim Fellowship), he has lately been covering the aftermath of the wars in Yugoslavia, with specific reference to the War Crimes Tribunal in The Hague. His other political books have included *The Passion of Poland* (1984) and *Calamities of Exile: Three Nonfiction Novellas* (yoking together stories set in Iraq, South Africa, and Czechoslovakia and published in 1998 by the University of Chicago Press). His "Passions and Wonders" series includes *Seeing Is Forgetting the Name of the Thing One Sees: A Life of Contemporary Artist Robert Irwin* (1982); *David Hockney's Cameraworks* (1984); *Shapinsky's Karma, Boggs's Bills, and Other True-Life Tales* (1988); and *Mr. Wilson's Cabinet of Wonder* (1995—a finalist for both the Pulitzer Prize and the National Book Critics Circle Award). A graduate of Cowell College of the University of California in Santa Cruz, he has taught there, as well as at Princeton University and at Sarah Lawrence, Vassar, and Bard Colleges; he is a longtime fellow of the New York Institute for the Humanities. He lives with his wife and daughter in Westchester County, New York.

Lawrence Weschler

A Miracle, A Universe

Settling Accounts with Torturers

The University of Chicago Press
Chicago and London

The University of Chicago Press, Chicago 60637
The University of Chicago Press, Ltd., London

University of Chicago Press Edition 1998

Portions of this work originally appeared, in different form, in the *New Yorker*.
Permissions acknowledgments may be found on page 303.

Printed in the United States of America
03 02 01 00 99 98 6 5 4 3 2 1

Library of Congress Cataloging-in-Publication Data

Weschler, Lawrence.
A miracle, a universe : settling accounts with torturers / Lawrence Weschler.
p. cm.
Originally published: New York : Pantheon Books, c1990.
Includes bibliographical references and index.
ISBN 0-226-89394-4 (pbk. : alk. paper)
1. Political persecution—Brazil. 2. Political persecution—Uruguay. 3. Human rights—Brazil. 4. Human rights—Uruguay. 5. Torture—Brazil. 6. Torture—Uruguay. 7. Civil-military relations—Brazil. 8. Civil-military relations—Uruguay. 9. Brazil—Politics and government. 10. Uruguay—Politics and government. I. Title.
[JC599.B7W47 1998]
323.4′9′098109048—dc21 97-52199
CIP

∞ The paper used in this publication meets the minimum requirements of the American National Standard for Information Sciences—Permanence of Paper for Printed Library Materials, ANSI Z39.48-1992.

Contents

In Memoriam

F.T.W.

(1928–1988)

A Living Wonder

Acknowledgments

In the first instance, once again, it was William Shawn, the editor of the *New Yorker,* who encouraged me to pursue this difficult and frightening topic, who allowed me to imagine I might not get permanently lost within it, and who in any case assured me that I'd have the space and time to struggle my way clear. As it happened, both the Brazil and Uruguay pieces actually appeared in the magazine after Mr. Shawn had left its helm. But the new editor, Robert Gottlieb, proved equally supportive and encouraging as I continued the work, and he helped see it through to completion. So that my first thanks go to both of them. Continuity was provided here—as in almost all the long pieces I've published in the magazine—by my own editor, John Bennet, whose even temper, uncommon ear, and uncanny common sense as usual rendered the processing of these pieces almost more of an education for me than their original researching. Peter Canby handled the exasperatingly tricky task of fact-checking the Brazil piece without ever seeming to show the slightest exasperation; Hal Espen performed similar service, with equally impressive poise and dexterity, on the Uruguay essays. Eleanor Gould, Elizabeth Macklin, Elizabeth Pearson-Griffiths, and Marcia van Meter all helped polish the prose during the final run-up to publication in the magazine.

But it was Tom Engelhardt, my editor at Pantheon, who helped shape these essays into a book—who helped me see the wider contours and then shape what we'd together seen. He's a uniquely gifted and centered reader, and it's a joy to be being read by him again.

There are several people I wish I could acknowledge from my stay in Brazil—a few of them I do mention by name in the body of the piece; the rest, however, didn't want me to mention their names at the time (for reasons which will become painfully clear), and I'm sure they wouldn't want me mentioning their names here either. I can, however, happily acknowledge the help of my steadfast interpreter in São Paulo, Anita Wright.

In Uruguay, on my first trip, my wife Joanna (seven months pregnant with our first child!) served as my splendid and indefatigable interpreter; on my second sortie, Patricia Pittman came over from Buenos Aires to fill in. In both cases, mere translation proved only the beginning of their contributions: much of the most valuable help came during the brief conversations we managed to squeeze in between interviews—evaluating what we'd just heard, anticipating what would come next, frantically revising our schedule, honing the questions, honing them further. The impress of their thinking and sensibilities is everywhere in these pages.

Many of the people who helped me most in coming to terms with the universe of issues involved in this complex and deeply troubling topic I quote at length in the pages that follow. However, I do want to express my particular appreciation here for the contributions of Dr. Inge Kemp Genefke and her colleagues at the RCT in Denmark; Jaime and Alma Wright and Cardinal Arns in São Paulo; Marcelo and Maren Vignar, Eduardo Galeano, Juan Rial and Carina Perelli, Luis González, Luis Pérez Aguirre, and Jo-Marie Burt in Montevideo; and Jorge Reiner, Carlos Varela, Louise Popkin, Martin Weinstein, Elio Gaspari, Pepe Zalaquett, Elaine Scarry, A. J. Langguth, and Aryeh Neier.

The John Simon Guggenheim Foundation extended me a fellowship at the outset of this work—when it wasn't yet clear what sort of work this would be—and that support proved catalytic.

My wife Joanna of course was invaluable in countless ways besides the merely linguistic. She is my sole support and my wise true friend. Finally, I need to mention our new daughter Sara, whose giggles and gurgles and bawlings and squirmings and snugglings and pleadings and wonderings and gaze—whose burgeoning humanity (a miracle, a universe)—haunted me through every hour of my work on these pages.

A MIRACLE, A UNIVERSE

Foreword

In the fall of 1988, a group of academics and lawyers and clerics and activists from countries as varied as Uganda, Argentina, South Korea, Chile, South Africa, Brazil, the Philippines, Guatemala, and Haiti gathered at the Aspen Institute's Wye Woods Conference Center, in Maryland, to try to puzzle through one of the most complicated issues facing polities all over the world as they try to move from dictatorial to democratic systems of governance—the question of what to do with former torturers still in their midst. In many cases, the receding security and military apparatuses, which were responsible for the preponderance of human-rights abuses during the previous regime, retain tremendous power—and they will not abide any settling of accounts. They demand blanket amnesties covering all violations committed during their tenure, amnesties designed to enforce a total amnesia regarding those crimes. The fledgling democracies thus face a harrowing challenge to a bulwark of their authority—the very principle of equality before the law—just as they are attempting to consolidate their rule.

Over and over again, the same sorts of issues get played out,[1] and over and over again, as the participants at the Aspen Institute conference began to realize, the same two imperatives seem to rise to the fore —the intertwined demands for justice and for truth. The security forces, of course, will abide neither, but if anything the desire for truth is often more urgently felt by the victims of torture than the desire for justice. People don't necessarily insist that the former torturers go to jail—there's been enough of jail—but they do want to see the truth established. Fragile, tentative democracies time and again hurl themselves toward an abyss, struggling over this issue of truth. It's a mysteriously powerful, almost magical notion, because often everyone already knows the truth—everyone knows who the torturers were and what they did, the torturers know that everyone knows, and everyone knows that they know. Why, then, this need to risk everything to render that knowledge explicit?

The participants at the Aspen Institute conference worried this question around the table several times—the distinctions here seemed particularly slippery and elusive—until Thomas Nagel, a professor of philosophy and law at New York University, almost stumbled upon an answer. "It's the difference," Nagel said haltingly, "between knowledge and *ac*knowledgment. It's what happens and can only happen to knowledge when it becomes officially sanctioned, when it is made part of the public cognitive scene." Yes, several of the panelists agreed. And that transformation, offered another participant, is sacramental.

I

A Miracle, A Universe

I might as well have been blindfolded—a possibility my driver had only half-jokingly considered—for all I was then able to gather or would later be able to recall about where we were going that day. São Paulo is Brazil's largest city and, indeed, with a population of almost thirteen million, one of the largest cities in the world. Before visiting, I'd envisioned a low, far-slung concatenation of villas and shanties. Blindfolded, I might have been able to continue imagining it that way. Eyes open, I found it indeed far-slung—wide and broad and as seemingly endless as Los Angeles—only it's almost all skyscrapers. Twenty- and thirty-story buildings ranged one beside the next, mile after mile, neighborhood after neighborhood—the very apotheosis of the Brazilian Miracle, that remarkable period in the late sixties and the early seventies when the country was relentlessly racking up annual GNP-growth rates of 10 percent and more. The urban centers amassed huge concentrations of wealth during that period and attracted vast influxes of migrants from the countryside, some of whom found low-paying jobs in the burgeoning industrial complexes that were powering the growth surge—but most of whom were relegated to meager existences in the dismal scrap-wood, tin-roofed favelas that came to ring the cities. Ring them and web them, for the favelas also sprang up along the side beds of the highways that coursed, like badly sclerotic arteries, into and out of the central cities.

For a while, as we drove that day, we were racing past some of those narrow bands of slums, but soon we turned off the highway and onto a series of side streets that wove in and out among the skyscrapers. My driver seemed to add a few extra curlicues to his route just to further confuse me. Presently, we turned in to a driveway and entered the courtyard of a fairly anonymous ecclesiastical institution of some sort. At one side of the building, we came to a stop, and the driver beckoned me out of the car. We entered the building through a back entrance, proceeded down a succession of blank, institutional-style corridors, and finally came up to an unmarked and unremarkable door. My guide reached into his pocket, pulled out a key, paused, gazed up and down the corridor to make sure he couldn't see any inopportune passersby, paused a few more moments to make sure he couldn't hear any, and then slid his key into the lock and opened the door. Once we were inside, he turned on the lights and said, "This, I believe, is what you came down here to see."

The room, medium length and fairly narrow, was entirely filled by parallel rows of gray metal bookshelves, upon which were ranged, from floor to ceiling, hundreds of light-brown cardboard filing containers, each container labelled simply with a handwritten number. The containers seemed to go on endlessly—thousands of them, as many of them as there were skyscrapers in the city outside. And, indeed, as I came to understand in the ensuing days, their contents documented another facet of the Brazilian Miracle.

I'd first met my guide in the fall of 1986, at a sparsely attended press luncheon in New York City signalling the publication of a book he'd been involved in putting together. He was a large, barrel-chested man in his late fifties with an expansive nature, an open, jowly face, a partly bald pate, long gray sideburns, and glasses. Several of the friends and colleagues who'd dropped by the luncheon to visit kept calling him Jim Wright, but most of the time, I learned, he goes by the name Jaime, and since most of the time he's in Brazil, the "j" is pronounced in the Portuguese fashion, as in "jam." Wright was born with dual American-Brazilian citizenship but gave up the American half in 1958 and considers himself wholly Brazilian. He and his wife have five children and five grandchildren, and all of them are Brazilian. His English is fluently American but is laced with some exotic inflections, no doubt as a result of his upbringing. He was raised in Brazil by American missionary parents from Arkansas, who took him back home on their furloughs. He attended college in Arkansas and went on to the Princeton Theological Seminary before returning to Brazil, where he has served three separate stints as executive for the Brazilian mission of the Presbyterian Church/USA.

The book he'd come to New York to help launch, *Torture in Brazil,* was an English translation of *Brasil: Nunca Mais* (Brazil: Never Again), originally published in Petrópolis in the summer of 1985. The jacket copy of the American edition describes the book as "a shocking report on the pervasive use of torture by Brazilian military governments, 1964–1979, secretly prepared by the Archdiocese of São Paulo." I hadn't had much time to look through it before the luncheon, but what I'd found was indeed shocking, not only because of its content—detailed accounts of torture used systematically by the Brazilian military against political opponents—but, even more, because of the sources of that content. I'd read other accounts of torture, in reports by Amnesty International, Helsinki Watch, and Americas Watch, for example, and, more recently, in the remarkable Argentine volume *Nunca Más.* But these reports almost always consisted of testimony by victims or witnesses which had been collected, as it were, after the fact—after the victims or witnesses had escaped or been released and were hiding or living in exile, or else after the regime concerned had fallen. In this regard, the Argentine volume is an exemplary model, largely consisting of the scrupulously ordered and painstakingly corroborated testimony of hundreds of victims and witnesses—testimony that began to be compiled within days after the fall of the Argentine junta by an official National Commission on the Disappeared. In fact, the establishment of the commission was one of new civilian President Raúl Alfonsín's first acts upon taking office, on December 10, 1983.

But *Brasil: Nunca Mais* was different, for it was based on the official records of the regime itself—verbatim transcripts of military trials which were never intended to be read by the public at large. Documents of this sort are never supposed to survive the fall of a totalitarian regime: in the rare cases where they exist at all, they're destroyed when the regime collapses. Marshall Meyer, who served as a rabbi in Buenos Aires for twenty-five years and was one of the members of Alfonsín's National Commission (though he's now moved back to New York City, where he heads the B'nai Jeshurun congregation, on the upper West Side), once told me how he and his colleagues rushed over to the headquarters of the SIDE, the Argentine military's secret security police, within days of the country's changeover to civilian rule, only to find the place gutted: they could still smell the ashes of the archives. The Argentine regime had had to abandon power in haste, in utter humiliation, following its ignominious defeat in the Falkland Islands war. The Brazilian military, on the other hand, had taken its time in taking its leave. The inauguration of the new civilian President, José Sarney, in the spring of 1985, had been preceded by a carefully calibrated, delicately cadenced transition—the so-called *distensão,* or relaxation, and then the *abertura,* or opening—which had been over a decade in the making. The Brazilian military authorities had certainly had time to clean up loose ends, to efface any embarrassing or incriminating pieces of evidence. And yet here that evidence was—*in their own words,* wrenched *from their own files.* These accounts of torture were thus doubly astonishing: first, in the indisputable authoritativeness—the undeniability—of the testimony; and secondly, in the very fact, the virtual scandal, that such testimony still existed at all.

Jaime Wright was listed as the translator of the American edition of *Brasil: Nunca Mais,* but it was clear from the introduction, by the Brazilianist Joan Dassin, that Wright had been heavily involved in the project from its inception. Indeed, although more than thirty people were involved at one stage or another in putting the book together, only two of them had allowed themselves to be identified at the time of its publication—Paulo Evaristo Cardinal Arns, who is the archbishop of São Paulo, and the Presbyterian minister Jaime Wright. At the press luncheon, Wright explained that the other people who had participated in compiling the volume not only had managed to keep the existence of the project absolutely secret for more than five years—the time it took to complete the work—but also had succeeded in keeping their own identities absolutely secret over the year and a half since the book's publication. Such secrecy had, of course, been essential to the project during the time when the military still held power in Brazil; however, it remained essential, they all agreed, because, though civilians were now nominally back in control of the Brazilian government for the first time since 1964, the military remained a powerful presence on the scene—only halfway out the door, as it were—and a continuous threat to come barging back in. Indeed, Wright informed us, the publication of *Brasil: Nunca Mais* had been followed a year later by that of a furious answering polemic, the work of a decidedly unrepentant lieutenant in Brazilian military intelligence, which was entitled *Brasil Sempre* (Brazil Always).

In subsequent meetings with Wright, I learned how this Presbyterian minister had become so intimately involved in a top-secret project of São Paulo's Catholic archdiocese. That relationship had its origins several years earlier. Jaime Wright's younger brother, Paulo Stuart Wright, had been a Christian student activist and had then become an assemblyman in the southern Brazilian state of Santa Catarina during the tumultuously reformist early sixties; he was, in fact, the first child of American missionary parents ever to attain such high political office in Brazil. He must have been effective at his work, for he was one of the first legislators to be stripped of their mandates in the weeks following the April 1, 1964, coup that brought the military to power. Paulo Wright fled the country, but the following year he smuggled himself back in and began to work in the underground, organizing peasant cooperatives and rural networks in, among other areas, Maranhão, José Sarney's home state. (President Sarney, for his part, was in those days a close civilian collaborator of the military overseers.)

"Paulo was teaching people how to stick together," Jaime Wright explained to me, "and to a military regime that's subversion." During that period, Jaime saw his brother from time to time ("I'd be in my office in São Paulo and the phone would ring and it would be Paulo saying to meet him at 2 P.M. in the Praça da República, and I'd know that that meant to meet at 3 P.M. in the Praça da Sé"); he never asked detailed questions about Paulo's organizing work, and Paulo didn't tell him much. ("That was partly for the security of his organization and partly for my sake, so I wouldn't have the burden of such knowledge.") This kept up for eight years, and then, one day in September, 1973, Jaime got another telephone call. *"Êle caiu,"* an anonymous voice said distinctly—"He is fallen"—and then the line went dead. Paulo had been "disappeared"—been abducted from the streets of São Paulo without leaving a trace. Jaime tried frantically to locate him in the military prisons, to no avail. He subsequently learned that his brother had been tortured and, within forty-eight hours, killed; indeed, he was eventually able to find proof of his brother's murder among the papers that the *Brasil: Nunca Mais* people ferreted out. But for years he knew nothing for certain and looked everywhere for the slightest scrap of information; to this day he has been unable to obtain either the body or any hint as to its burial site.

During his efforts to obtain information about his brother, Wright, to his chagrin, had found his colleagues in the various Protestant hierarchies of little help. Many of the Protestant churches in Brazil had "acculturated with a vengeance," as he puts it; the more solidly established Protestant denominations often attracted nouveau-riche beneficiaries of the Brazilian Miracle and hence were tacit supporters of the military regime. This was true to a large extent of the Brazilian Presbyterian Church. (Wright makes a clear distinction between the position and work of that church and those of the Presbyterian Church/USA in Brazil.) Some of the more evangelical groups, like their Pentecostal sponsors back in the United States, were, if anything, more shrilly anti-Communist than the regime itself. For that matter, the security apparatus of the regime was known to include an inordinately high proportion of Protestants. By contrast, Wright, in his quest for information about his brother, was able to enlist considerable support from Cardinal Arns, who had been displaying a progressively more forthright and assertive stand regarding the military regime's use of torture on its political opponents ever since his appointment to the leadership of the São Paulo archdiocese, the world's largest, in 1970. Wright speaks glowingly of Cardinal Arns. "To begin with, Cardinal Arns is a Franciscan, and the Franciscans, with their vows of poverty, seldom aspire to become bishops. He has a deep knowledge of the Scriptures, which he memorized as a boy. And he has a pastoral heart: he is moved by deep compassion in the face of violence and persecution. I tease him by telling him he's a Protestant in disguise—a true Protestant." (Wright has often commented on the way his fallen brother Paulo was to a certain extent replaced in his life by this second Paulo, the Cardinal.)

In the years after 1973, Jaime Wright and Cardinal Arns worked ever more closely together on the desperate human-rights issues facing their flocks. In October, 1975, when Wladimir Herzog, a popular and widely respected São Paulo television journalist, died under torture, his colleagues convened a special ecumenical service in his honor at the São Paulo Cathedral. Cardinal Arns agreed to preside, while a distinguished rabbi represented the Jews (Herzog was a Jew) and Jaime Wright represented the Protestants. ("Well," Wright says, " 'represented' isn't quite the right word: none of the other Protestant leaders would accept the invitation.") Over eight thousand people filled the cathedral for the Herzog service, with a crowd of thirty thousand more spilling out into the surrounding plaza, and the event is considered crucial in sparking the resurgence of an independent civil society in Brazil in the decade that followed. A few years later, Wright and Cardinal Arns collaborated on another decisive gesture. They and several fellow human-rights activists decided to gamble that on the occasion of President Jimmy Carter's state visit to Brasília the regime would be reluctant to engage in outright censorship; they chose that day—March 29, 1978—to place in *Folha de São Paulo,* one of the country's leading newspapers, a two-page spread detailing the military's record of tortures, disappearances, and other human-rights violations. The text included the first published mention of the facts surrounding the abduction and disappearance of Paulo Stuart Wright (along with a small photograph of him). "The sudden lifting of censorship like that, for one day—it literally took one's breath away to see it," Wright recalls. "Whatever may be said about Jimmy Carter's performance back in the United States, you have to appreciate the effectiveness of his foreign policy abroad. In Brazil, in particular, his Administration's sustained pressure was a major factor in the regime's ongoing liberalization."

In 1978, Wright also completed his third term as executive of the

Presbyterian Church/USA in Brazil and received permission to work even more closely with Cardinal Arns. "As far as I know," Wright told me, "I am the only Protestant minister who works inside the Catholic Church at the invitation of a cardinal." He has an office in the Curia building, right beside Cardinal Arns's, and the Cardinal has on occasion referred to him as "my auxiliary bishop for international affairs and human rights." Indeed, Wright is so deeply trusted by Arns that he participated in the drafting of the sermons that the Cardinal's office prepared for Pope John Paul II during his visit to São Paulo in 1980.

In March, 1979, the wary, gradual, fitful process of military liberalization, which had been under way for several years during the Presidency of General Ernesto Geisel, entered a new phase with the inauguration of Geisel's chosen successor, General João Baptista Figueiredo. (It was at this point that the *distensão* began turning into the *abertura.*) The institutionalized practice of torture against opponents of the military had been on the wane for some time, but military officials were concerned about an eventual investigation into and retribution for their earlier human-rights abuses. In fact, the prospects for any further liberalization were momentarily frozen, pending the resolution of these concerns. Against this backdrop, President Figueiredo, as one of his first initiatives, promulgated a plan for a so-called mutual amnesty. For several years, there had been a rising cry on the part of civil society, led by Cardinal Arns and his associates, among others, for a complete amnesty of those accused of political crimes—both exiles and prisoners. Figueiredo now acceded, in part, to these demands (there were several conspicuous loopholes in his initiative), but he coupled this gesture with another, offered in a sudden spirit of ostentatious magnanimity: a blanket amnesty for any state security agents who might otherwise someday become liable to charges arising from their human-rights violations. Indeed, his edict was drafted in such a way as to foreclose even the possibility of any future official investigations into the behavior of the security forces between 1964 and 1979. Bygones were to be bygones: the book was closed. The *abertura* could proceed.

For the regime's thousands of victims and their families and friends, however, closing the book wasn't going to be so easy. Furthermore, for

Jaime Wright, Cardinal Arns, and several of their colleagues, allowing the book to remain closed would prevent any future understanding of what had happened in Brazil between 1964 and 1979 and what its happening had meant—an understanding without which, they feared, the country would forever be liable to a harrowing reversion. It was during this period that Wright and a very small group of his colleagues hit upon a daring plan.

"To understand what we set out to do in 1979, you have to understand something about the unusual nature of the military dictatorship in Brazil," Wright told me. "The Brazilian generals, you see, were technocrats. They were intent on doing things by the book, on following the forms, even if the results were often cruel and perverse. For example, they were obsessed with keeping complete records as they went along. They never expected anyone to delve into those records—certainly not in any systematic fashion. They never imagined they'd be held accountable to anyone. But the forms, the technicalities, required complete and well-ordered records, so they kept them. Now, in the early stages of an internee's *processo*—that's the Portuguese word for a military court proceeding—the authorities often had recourse to torture. This was partly because they were eager to extract as much information as quickly as possible so they would be able to make further arrests before the prisoner's friends and comrades could learn of his arrest and cover their tracks. But it was also an almost traditional reflex, going back to the days of slavery and the Inquisition. A confession was extracted through torture, and its truthfulness was conclusively affirmed when the victim signed the written version of his statement. About a third of the *processos* eventually came to semi-public trial before one of twelve five-judge military tribunals operating throughout the country. (The other two-thirds never made it that far.) At that point, the prisoner or his lawyers sometimes denounced the supposed confession as having been obtained under duress. It's amazing, when you think about the risks involved—after all, these prisoners could expect to be given back over to their jailers following the trial—that anybody ever chose to make such a denunciation. But, from what we've been able to ascertain, about 25 percent of the prisoners did. Anyway, in such cases the judges would dutifully listen as the defendants described their tortures; the judges would then summarize these accounts and order the court reporters to enter the summaries into the record. Everything was done by the book. And then the tribunals would hand down their decisions. Once in a while—admittedly, very rarely—they'd actually find the defendant innocent. But it didn't really matter, because either way the losing side would appeal the case to the Supreme Military Court in Brasília, which would almost invariably find the defendant guilty after all. In the process, though—and this became very important for us—all the transcripts and files of all the cases were transferred from the various provincial tribunals to Brasília, where they were carefully catalogued and stockpiled in the archives of the Supreme Military Court.

"It therefore occurred to us, back in 1979, that the regime's own records would include detailed sworn testimony regarding the use of torture throughout the period of military rule—if we could only get at them."

The 1979 amnesty law ironically provided Wright and his colleagues with a pretext, because lawyers were now being permitted access to the archives, though only on a piecemeal basis, as they prepared amnesty petitions on behalf of their still imprisoned or exiled clients. Lawyers were allowed to take out individual files for twenty-four-hour periods, after which they had to return them. Wright and his colleagues quickly realized that under this pretext they might be able to photocopy a sampling—perhaps even a significant sampling—of the Supreme Military Court's own records, thereby laying the groundwork for an unimpeachable study on the subject of torture in Brazil.

"The idea actually first occurred to a few of the lawyers who had been courageously working on behalf of political prisoners all during the military dictatorship," Wright explained. "They broached the idea to me, and we had some initial discussions about it. I think the decisive moment came one afternoon in August, 1979, when a few of us went out to the airport to greet Paulo Freire, who was returning after a fifteen-year exile." Freire was a distinguished Brazilian educator who advocated teaching peasants and the urban poor to read and write as a means of "consciousness raising"—his phrase (in fact, he coined the phrase). He was especially influential during the fifties and early sixties in the state of Pernambuco, in the destitute northeastern section of the country, where he taught at the state university. After 1964, he'd first gone to Chile, from which he'd had to flee in 1973, at the time the Allende government was toppled. He went on to Geneva, and from his base there he helped to establish literacy programs in the former Portuguese colonies in Africa—Guinea-Bissau, Angola, and Mozambique.

"Many of the exiles were now beginning to return," Wright continued, "so there was a certain amount of joy, but we were also trying to figure out some way to make sure that these horrors would not themselves return someday, with people like Freire having to go right back into exile, or worse. So we sat there in the car mulling over the implications of the existence of that archive, and the chances of our having access to it. One of the passengers in the car was a member of the staff of the World Council of Churches, visiting Brazil from the WCC's headquarters in Geneva, and he became enthusiastic about the idea. We hatched the whole plan right there in the car, waiting for Freire. We realized, of course, that everything would have to be handled with the utmost secrecy. The next day, I went into the Cardinal's office and presented the plan to him. He immediately endorsed it, and volunteered his personal sponsorship. He agreed that it would be a good idea to approach Philip Potter, the general secretary of the World Council, for assistance in funding the project, and he signed a letter to Potter that we'd drafted in the car the day before and which the WCC envoy hand-delivered a few days later, on his return to Geneva. Potter's response was immediate. He set about fund-raising right away, and we received our first contribution—about $25,000—the following month." The WCC's ongoing secret financial support for the project eventually constituted one of the largest individual grants in its history—over $350,000.

By the beginning of 1980, the secret collaborators had hired their first staff members and rented a little suite in a nondescript office building in Brasília. "No sign on the door," Wright recalled, "and, inside, just three leased photocopying machines. We had twelve lawyers working with us who on a seemingly random basis began systematically checking out files from the archive. Our staff put in ten-hour days, seven days a week, copying page after page. The lawyers would then return the originals, as required, thus allaying any suspicion. There were 707 cases in all in that section of the archives, involving over 7,000 defendants. You could check out a whole case at a time, and I remember one time a lawyer arrived with a case consisting of more than two dozen volumes, weighing over eighty kilos. We'd initially hoped to be able to photocopy a scientific sampling of the cases in the archive—we certainly didn't expect to be able to continue on such a basis without being discovered for long. We were transporting the photocopies out of Brasília almost immediately, storing them in São Paulo and already starting to process them there. We just resolved to keep photocopying until we were somehow forced to stop. Eventually, we'd copied half of the archive—way more than we ever expected—and then, one day, after over three years of photocopying, we realized, to our astonishment, that we'd managed to copy *every single file* in their entire holdings —over a million pages! We had duplicated the entire universe of documents in the archive."

Wright's story was beginning to sound like a fantasy out of Borges. (Though not perhaps from Borges's life: for while the inspired scheme to replicate an entire archive would certainly have appealed to the "Library of Babel" side of the late Argentine master, the fact is that through most of the sorry recent history of his own country Jorge Luis Borges maintained a studied, almost imperious indifference to the wretched tortures and disappearances occurring all about him. Not his concern, he kept telling visitors who urgently tried to enlist his considerable moral authority in the fight against the Argentine junta. That is, until late in the game, when, remarkably, he seemed to switch over entirely: during the last years of the junta—and, to his credit, well before the Falklands fiasco—Borges began making modest but firm statements deploring the tortures and condemning the torturers, statements that resonated all the more loudly for the troubling silence that had preceded them. And, curiously, his concern over this issue, when it finally did surface, had a very un-Babel-like quality: once, when a visitor began reciting a litany of terrible recent human-rights cases, as if to emphasize and reemphasize the dimensions of the horror, Borges interrupted him after the first, saying "Stop—one is already too many.")

In New York, Wright told me more of the saga—and there was a lot more: how the team had catalogued the million pages, transferred the data to computers, reduced the material to an initial seven-thousand-page report, and then reduced that report to the summary digest; how it had procured a publisher for that digest and sworn him, too, to secrecy; and, for that matter, how the team had managed to do all this and keep the project a secret till the day the book suddenly just appeared in bookstores. And then what happened after that. But I was already hooked. I'd made up my mind: I wanted to go to São Paulo and talk with as many of the participants in the project as I could track down. Wright was dubious. The secret had held this long. Except for him and Cardinal Arns, none of the participants had thus far spoken with any members of the press about the project. I explained that I didn't want or need to know their names, only their stories, and eventually Wright agreed to see what he could do—he would talk to some of his colleagues and find out whether anyone would be willing to talk to me on that basis. But he wasn't making any promises.

When I arrived in São Paulo, about a month later, Wright's initial news wasn't at all good. The Cardinal, with whom he'd hoped to arrange an interview for me, had been called out of town; I might, if I liked, leave some written questions and he'd answer them in writing when he got back, but that was the best we were going to be able to do. (I did, and he did.) As for the other principals, there were a lot of problems. For one thing, although more than thirty people had worked on the project at some point, most of them didn't know that they had. The project's coordinators had so cleverly divided up the tasks that most of the participants were unaware, even after the book came out and began generating headlines, that that was what they'd been working on. In particular, this was true of the people who had photocopied the million pages; for all they knew, they were just working for some especially compulsive lawyers. And it would naturally be impossible to approach any of those people, because doing so might retroactively unravel the project's entire security scheme. As for those who had *knowingly* participated in the project, Wright had broached the subject to some of them—including a man who had been one of the chief organizers and would have proved an especially valuable source—and had found their reluctance unshaken and unshakable. This chief organizer, for example, asked how they could be sure that I wasn't a CIA agent out to break their security—a concern I was in no position, finally, to assuage. A week before my arrival, a one-day general strike had been called in Brazil to protest recent economic developments—the first such strike since the return of civilian rule—and the military had responded by turning out in force, patrolling the streets and staring down the workers. That had left people pretty spooked: to many Brazilians, including some of the project's organizers, such a show of military muscle hardly boded well for the fragile renascent democracy. And it further stoked the anxieties of some of the people I had hoped to talk to. Beyond that, Wright suggested that in some instances we were dealing with what he called *paranóia remanescente.* Some of the participants in the project had themselves been tortured—going through the material, they had occasionally come upon their own cases—and these participants were especially reluctant to jeopardize the project's heretofore pristine security.

Wright gave me the names of some people who would be able to furnish me with background on the public context of the project—lawyers who had defended prisoners before the military tribunals, journalists who had taken a particular interest in the book when it came out, priests who were continuing to work against ongoing ill-treatment of common criminals (a scandalous problem), and so forth. He agreed to give me further details on the mechanics of the project as he recalled them, provided I understood that there were many questions he would not be willing to answer. And for a few days we proceeded along those lines. I told him I'd try to develop contacts with other members of the team on my own, and he wished me luck.

And then I did get lucky—ridiculously lucky. Through a chain of coincidences too bizarre to go into, I located one other team member, and this person agreed to talk to me. After that, the ground rules changed slightly. Although Wright still declined to supply me with any fresh leads, he agreed to confirm the validity of any correct leads I might develop for myself; furthermore, he agreed to speak with any further participants I myself might be able to locate, and to provide them with his evaluation of my credentials and my character, for whatever that might be worth. Wright has a terrific poker face—I could see how *he* was able to keep things a secret right up through publication. I never got anything from him that he didn't intend me to get. Actually, poker isn't quite the right analogy: the image that kept flitting through my mind during our conversation was of that kids' game Battleship. "C-8," I'd say, in effect, and he wouldn't flinch: nothing, no response at all. "How about D-6?" I'd ask, or words to that effect. "Well, there," he'd in effect reply, "you've hit one of my destroyers."

So we proceeded on that basis, and if I wasn't able to interview everyone I might have liked to I was still able to talk with several people, both in and outside the project, and to develop the following account. (I have disguised some details to protect the security of the project, which, I believe, remains untarnished.)

I don't know why, but it took me a while before I fully grasped one of the key facts about this project: Cardinal Arns was completely out on a limb. He had not consulted with his fellow-bishops before or after giving his go-ahead, nor had he sought permission from the Vatican; indeed, the Vatican never knew about the project. Arns had told the team members that if anything went wrong he would assume personal responsibility. They, for their part, had told each other that if anything should go wrong they would all endeavor to keep his name out of the scandal. And it would have been an incredible scandal. "The biggest crisis in the history of church-state relations in Brazil" is how one of the team members described the stakes for me one day when I asked what would have happened if their project had been uncovered while the military was still in power. One of the reasons Arns and Wright went to the World Council of Churches for funding was that while Arns could provide the team with a moral umbrella and a certain amount of physical shelter, he could not draw on any substantial Catholic funds without provoking the suspicion of a large and perhaps not entirely sympathetic Church bureaucracy. For that matter, Potter, in Geneva, was out on a limb of his own, for he and a select few of his colleagues at the WCC were spearheading the funding for a major secret operation in Brazil without informing any of their member churches in Brazil, several of which, as I've suggested, might not have been altogether supportive of the initiative, either.

I spent a lot of time during my first few days in São Paulo talking to people about the evolving response of the Brazilian Catholic Church to the military dictatorship—and, in particular, about Cardinal Arns's central role in that evolution. On the plane down, I had read a then-unpublished manuscript by Ralph Della Cava, an American scholar with a passionate interest in and knowledge of this subject. "The Brazilian episcopate in the last three decades has emerged as the most pastorally innovative, organizationally complex, and theologically progressive episcopate in the world," he'd written. "The two most powerful visions of the future of the Catholic Church are those of the Brazilian episcopate and John Paul II." Della Cava argued—and people I spoke with in Brazil agreed—that the emergence of this powerful alternative vision, which is loosely defined as "liberation theology," was a gradual process and was still incomplete. That is to say, all along there were important elements of the Brazilian episcopate—the world's third largest (after Italy and the United States), with over 350 bishops—who cherished a more traditional, authoritarian, conservative, and elitist role for the Church (the sort of role staked out by the Argentine episcopate during those years, for example). But during the fifties some very progressive alternative visions of the Church's overriding responsibility toward the poor began to be articulated in the northeast, the most desperately impoverished section of Brazil. People like the dynamic archbishop of Olinda and Recife, Helder Câmara, and, especially, church workers lower down in the hierarchy were upending what they saw as the Church's traditional bias in favor of the rich landed classes and their status quo. It was in this region that some church workers began fashioning the now world-renowned *comunidades eclesiais de base,* or CEBs —small, grassroots church communities. These communities were often leaderless, or, rather, were self-leading; without the leadership of priests, that is—a circumstance that particularly threatened Church conservatives (and one that came under increasingly skeptical scrutiny after the election of John Paul II). During the sixties and seventies, the CEBs came to articulate some of the most radical "people's" critiques of the Brazilian capitalist order and its staggeringly lopsided distribution of wealth. Back in New York, Alfred Stepan, a noted Brazilianist, who is the dean of Columbia University's School of International and Public Affairs, had spun out a nifty piece of speculation for me: "In a sense, the whole notion of 'consciousness-raising' had its origins in the Brazilian northeast during the mid-fifties, with people like Paulo Freire and Helder Câmara. By the early sixties, it had reached Chile, and from there it made its way up, by the mid-sixties, to Ivan Illich, in Cuernavaca, and from there it filtered on up, by 1968, into the pages of the *New York Review of Books.*" He paused. "That's perhaps a bit facile, but not entirely off the mark."

Some of the initial manifestations of liberation theology were beginning to make their presence felt in Brazil's urban centers during the reformist upsurge of the early sixties, and especially during the later stages of João Goulart's Presidency (1961–1964); there was a good deal of grassroots Catholic support for Goulart's populist-protosocialist initiatives. But the vast majority of the Catholic hierarchy still viewed those initiatives with profound suspicion. Like the middle and upper classes, whose concerns they overwhelmingly reflected, most Brazilian bishops of the time were fiercely anti-Communist and were deeply troubled by what they perceived as Communist inroads into Goulart's Administration. They generally applauded the April, 1964, coup that overthrew Goulart—or, at least, they extended the military their tacit support. The military, it was hoped, would clean up the mess, prune away the excesses, set things back on the straight and narrow, and then bow out. The years that followed, however, tended to radicalize large sections of the episcopate. More and more Brazilian bishops translated the lessons of Vatican II and the follow-up Conference of Latin-American Bishops in Medellín, Colombia, in 1968, into the necessity for solidarity with the country's poorest members—who, after all, were its vast majority. They began to speak of a "preferential option for the poor"—a notion that a few years earlier might have been branded as verging on the heretical. Interestingly, Pope Paul VI tended to support these tendencies—or, at any rate, he was not threatened (as John Paul II later appeared to be) by the growing autonomy of the Brazilian episcopate. It was Paul VI, for instance, who now moved to replace the conservative archbishop of São Paulo, Agnelo Rossi, with the more moderate Friar Paulo Evaristo Arns. (When Arns, who had been serving as auxiliary bishop of São Paulo since his consecration in 1966, travelled to Rome in 1970, he was asked by several influential Catholic groups in the archdiocese to deliver to the Pope a petition protesting Cardinal Rossi's overfriendly relations with the military. Paul VI responded by kicking Rossi upstairs, summoning him to Rome, where he became, in effect, the mayor of the Vatican—and then ordering Arns himself, who had requested assignment to the impoverished Amazon region, to take full command of the archdiocese of São Paulo instead.) The Brazilian episcopate of the seventies was by no means united in its openness to liberation theology; the staunchly anti-Communist archbishop of Rio, Eugenio Cardinal Sales, for example, was a longtime friend and ongoing supporter of the military, and he had many allies in the bishops' conference. But increasingly the Brazilian Catholic Church came to represent a uniquely independent haven within the country—one beyond the absolute control of the military, and constituting the nucleus, as it were, of a resurgent civilian society. In this transformation Cardinal Arns played an important role almost from the start of his archbishopric.

His first act as archbishop made quite an impression (I was told about it several times): he had the archdiocese sell the palatial residence to which he was entitled and use the proceeds to build community centers, which were then put at the service of the CEBs operating in the São Paulo area, and he moved into a far more modest dwelling, in which he still lives. As archbishop, he became increasingly active in his support of the labor unions that were trying to reestablish themselves in the huge industrial belt surrounding São Paulo following years of withering repression. He authorized churches to be used as meeting halls for workers' rallies, and at one point (another story I heard repeatedly) he visited a government compound that had been occupied by landless squatters and that was under siege by military troops. "Don't touch me," he warned an officer who tried to block his way as he approached, bearing soup and bread. "There are children in there. If they were your children, you'd want me to help them. Let me pass." And the officer did.

But Arns was perhaps most daring and outspoken in confronting the regime on the issue of torture. Upon being named archbishop, he made a special effort to start visiting some of the local prisons, and it was perhaps in them that he first encountered evidence of the widespread physical abuse of political prisoners. This was the period—as *Brasil: Nunca Mais* later established—when the military terror was reaching its peak; and hardly anyone else was speaking out against it. In January, 1971, only two months after Arns's installation, two São Paulo church workers were detained by military authorities. Arns went to General Humberto Mello, the military commander of the São Paulo region, to plead their case, and was assured that they were being well treated. A few days later, however, he was able to verify that they had been subjected to terrible brutalilty. In a sermon the following Sunday—a sermon that was either read or posted in every church in the archdiocese—Arns denounced their "ignominious torture." It was the beginning of an ever more consuming crusade.

Not everybody today celebrates that crusade. I spoke with one important mainstream editor who expressed decided skepticism. "I don't know him well, but I don't especially like him," he said when I asked what he thought of Arns. "He is, for one thing, a Franciscan. There is in the Church this distinction between secular cardinals, who come from society and are men of the city, and friar cardinals, who come from the cloister and to an extent stand aloof from the city. Cardinal Arns is very tough. The moment he saw that Mello was playing him for a fool, he started to fight. 'My point is that people are being tortured in the jails of São Paulo,' he said, over and over again. Which was all very fierce and glorious. *My* point, though, is that in order to have this kind of cardinal you need the other kind, like Cardinal Sales, the archbishop of Rio, who talks to the regime, who keeps the channels open, who works quietly behind the scenes. Sales saved dozens of lives, and I don't think Arns saved a single one. To Cardinal Arns we perhaps owe the fact that we no longer have political torture in Brazil today. To Cardinal Sales we owe the fact that this and this and this individual are still alive. It's not as pure a choice as it might seem."

I tried this formulation out on several other people. Some agreed—while insisting that Cardinal Arns's was still the preferable option—but others didn't buy the premise. "Cardinal Sales was the military's best friend on this issue," Della Cava told me when I spoke with him. (He happened to be in Brazil while I was there.) "He tended to operate through personal contacts rather than public statements. This in no way diminishes the fact that Sales did occasionally intervene and did save some lives. But can your editor friend produce evidence that Arns failed to save lives? Arns was absolutely crucial in helping to crystallize a civil resistance to the military, and had there not been such a resistance we might well have had many more years of torture—and who's to say how many more lives would then have been lost?"

It was Della Cava who suggested to me that Wladimir Herzog's death had been the key development in that crystallization. "By 1975, there had been all sorts of instances, but none of those individual cases had galvanized the country. I later had occasion to ask Cardinal Arns, 'Why him? Why did you make such an issue of Herzog?' He replied that he'd received a few calls about the case shortly after Herzog's arrest, urging him to intervene. He'd called on the governor and on the commander of the Second Army, and both of them had assured him that everything was OK, nothing was going to happen. So he relented. And then, a few days later, Herzog turned up dead: people were just presented with the corpse. Cardinal Arns told me how shaken this had left him. He questioned whether he had done enough, and he had this sense of at least having to do something more now. He couldn't allow the incident to go unsung. So he presided at that Mass—the thousands of people showing up, with the police cameras all clicking away—and he made of it the turning point for the society."

I asked Della Cava to describe the Cardinal.

"He's a smallish man," Della Cava said. "Five seven, maybe five eight. Very earnest, fairly humorless. An intelligence a cut above most of the rest of us. A high-pitched voice. One wouldn't imagine him a great orator. He's not particularly charismatic or dramatic—not like Dom Helder Câmara, who hardly has to lift an eyebrow to draw a sigh from the crowd. No, his strength grew out of a situation in which everyone knew that something was rotten and nobody would say it. And then along came this Mr. Everyman—a man like us: not tall, not powerful, not charismatic—who spoke with clarity and immediacy and truth. A man, that is, who rose to the occasion. And now, today, with the occasion having to a degree passed and the issue abated, one again sees him for what he is—a decent, hardworking cardinal trying to help make this city of thirteen million people function."

Among the Cardinal's greatest fans, it turned out, was Philip Potter. One afternoon, I telephoned him from my hotel. He was no longer in Geneva, having retired as the World Council of Churches' general secretary in 1984, after twelve years of service. A native of the island of Dominica, in the Caribbean, he had been the WCC's first Third World leader, and he'd now returned to the Third World and to the teaching of theology, his first love. I tracked him down in Kingston, Jamaica, where he is currently a lecturer at the United Theological College of the West Indies. A Methodist minister, he initially rose through the ranks of a Christian youth movement, the World Student Christian Federation, directing it for many years before becoming the leader of the entire WCC. I had been told that he was a masterly administrator and a master scholar. He is fluent in French, conversant in German, and reads Latin, Hebrew, and Greek. He'd been described to me as a large, tall, and imposing figure of a man, a very dark-skinned West Indian, and his voice now, over the phone, was at once genial, authoritative—and richly deep. "When I first heard the proposal, my response was immediate and positive—especially coming, as it did, from that particular group of colleagues," Potter recalled. He went on to tell me that the WCC had a longtime interest in human rights, going back to 1948, when the organization had been instrumental in the United Nations negotiations that culminated in the Universal Declaration of Human Rights. "Torture, of course, is a critical issue for us," he explained. "It's an element that goes to the heart of what we believe, for it involves destroying a person's dignity, taking away his possibility of affirming or denying, of swearing truthfulness, and emptying him of his humanity and turning him into a jellyfish. We realize, too, as Christians, that the churches in the past have not had a brilliant record in this regard—either in terms of the torments associated with the Catholic Inquisition or in terms of the various Protestant analogues. And we in the Third World understand this especially deeply. So we saw this project as a test case—not so much an indictment as a warning, a prophetic challenge in the biblical sense, as if to say, as the title eventually did say,

'Never again.' It was for us a matter of deep gratitude that there were people with the evident courage to accomplish this task and to do so in the proper spirit, with dignity and without a feeling of hatred or vindictiveness. We hoped this could be a model for how this sort of work should be done elsewhere, and we were eager to support it."

Potter had known Jaime Wright since school days, and had known his brother Paulo as well, because Paulo had worked with the World Student Christian Federation. The WSCF had been slated to convene its quadrennial meeting in Brazil in 1964, he recalled, and had had to change over to Argentina at the last moment because of the coup. Potter said he'd taken a special interest in Brazilian developments since then, although, as he pointed out, the WCC's interest in human rights was worldwide: "South Africa, Eastern Europe, Korea, Uruguay, Chile . . . In Santiago, for example, the WCC has been a longtime co-sponsor of the work of the Catholic Church's Vicariat of Solidarity, one of the principal independent counterforces to General Augusto Pinochet's dictatorship."

I asked Potter about Cardinal Arns.

"Ah, yes," he said. "My good friend the Cardinal. We're the same age, sixty-five—I'm just a month older. What can I tell you? He's a man of tremendous sanity, with an incredibly quiet but unalterable strength—a very rare personality. A Franciscan. I'm very fond of Francis; I often went to Assisi. I very much like this style—of simplicity, of a light touch. Over the years, the Cardinal and I have enjoyed telling each other stories of our adversities in which all we could do was to stand our ground in the face of the storm, to weep and laugh and pray and sigh to the birds and the flowers, as St. Francis would. We used to encourage each other very much." Potter recalled a visit he'd made to São Paulo in July of 1979—just a few weeks, as it happened, before the hatching of the photocopying scheme. He'd gone to São Paulo to help dedicate a large Pentecostal church. "The Cardinal had been unable to make it to the ceremony itself—he'd called in advance to apologize—but he arrived soon afterward, and found me surrounded by television reporters who were trying, with considerable linguistic difficulty, to conduct an interview. He volunteered to serve as an interpreter—translating my French into Portuguese—and that's how the interview went out that evening over Brazilian television: the words of the general secretary of the World Council of Churches being translated by the head of the Catholic archdiocese." Potter was silent for a moment. "Here in the islands we have a phrase that applies equally well to Jaime Wright and Cardinal Arns—we say that such people are 'filled with grace, grits, and gumption.' They both needed all three for this project."

I asked Potter what he had done when he received the Cardinal's letter.

"We realized immediately that we'd have to move very quickly and with the utmost discretion. There was no saying how long the group would continue to have access to the materials—or, for that matter, how long it would be before the materials themselves were destroyed. Everything was done quietly—nobody asked any questions. In the ecumenical movement, we've had all sorts of experience with this sort of discretion—going back to the Nazi days, when we were smuggling people out of occupied Europe. One simply takes responsibility oneself and tries to involve as few people as possible and to shield as many as possible from the harassments to which unnecessary knowledge might subject them. We got in touch with colleagues in Europe, the States, Canada, New Zealand, Australia . . . "

How, I asked, did he describe the project when he was phoning potential contributors?

"Oh, no, on a matter like that, we'd never have recourse to the phone—or even, if we could possibly avoid it, to writing. Whenever we could, we dealt in person. The WCC is a very open organization, but when it comes to people in danger we watch things very carefully. Everything is done on trust. It's part of our Christian heritage. In matters like that, you realize that the world cannot really function except through trust—trusting that people will be truthful and circumspect. Did you know that in Hebrew the word for trust and the word for truth have the same root—*aman*? You see it, too, of course, in the English word 'amen'; which is to say 'I believe, I trust, I commit.' The Greek word for truth is *aletheia,* which means 'not covered up': *a-letheia*. When Jesus says 'I am the light of the world,' he is referring to that sense of uncoveredness. You shall know the truth, and the truth shall make you free. One of the particularly nice things about this project was the way we were able to combine the two meanings, for it was precisely through trusting people that we were able to bring great and important things to light."

Arns and Potter got a scare early in the game—and ironically it came precisely from trusting too much to writing. One morning, I was over at Wright's house, a modest but comfortable two-story dwelling on a small lot in the Brooklin Paulista district, about half an hour's drive from downtown—on a street that at one time had evidently consisted of many such houses, though now it seemed to be giving way to skyscrapers all around. Wright was looking through a relatively thin file of papers documenting the progress of the project, trying to reconstruct the chronology of its funding. "Ah, here's something," he said, pulling out a letter. "Apparently, both the Cardinal and Potter felt the need for at least one written communiqué, to cover their flanks, as it were, when the project was just getting started. So here you have a letter dated June 23, 1980, from Potter to Cardinal Arns, marked 'Confidential,' referring to that WCC envoy and me by name, and continuing, 'It is with the greatest pleasure that I am able to confirm that we have already been able to raise the major part of the funds necessary for your special project. Given the great importance that surrounds the project for Brazil and the Brazilian churches, we hope to be able to contribute to the dissemination of the results to member churches all over the world for reflection.' Well, as you can imagine, the news about the success of the fund-raising was very gratifying, but one morning a few weeks later I was stunned to find the letter, in its entirety, including the references to the WCC man and me, published in the archdiocese's widely circulated newspaper, *O São Paulo.* It ran under a nice headline about ecumenical relations. I must say this was the only time I had to chastise the Cardinal. I stormed into his office and said, 'What on earth were you doing, publishing this letter?' He looked up at me and stammered, 'It was *published?*' Apparently, one of his assistants—and the point is, virtually none of his assistants had been informed about the project—had found the letter lying among his papers and just thought it would make a nice item in the newspaper. We had a real scare there, but, thankfully, the readers weren't very alert, or maybe it was just a question of who bothers to read about improving ecumenical relations. At any rate, the incident passed and nothing happened."

While that crisis came and went, the photocopying in Brasília had begun in earnest. Although I was never able to talk with any of the photocopyists themselves, I did get a chance to speak with the man who set up and ran the Brasília operation. He recounted for me how the group rented space in a downtown Brasília commercial building that was otherwise given over to offices for lawyers, doctors, dentists, exporters—and, indeed, a few copying places. With the group's three photocopying machines running pretty much around the clock, its office was occasionally mistaken for a regular copying place. "People would come in and want us to copy their books or manuscripts or receipts—especially late, after all the other places had closed and we were still going. We'd explain that we weren't a commercial operation, but they'd insist, and in order not to cause a scene or draw undue attention we developed a policy of simply accepting such orders, charging the going rate, and plowing the proceeds back into the project. Unfortunately, at one point we discovered that one of our staff members was pocketing these random windfalls, so we had to let him go. But mostly we didn't have any problems, and we were working at such a pace—after all, we had only twenty-four hours to get the files back to the archive—that our people didn't have time to really study the documents we were having them copy or to develop any notion of what sort of project they were engaged in."

The Archive of the Supreme Military Court was in the basement of a fourteen-story, glass-walled building entirely given over to the offices of the military courts. (That building in turn faced a plaza surrounded on all sides by other sorts of court buildings—civil, commercial, administrative, and so forth. Brasília was of course one of the world's newest and most highly planned cities, having been invented from scratch in 1956 and inaugurated in 1960, just four years before the coup.)

Only archive functionaries had access to the stacks, and they sat at their posts in a semicircle of desks in the vestibule just inside the archive's entrance. The way the ground rules worked, lawyers who were certified to practice before the Supreme Military Court could request specific files bearing on cases upon which they were working; the circumstances of the amnesty provided a fairly wide latitude in this respect, since tangential cases might conceivably have a bearing on any specific case. They'd fill out an application, the functionary would go back and retrieve the files in question, and the lawyer would check out the material by signing a large bound ledger. "At first, there were only three of us lawyers who were checking things out, beginning with cases with which we were familiar," my informant said. "But the ledger itself quickly began to look suspicious, with the same three signatures appearing over and over. So we enlisted the help of several other lawyers—people we trusted, and who trusted us. We didn't tell them why we needed the files—just that we did. They didn't ask questions but helped us by getting the files we asked for out of the building, delivering them to us, and returning them the next day. Some functionaries were more cooperative than others—some were downright hostile—so we tried to approach the cooperative ones. There were times when none of them were there, so that was always a moment of tension—descending into the basement and ascertaining who was on duty that day. If none of the sympathetic clerks were there, we simply had to skip it for a day or two. We had no way of knowing what we were after—how many total cases existed back there in the stacks, how they were organized, how they might be called up. But we were gradually able to cultivate some inside contacts—inside the court system—who, again, didn't know exactly what we were after but were willing to help us with regard to specific questions. The project would have proved impossible without their assistance—we wouldn't have known what to ask for, nor would we have been able to determine when we'd retrieved everything. After the book was published, several years later, the court administrators were furious over the breach in their security: they realized that we had to have had some inside help and they ended up transferring everyone, all the functionaries, to other assignments. But our contacts never expressed any resentment to us, and as for the others. . . ." My informant's voice trailed off and he smiled.

I asked him if there were any close calls during that phase of the operation.

After a pause, he replied, "One time all our photocopying machines had broken down, for some reason or other, just on the day when we'd arranged to check out a particularly important and unusually bulky case, consisting of dozens and dozens of files. On the spur of the moment, we decided to fly them down to São Paulo and do the copying there overnight and then fly them back in the morning. It was going to be a tight call making the various flights. Anyway, we loaded the files into the front of a VW bug—they entirely filled its trunk—and set off for the airport. Only, naturally, we got a flat tire. We were quickly surrounded by all sorts of friendly passersby, eager to help—in particular, several soldiers and policemen. Both the jack and the spare were in the trunk, under all the files, and we couldn't open the trunk to get at them with all those people around. They couldn't understand why we were so eagerly turning down their help; the clock was ticking, and they weren't leaving. They wanted to help—they were insisting on helping. In retrospect, it was a comical scene, but at the time it was nerve-racking. We had to concoct all kinds of crazy stories about why we needed to be alone. The people finally left, grudgingly. Then we had to empty the trunk, pull out the spare and the jack, and reload the files—all this in record time. When we were finished, we didn't have any place to put the flat, so we ended up driving the rest of the way to the airport with the tire in the back seat. But we made it. And somehow our security held."

The files weren't exactly easy to copy. They consisted of Dickensian folders, bulging with papers of different sizes, all clamped together by metal braids. "Either you had to disassemble the folders, copy their contents, and then—this was the hard part—reassemble the contents back onto the braids," my informant recalled. "Or you had to be some sort of muscleman, pressing the pages in the still-assembled folders down onto the glass surface, page by page. Either way, it was quite a production." But the copyists persisted, and the project lumbered inexorably on.

"Toward the end, when we were about 90 percent done, the administrators at the archive must have started getting suspicious," my informant continued. "They couldn't figure out what was going on, but they suspected that something was. So, from one day to the next, they cancelled everybody's lending privileges, and decided to send all the files back to the provincial archives from which they'd come. That way, they figured, they'd solve any possible problems. Only, they forgot to cancel lending privileges at the provincial archives, so we just ended up sending people to the various outlying districts to check out and copy the few cases we still needed."

Very early in the project, the organizers realized that they had to get the copied pages out of Brasília and down to more secure quarters in São Paulo as quickly as possible. Growing stacks of highly classified documents moldering away in an unsecured office in Brasília—the capital of the military regime—would have constituted a security disaster just waiting to happen. They initially packed the photocopied pages into boxes and put them on overnight buses headed down to São Paulo, where they had someone retrieve them at the station. But the buses took more than sixteen hours in the best of times, and were frequently subject to unexplained delays, and the nerves of the people responsible for this phase of the operation were being frayed raw. So they shifted over to more expensive but less anxiety-provoking air freight. The boxes were still out of their physical control, but for shorter, more predictable periods. In order to downplay any suspicions, the organizers used several different companies and airlines. And, somehow, there weren't any hitches, and everything arrived.

"Technically," Jaime Wright suggested to me one afternoon, "we weren't doing anything illegal." He paused for a moment. "Or, anyway, I suppose it might have been possible to try and argue things that way." He explained that the documents in the archives were public records, that they had been checked out legitimately by people who were entitled to check them out, and that they had been returned in their entirety and on schedule. Precisely what one was allowed to do with them while they were in one's possession had never been spelled out in the law.

But the hazards involved with this project were never ones associated with technical interpretations of the law. Technically, the military themselves had been in violation of all sorts of laws—including laws of their own formulation—all during the years since the coup. They were not going to be terribly impressed by subtleties of legal precision if the project should ever come to light.

True, the *abertura* was continuing all through the period that the secret team was engaged in its project, between 1979 and 1985. But that ongoing process of liberalization was in perennial jeopardy. There was never any inevitability about it, and certainly not about its culmination in an orderly transfer of power to an opposition civilian President. Alfred Stepan, of Columbia University, who interviewed dozens of officers during trips to Brazil in 1981 and 1982, recently wrote, "While only a distinct minority [in those years] wanted a military President in 1985, virtually none of them thought that the opposition could or should gain the Presidency in 1985. The overwhelming sentiment within the military was that the opposition could not realistically contemplate power until the pro-regime President selected via the upcoming electoral college finished his term in 1991."

Each time the opposition seemed on the verge of political gains—before the municipal elections in 1980, or before the congressional and state gubernatorial elections in 1982, or through all the maneuverings that led up to the indirect Presidential vote by the electoral college early in 1985—the military authorities evinced extreme ambivalence: it was not at all clear that they were going to allow matters to proceed, and in 1980 they didn't (those elections were cancelled). As late as April, 1984, the Army suddenly took over the streets of Brasília once again in a momentary fit of misgiving. In addition, ongoing labor unrest, especially in the industrial belt around São Paulo, occasionally provoked reversions to patterns of military repression.

If the photocopying team was working in an incredibly charged and precarious environment vis-à-vis the state authorities, its safety was still further jeopardized by the activities of renegade elements from some of the regime's earlier incarnations. Ever since 1975—the Herzog case was a catalyst in this regard as well—the officers who were allied with President Geisel and then with President Figueiredo had been trying to rein in the excesses of the military police and security services. One can debate the extent to which what was involved here was a mysteriously renascent sense of concern about human rights among certain high-level officers—or, rather, less mysteriously, merely a power struggle among competing factions in the military hierarchy. In any event, by the late seventies the faction that seemed to be losing—the once omnipotent security apparatus—was increasingly resorting to acts of clandestine terror in an attempt to destabilize the situation and undermine the apparent winners. (In this sense, Brazil in the early eighties was not unlike France during the late fifties, when the Algerian crisis was moving toward its climax.) Throughout 1980, there were bombings of newspaper stands carrying opposition papers. That same year, a mail bomb sent to the president of the Brazilian Bar Association killed his secretary. On April 30, 1981, two active-duty security officers in Rio were blown up in the parking lot outside a packed concert hall when a bomb they were attempting to smuggle into the hall (in which a leftist pre-May Day celebration was under way) exploded prematurely. The people engaged in these right-wing acts of terror had earlier been the very torturers whose careers the *Brasil: Nunca Mais* team members were attempting to document. There can be little doubt that if they had ever found out about the archdiocese's secret project they would have derailed it by any means necessary.

One day, in a conversation with Elio Gaspari, who is the deputy director of *Veja,* Brazil's foremost newsweekly, and is as cool and temperate an analyst of the Brazilian scene as one is likely to encounter, I asked whether he would use the word "courageous" to describe the members of the project.

"Absolutely," he replied, without a moment's hesitation.

What, I asked, had they been risking?

This time, he didn't even let me finish the question. "Life," he said.

Little by little, week by week, the million pages were being brought together in the project's secret storehouse in São Paulo. As soon as each new shipment arrived, its processing began. I had an opportunity to talk with several of the people involved in this phase of the operation, and learned some of its details.

First, every page would be microfilmed, on a machine "borrowed" from a local university without its administrators' knowledge. One person did the microfilming of the entire million pages. The reels began adding up—they eventually totalled over five hundred—and the team members resolved to smuggle batches of them out of the country as often as they could. They wanted to make sure that no matter what happened to the project, as much of the documentation as possible would survive in some form for future witness and as a subject for research. One person was responsible for spiriting the batches away to Geneva—several dozen reels at a time in the bottom of a tightly packed suitcase. He would return from each trip with additional funding for the project stuffed in a money belt. "Hundred-dollar bills," he told me. "Terribly inconvenient. Ten or twenty thousand dollars ends up being a real wad. You'd think they'd print more currency in big denominations, if for no other reason than to facilitate financing the Contras. Anyway, I'd return with these bulging wads wrapped around my waist. We hardly ever had any problems. Once, though, in Frankfurt, as I was making a changeover on my way back home, everybody in the plane was subjected to a thorough search. The security guard quickly zeroed in on my bulge and asked 'What's this?' I just said 'Money' and he seemed satisfied. They must have been looking for some sort of terrorist. Still, I sweated the whole flight back, imagining that the German police might have called ahead to warn the Brazilians, and not knowing what might be awaiting me when I disembarked. As it happened, nothing was."

One person told me that "chocolate" was the code word. "Whenever we wanted to ask one another about the microfilm or the money, we'd refer to it as 'the chocolate.' 'Has the chocolate come yet?' 'Did he take them the chocolate?' 'Love that Swiss chocolate.' It wasn't a very sophisticated code, and things could get confusing. Sometimes people talked about chocolate and all they meant was chocolate: one time somebody came barging in saying, 'Now, who's gone and eaten all the chocolate?' and I nearly had a heart attack."

The fact that the project was being secretly funded in dollars presented its coordinators with an ironic windfall during the early eighties, when Brazil was experiencing triple-digit inflation. (The economy's headlong deterioration was one reason the military was under such pressure to relinquish authority, and one reason it seemed willing to consider doing so.) This inflation doubled, and even tripled the spending power of these investigators busy documenting the abuses of the very military whose policies, for years unchecked by any independent criticism, had brought about the fiasco.

Once the files had been microfilmed, they were archived. The file on each case was assigned a classification number, on the arbitrary basis of when it had entered the collection. This number, which was, of course, different from the number that the file had been assigned in the Supreme Military Court's archive, was the one by which that file would always be referred to in the Brasil: Nunca Mais documents. This arrangement would help to disguise the nature of the project should any individual facet of it come to light.

Once the files were archived, they were ready for data processing. Some of the team members were computer specialists, and they had designed incredibly thorough questionnaires, which a battery of staff members (the largest single contingent in the project) now began filling out: the defendants' names, ages, affiliations, professions, and so forth; the sites of alleged activity, and of pretrial incarceration; the nature of the charges; the date, the length, and disposition of the trial; the names of the security agents, investigators, prosecutors, judges. For five years, one woman had a single job: to go through the million pages and extract every single piece of testimony of torture, verbatim. The extracts were the subject of an even more detailed questionnaire: the type and duration of torture; the site and physical description of the torture center; the description, rank, service branch, and, where possible, name of each torturer.

Again, the work was parcelled out in such a way that the individuals doing it rarely had any idea of the wider contours of the enterprise. "After each phase of the project, that phase's entire crew was dismissed and a new one taken on," one of the São Paulo coordinators explained to me. "Thus, after one crew finished filling out the questionnaires we had another one transcribe the results—just a sequence of numbers, after all—onto computer diskettes." The project was using two Prológica CP 500 computers, Brazilian knockoffs of the Tandy TRS-80: the data eventually filled over a hundred diskettes. "Another crew was subsequently brought in to manipulate the data—to analyze the intersection of, say, Category 37 and Category 61, or determine how often Factor 22 appeared in Subgroup B-7." The project eventually generated over a hundred and twenty statistical tables.

And, all the while, the secret held. In every case, the staff members were hired on the basis of personal acquaintance and trust, even though most of them would have no knowledge of the sort of project they were engaged in. (One of the São Paulo organizers told me that of the twenty people engaged in the phase he'd supervised only two had been able to deduce the fact of their involvement after the book was published.) The coordinators, for their part, exercised phenomenal self-restraint: not one of those I spoke with had informed even his or her spouse of the nature or status of the project the entire time it was going on. As Wright had said of his brother's silence, this was as much for the protection of the one kept in ignorance as it was for the security of the project. Even at this late date, many family members are ignorant of important aspects of their spouses' or parents' involvement. Wright's wife, Alma, kept an ear demurely cocked from a neighboring room through most of my interviews with her husband, and toward the end of our sessions she commented that a lot of what he was saying was news to her.

Nevertheless, the São Paulo team had three close calls—or, at any rate, acted on the assumption that it had had them—each time transferring the entire operation from one base to another overnight. One was when members of the team recognized a plainclothes policeman scrounging around a nearby courtyard; another was when an unlisted phone they kept exclusively for outgoing calls suddenly rang one day. "The third time," one of my informants recalled, "happened when one of our researchers became a convert. The court archives often included all sorts of background material, and in this one instance our researcher was inventorying the case of a fairly obscure and now decimated leftist organization. He became more and more engrossed in the group's politics, reading its manifestos, which were included among the documents. One day, we noticed that an entire file container was missing from our shelves. People were under strict instructions never to remove anything from our storehouse, so we had a real fright. A couple of us paid a call on this guy at his home, and he admitted to having the file right there by his bed—he'd just really gotten into it. He apologized, gave us back the file, promised it wouldn't happen again. This was on a Friday. Over the weekend, we found a new base and transferred everything—all the metal shelves and the cardboard containers and the computers and the filing cabinets. On Monday, this man showed up for work at the usual place, and the work had disappeared into thin air. Our response may have been a bit extreme, but we just couldn't take any chances."

Each time the project had to pick up and move on the spur of the moment like that, Cardinal Arns found them a new niche, in some out-of-the-way church building. In his written answers to the questions I'd provided for him, Arns hardly ever displayed any humor, but in reference to this subject he noted wryly, "Being the Archbishop helps."

➾➾➾➾➾➾➾➾

During a case tried before the Council of Military Justice in Juiz de Fora in 1970, the military judge ordered his stenographer to record the contention of Ângelo Pezzuti da Silva, a twenty-three-year-old student, detained in Belo Horizonte and tortured in Rio de Janeiro, that "tortures are an institution, given the fact that the defendant was an instrument for practical demonstrations of this system, in a class in which more than 100 sergeants participated and whose teacher was an officer of the Army Police, called Lt. Ayton; that in this room, while slides about torture were being shown, practical demonstrations were given using the defendant . . . and other prisoners in the Army police as guinea pigs."[2]

In a case in Belo Horizonte in 1970, Augusto César Salles Galvão, a twenty-one-year-old student, testified concerning one common form of torment to which he'd been subjected: "The parrot's perch consists of an iron bar wedged behind the victim's knees and to which his wrists are tied; the bar is then placed between two tables, causing the victim's body to hang some twenty or thirty centimeters from the ground. This method is hardly ever used by itself: its normal 'complements' are electric shocks, the *palmatória* [a length of thick rubber attached to a wooden paddle], and drowning."

José Milton Ferreira de Almeida, a thirty-one-year-old engineer from Rio, was able to give a military tribunal trying his case in 1976 a fairly sophisticated technical description of an electrical device used during his tortures: "There was a machine called 'the little pepper,' in the torturer's language, which consisted of a wooden box; inside there was a permanent magnet, in whose field a rotor turned, and from its terminals a brush collected electrical current that was transmitted through wires attached to the terminals already described; this machine produced around 100 volts and a considerable electrical current, or something like 10 amperes . . . this machine was extremely dangerous because the electrical current increased with the speed of the rotor as it was turned by the crank . . . the machine was applied at a very high speed, then suddenly stopped and turned in the opposite direction, thereby creating a counter electromotive force that doubled the original voltage of the machine."

Ferreira de Almeida also gave his judges a vivid account of how he "sat down in a chair known as 'the dragon's chair,' an extremely heavy chair, whose seat is a sheet of corrugated iron; on the back part there is a protuberance where one of the wires of the shock machine can be inserted [and] in addition to this, the chair had a wooden bar that pushed your legs backwards, so that with each spasm produced by the electrical discharge your legs would hit against the wooden bar, causing deep gashes."

In 1973, Leonardo Valentini, a twenty-two-year-old metalworker, told his military tribunal in Rio that there was also, in his cubicle, to keep him company, a boa constrictor called Miriam.

Fernando Reis Salles Ferreira, a forty-eight-year-old airline worker, told the military judges at his 1970 hearing in Rio how "they continued to torture him with inhuman methods, such as the position of 'Christ the Redeemer,' with four telephone books in each hand, on tiptoe, naked, with beatings on the stomach and on the chest, forcing him to stand erect."

In 1973, before the military court in Ceará, Maria José de Souza Barros, from the rural area of Japuara, testified "that they took her son to the woods and beat him so that he would tell about her husband; that the boy . . . is nine years old; that the police took the boy at five o'clock in the afternoon and only brought him back around two o'clock in the morning."

César Augusto Teles, a twenty-nine-year-old driver, told his judges how military security agents tried to get him and his wife to talk: "On the afternoon of that day, around seven o'clock, my two children, Janaina de Almeida Teles, five years old, and Edson Luiz de Almeida

Teles, four years old, were also abducted and brought to the [headquarters]. We were then shown to them in our torn clothes, dirty, pale, covered with bruises. . . . Threats that our children would be molested continued for several hours."

A twenty-nine-year-old bank worker named Inês Etienne Romeu testified, "At any hour of the day or night I suffered physical and moral assault. 'Márcio' invaded my cell to 'examine' my anus and confirm whether 'Camarão' had practiced sodomy with me. This same 'Márcio' obliged me to hold his penis, while he contorted himself into obscene positions. During this period I was raped twice by 'Camarão' and was forced to clean the kitchen completely naked, while listening to wisecracks and obscenities of the worst kind."

The stenographer at the 1972 military trial in Rio of twenty-nine-year-old Maria do Socorro Diógenes recorded that on one occasion "the accused, together with another defendant in this legal proceeding by the name of Pedro, received electric shocks, applied by the police, who forced the accused to touch Pedro's genital organs so that, in this way, he might receive the electrical discharge."

In 1970, Luiz Andréa Favero, a twenty-six-year-old teacher detained in Foz do Iguaçu, described to the military court what had happened to his wife: "The accused heard the screams of his wife and, after asking the police not to ill-treat her in view of the fact that she was pregnant, they all laughed at him. . . . On the same day, the accused received word that his wife had suffered a hemorrhage and, later, it was ascertained that she had had a miscarriage."

The court stenographer recorded in 1972 that João Alves Gondim Neto, a twenty-five-year-old student, told the Fortaleza military court that, "while he was at the barracks of the 23rd BC [Riflemen's Battalion], he was visited by someone who was seeing all prisoners, and that he is sure that he was a medical officer of the 23rd BC; that the defendant was urinating blood at that time because of beatings on his kidneys; that said person not only refused to medicate him, but also advised the torturers what parts of his body could be hit without leaving a trace."

A twenty-four-year-old student named Ottoni Guimarães Fernandes Júnior testified that "among the police officers there was a doctor whose function was to revive those who were being tortured so that the torture process would not be interrupted; [Fernandes Júnior] remained two and a half days on the parrot's perch where he fainted several times . . . on those occasions injections were applied by that same doctor . . . the doctor gave him an injection that produced a violent contraction in his intestines."

A thirty-year-old São Paulo economist named Vinicius José Nogueira Caldeira Brant testified, concerning the fate of a fellow-prisoner, Eduardo (Bacuri) Leite, "that he was taken out [of the solitary cell next to his] before dawn on 27 October, three days after newspapers had published the news of his escape, and that it is public knowledge that Bacuri was assassinated with refinements of perversity."

On November 7, 1975, the journalist Rodolfo Osvaldo Konder, a codefendant in the same proceedings as the journalist Wladimir Herzog, whose martyrdom provoked the great Mass at Cardinal Arns's cathedral, testified about an episode a few weeks earlier in prison: "Someone turned on the radio and Wladimir's screams became mixed with the radio sounds. I well remember that during that phase the radio gave the news that Franco had received last rites, and that fact was recorded in my mind because at that very moment Wladimir was being tortured and was screaming."

And all of it was noted, and all of it was taken down, all of it preserved, and all of it lay buried in the archives of the Supreme Military Court: there and (or so the security agents and the judges and the generals comfortably assumed) nowhere else.

❯❯❯❯❯❯❯❯

The thing I couldn't figure out was what the judges were doing having the stenographers write any of this material down in the first place, let alone what the military archivists were doing preserving the transcripts once they'd been recorded. For that matter, I was having a hard time imagining what those trials must have been like at all. While in São Paulo I took my sense of bafflement to several lawyers who'd defended prisoners at one time or another before the military courts and endeavored to have them help me past my confusion.

"First of all, you have to understand that military justice had two phases," one of the lawyers explained to me. (Even they were reluctant to have me identify them by name, in view of the possibility that a reempowered military might one day look less than favorably on their having described its workings in detail.) "A suspect would be arrested or abducted by one of the various security units—the DOI or the OBAN, or whatever—and held incommunicado for weeks, or even months." (The OBAN, or Operação Bandeirantes—named in honor of the *bandeiras,* who were historical Brazilian explorers and treasure hunters—originally evolved in São Paulo as an extralegal enterprise, only semi-officially related to the military, although it was in fact staffed by security personnel from all the military branches and also by the police. Funded by contributions from local businessmen and multinational corporations, including Ford and General Motors, the OBAN, because of its extralegal status, had great flexibility and impunity with regard to methods of interrogation, and its "successes" in battling "subversion" meant that, from 1970 on, its structure served as a model for the creation of DOI-CODI units—Information Operations Detachment/Center for Internal Defense Operations—which then sprang up all around the country, under a centralized Army command.) "During that time, the suspect would be brutally tortured, and, presumably toward the end, forced to sign some sort of written confession," this lawyer continued. "Except for the confession, no record was kept of those proceedings. The DOI and the OBAN, I assure you, weren't taking any notes. Only after the security unit had finished with a prisoner would it hand him over to the military courts for processing, and only then could we, as lawyers, get access to our clients."

Another lawyer told me, "Normally, our first contact would come at the police station to which our client had been transferred. Usually, we'd meet in a small room with two policemen present, listening, though technically they weren't allowed to be there, even according to the rules of military justice—they just wouldn't leave. You could often see the physical evidence of torture. You'd quietly, cautiously try to get the prisoner to tell what had happened. Sometimes prisoners would just sit there crying—unable to do anything but cry. Sometimes they'd refuse to speak. Once in a while, they'd whisper, 'I was tortured, but don't tell anyone or they'll torture me again—they said so.' Or they'd be reluctant to denounce the torture because they hoped that such forbearance would earn them greater leniency from the judges. Some of the lawyers themselves advised such tactics. We, however, would urge them to denounce the torture—'There can be no defense of human rights without denunciations of violations,' we'd say—but often the prisoners just couldn't go through with it. One had to be really brave to do so."

The Brasil: Nunca Mais project's tabulations revealed that denunciations of torture occurred in some 25 percent of the cases in their files. I asked one lawyer what percentage of the clients he represented had in fact undergone torture, whether or not they denounced it. "As far as physical torture goes—beatings, drowning, shocks, that sort of thing—not everyone went through that," he replied. "But there were cases in which a person would be kidnapped from his home in the middle of the night, taken to an unknown place, kept there for three months, and forced to listen to people's screams every night, and then, even though he himself had suffered no violence, he'd sign a confession. And there were cases in which they'd arrest the man's wife in front of him and drag her away, without touching him, and he'd sign a confession. It depends on how you define torture."

Well, I suggested, what if you define torture as any form of coercion which compels someone to confess to something he would otherwise not have confessed to?

"O.K.," the lawyer replied. "By that definition, all my clients were tortured."

The prisoners would be brought before a standard military tribunal, consisting of five judges: four military officers without any legal background, who were on temporary assignment, and one civilian—the *togado,* or "robe-wearer"—who was a judge. Also in the room would be the prosecutor and the defense lawyer, both of whom were civilians; the defendant; and the court stenographer. The proceedings were technically open to the public, but they took place in military buildings and one had to leave one's ID at the entrance. I asked a lawyer whether people would come in off the street to observe the trials. "Never," he replied. "They wouldn't even walk on the same side of the street."

Before the trial got under way, the prosecutor would enter the defendant's signed confession in the record. This was in itself a violation of the Code of Military Justice, which, like the Brazilian civilian code, stipulated that only uncoerced confessions given in person before the judges were considered admissible as evidence. At the trial, the defendant might renounce his confession, saying that it had been coerced by torture. "The judges would then invariably all make disgusted faces," one of the lawyers recalled, "scowling, and saying, 'Don't write it down—it's a lie.' " The defense lawyer would appeal to the president of the court (the senior of the five justices), and the president would thereupon dictate, in his own words, a summary of the defendant's testimony. "Sometimes that summary was extremely sketchy," the lawyer recalled. "The defense lawyer would then insist on a more thorough transcription. Sometimes we'd have to insist very hard, and sometimes even that wouldn't work. But in a later phase of the proceedings the defendant would be asked if he had anything more to say, and we'd have prepared him to say yes and present the court with a written version of the denunciation, which then had to be entered in the record."

I asked one lawyer what impact such denunciations had on the progress of a case.

"Once in a while, some of the judges were shaken. Once in a while, they ordered a corroborating medical exam. But usually the denunciation had no mitigating impact on sentencing at all. In fact, in some cases it only inflamed the judges. 'The defendant is not happy just to be a subversive,' they might declare. 'He insists on further abusing the law by showing contempt for the court with his filthy lies.' "

In any event the verdict would always be appealed to the Supreme Military Court, in Brasília, by the losing side. That body consisted of fifteen judges—four generals, three Air Force commanders, three admirals, and five civilians—ranged behind a horseshoe-shaped bench. " 'Mules' justice,' we'd end up telling each other, when, as usual, they ruled against us," one lawyer said.

The defendant himself would not be present at these proceedings—only his lawyer. "The judges on the Supreme Court had life appointments," another lawyer explained. "They'd sit at their horseshoe bench, with the president of the court—who was elected by his fellows every few years—at the base of the U, the youngest, newest members to his left, and then the older members coming up on the right side, the most senior sitting directly to his right. The more junior members of the court, who had more recent nonjudicial military exposure, tended to be the most hard-line. We'd pitch our arguments to the more senior ones, who, as time passed, tended to distance themselves more and more from their purely military identifications. One judge in particular seemed open to our denunciations of torture—he would ask for more information, and so forth. He was never elected by his fellows to the court's presidency, he stopped getting invited to the group's Christmas dinners, and when his daughter, fairly late in the dictatorship—in 1981—scored first in the state bar exam, she was denied employment as a judge or a prosecutor. She has since become active in the human-rights movement."

One lawyer said, "The Supreme Military Court Building in Brasília was a strange place. Its modernist façade with blue-tinted glass made you think when you were inside looking out that it was perpetually raining. It was inaugurated during the presidency of Emílio Médici"—between 1969 and 1974, the period when torture was at its worst—"and the judges had only reluctantly transferred to Brasília from their much more comfortable quarters in Rio. In fact, they'd transferred their quarters with them, so that inside this modern glass shell everything was antique, dark wood, neocolonial. Hanging on the wall above the place where the court president sat in the public hearing room was a large crucifix. All the military tribunals were overseen, as it were, by crucifixes, but this one, which the judges had brought up with them from Rio, was especially ornate, and portrayed Christ's death agony with exceptionally gruesome realism. It proved quite a presence during much of the testimony."

I asked the lawyers I talked to, and other observers, why the judges had allowed the denunciations of torture to be entered in the record and then allowed the records to be preserved. Some of the lawyers couldn't comprehend my question. "What do you mean?" they'd counter. "It was the law—they had to." Alfred Stepan, back at Columbia, had suggested that "Record keeping like that is part of a long Iberian tradition of thoroughly recording acts of state, which, as acts of state, could not by definition be viewed as suspect or illegal. England and the United States," he continued, "are by contrast at the bottom of the list of states that require charters and records for everything. The Iberians have a strong tradition of the state's noting, monitoring, recording. Remember, Brazil itself was founded by the state, not by its colonists, so there's never been a particularly robust civil society."

"If the judges had refused to enter the denunciations in the record, the defense attorneys would have probably just got up and left," one lawyer suggested. "The judges didn't want things to descend to the level of farce. There was a sense of minimum obligation. But recording the testimony was as far as it went. They hardly ever pursued an investigation of the charges, launched prosecutions against repeatedly mentioned torturers, or altered the outcome of cases." Somebody else told me, "There's a common Brazilian expression—'For friends, everything. For enemies, justice.' They didn't think they were doing anything wrong."

"Remember," Ralph Della Cava advised me, "all this was occurring in a broader context, in which the military were all along reluctant to make a final break with the previous constitutional order. They saw themselves as the protectors of one interpretation, anyway, of its continuity. Even when they were ruling by decree, there were various constitutions still in varying degrees of effect. They even continued to permit political parties. I mean, they defined which political parties would be allowed and what they'd be allowed to advocate, but they didn't ban them outright. For some reason, that façade was important to them."

"They never dreamed that any of this would be used against them," Jaime Wright commented. "They never imagined they'd ever lose power."

"They were like the Nazis," another of my informants said. "They imagined that they were laying the groundwork for a civilization that would last a thousand years—that, far from having to justify themselves for occasional lapses, they would be celebrated by all posterity for the breadth of their achievement."

"The Brazilian military are very efficient," I was told. "They always keep records. There are records for rebellions going back to the eighteen-hundreds and the seventeen-hundreds, although many of them are in archives in the United States, spirited off like the Elgin marbles. Of course, more recently the military have destroyed such records whenever they were leaving power. They did so in 1945, for instance."

"The judges no doubt assumed," one of the lawyers told me, "that the same thing would happen this time that happened in 1945—the records would all be burned, and they themselves, of course, would be immune. In fact, the records probably would have been destroyed this time, too, if not for the Brasil: Nunca Mais project. It's surprising that they were still around as late as 1979. Probably the military people were waiting till power was transferred to a civilian legislature, over which they would still have had considerable influence, and which they could have pressured to pass some sort of classified-archives law, wherein all top-secret papers of a certain sort would be reviewed and destroyed every two years—something like that."

"Face it," another of the lawyers suggested. "Dictatorships are men's creations, and they, too, make mistakes."

Wright closed the door, turned on the light, and said, "This, I believe, is what you came down here to see." We were standing in the final storehouse, the one they'd suddenly had to transfer everything to on the Weekend of the Convert. Rows and rows of gray metal bookshelves—hundreds of light-brown cardboard filing containers ranged one beside the next. "We tell the people who work here in the building, the janitors and so forth, that these are just some of the Cardinal's personal papers, and that seems to satisfy them."

We opened several of the containers: nothing particularly surprising—just several hundred xeroxed pages in each one. Occasionally Wright would pause to read out a passage of testimony. (For instance, that of a twenty-year-old journalist from Rio, Miriam de Almeida Leitão Netto, who contended at her 1973 hearing, according to her judge's paraphrase, "that despite her being pregnant at the time and her torturers being aware of it, she was left without food for several days, and that the persons conducting the interrogations let dogs and snakes loose on her," and so forth.)

"Here is an interesting and especially valuable offshoot of the main project," Wright said, pointing out six gray metal filing cabinets. He opened a few of the drawers, revealing a sequence of manila folders, numbered 1 through—he slid open the last drawer—10,170. "The military prosecutors would enter all sorts of tangential confiscated documents as evidence during their inquests of the various leftist groups," he explained. "Pamphlets, manifestos, booklets, correspondence. So, as we were collating our million pages, we removed the photocopies of all such documents and gathered them together here. This, therefore, constitutes without doubt the world's most complete archive of literature and ephemera produced by the Brazilian left during the sixties and seventies. Even the Supreme Military Court doesn't have anything to match this collection, since there the documents are all scattered among the seven thousand different cases." The collection is indexed and cross-referenced, according to five different classification schemes.

"Over here," he continued, taking me around to the other side of the storeroom, "are our two computers." They were desk-top models. "And then over here is a copy of the initial report we were able to generate using them. Project A, we called it."

Project A is a comprehensive, 6,946-page survey of the material in the million pages. It was essentially put together by three of the principal coordinators of the entire Brasil: Nunca Mais project and constitutes the core of their achievement. It includes more than a hundred and twenty statistical tables and also exhaustive lists in several subject categories. It consists of twelve volumes, bound in black leather, and has been published in a run of thirty complete sets. One set will be housed at Columbia University; another will be available at the World Council of Churches headquarters in Geneva, which already has a complete set of the million pages in microfilm; and there will be a complete set in the library of each of the major universities throughout Brazil.

"Here, for example," Wright said, reaching toward the shelf, "are three volumes—let's see, twenty-seven hundred pages—collectively entitled *As Torturas* (The Tortures). These contain the verbatim transcripts of all 1,843 denunciations of torture found in the collection. Each entry is headed with a box giving the name of the victim and denouncer (for instance, this one, No. 1635, is Rosalina Madeira Wetten), along with occupation (in her case, *dona de casa,* housewife), age (sixty-one), year of trial and denunciation (1977), site of torture (DOI-CODI headquarters in Rio), and then the details of where the original transcript of the testimony can be found in the archives. This woman's testimony goes on for three pages. Some are longer, some shorter." (Mrs. Wetten, a heart patient, had been kidnapped by four strangers while on an errand on behalf of her diabetic daughter—who, incidentally, was kidnapped the next day in a separate incident. Mrs. Wetten was forced into a car, hooded, taken to a cell and forced to undress in front of five male strangers. She found this particularly humiliating: a shy woman, she told the court that she didn't even undress in front of her husband. She was compelled to stand for hours without being offered food or drink, submitted to some sort of mechanical torture which left her scarred, and then eventually taken out of the cell and dumped in a strange neighborhood.)

Setting those volumes aside and reaching for another, Wright said, "Here is a volume called *Os Atingidos* (The Victims). This one contains over three hundred pages of computer readouts listing the names of 17,420 individuals who were caught up in the military-justice system in one way or another. We've divided them into four categories: those charged and taken to court (it is exclusively from this group that we've been able to extract the transcribed denunciations); those charged but not taken to court; witnesses who were arrested but not themselves charged; and others, not necessarily witnesses, who were arrested and required to depose." Each single-line entry lists an individual's name, sex, age, occupation, group or party affiliation, and Brasil: Nunca Mais case number, and gives a brief history of his or her case's transit through the military-justice system. There were about sixty entries per page. Some names appeared more than once; this meant that those people had been subjected to more than one inquisition. The military justices in Brazil apparently didn't subscribe to the doctrine of double jeopardy.

"This," Wright said, taking down another volume, "is *Os Funcionários* (The Functionaries). Again, these are simply computer readouts, divided into several categories. First come the torturers. Here we have about a thousand entries, but many of them are multiple listings—versions of the same name appearing in several denunciations. That's what these brackets along the side indicate. For instance, here is this fellow Ailton, a real monster—he shows up more than twenty times. Each entry provides the rank, service, and name as they were listed in the denunciation, the site of the torture, the year, the number of the denunciation (that refers to the 1,843 verbatim transcripts in the first three volumes), the Brasil: Nunca Mais case number, and then, over here, whenever we were able to ascertain it through additional research, the torturer's full name and identification. All told, there are 444 different names. Other lists in this volume document all those who participated in arrests, roundups, and investigations; those who were in charge of investigations; the medical examiners . . . Now, that's an interesting list—doctors who either participated in torture or signed death certificates. We don't give out this list, because it can be misleading. Some of these doctors were faithful to their Hippocratic oath and did not collaborate; if they were required to perform an autopsy, for example, they accurately recorded the cause of death—something a lot of doctors did not do. Others were especially notorious—this Isaac Abramovitc, for instance, or this Harry Shibata. Their names, as you can see, just keep showing up again and again. Let's see, other categories: lists of collaborators and informers; lists of all the members of repressive organizations, federal and state; those who acted as court recorders, stenographers . . .

"Here, look at this! Fascinating names keep popping up. Here we have Dulcidio Wanderley Boschilia, a first sergeant serving as court recorder in the São Paulo district in 1971 and 1972. Today, he's one of the top soccer referees in the country. There was a big item in the paper about him. He's a good referee, too; the military training helped. There was no way he could have avoided serving as a court reporter—it was just his assignment and in itself it wasn't anything bad. In fact, as I recall, he was a good stenographer.

"Let's see, what else? Oh, yes, finally, a list of all the judges in the military courts. I had to type the page numbers on all these pages, and some names would just catch my eye. Now, keep in mind that for officers to be eligible to serve as judges they had to have attended military school, and that means that they often came from military families, and the families often revealed something of their politics in their choice of children's names. So, here, look at this one, a Navy lieutenant commander—Hitler de Oliveira Mota. Or this one, an Army major—Mussoline da Silveira Soares."

Wright reached for another volume, entitled *Perfil dos Atingidos* (Profile of the Victims). "Here we've analyzed the ideology, group affiliations, and professions of the victims. This volume is more descriptive—it's not just lists. It includes a remarkable piece of work—a long historical survey that culminates in this chart here, 'An Organogram of the Left,' which documents the progressive fragmentation of the left, in the face of government repression, into close to fifty factions and subfactions." The chart looked something like a gaga family tree, with each branch dated and leading to another initialled subgroup, with its own abbreviated destiny. Wright said, "If there's any humor in the project, I suppose it's in this section—all the petty faction fights. But it's a dark humor. You can imagine how effective they might have been if they had stayed united. Instead, it was no contest—the regime had an overwhelming advantage."

Wright pulled down another volume—*Os Mortos* (The Dead). "Here we have each recorded instance in which someone testified about the death of a political activist or prisoner. These deaths were often officially attributed to car accidents or attempted escapes, but this testimony shows that the deaths were more often than not the result of torture." Wright flipped through the pages. "A hundred and forty-four cases." He paused when he came to three brief transcript excerpts devoted to the fate of Paulo Stuart Wright. In the back of the volume was an appendix listing 125 people who had disappeared and whose fate was not documented in any way.

Wright reached for yet another volume. "This one consists of a detailed statistical survey of all the different types of torture found among our base of 1,843 denunciations. We were able to isolate 283 different types of torture. They're listed in alphabetical order in this chart, along with rate of incidence, and then subdivided by type. There's moral/psychological, general physical, and physical specific, which is subdivided into sexual; electrical; with instruments for cutting or burning; with mechanical instruments, such as the '*coroa de Cristo,*' or 'Christ's crown,' in which a metal band is squeezed tighter and tighter about the victim's forehead until the skull cracks; edge-of-death tortures, such as drowning; and combined tortures, as when a person was doused with water in order to heighten electrical conductivity. And then there are the atypical tortures—cockroaches inserted in the anus, being forced to ingest large quantities of salt and then denied water for several days, being forced to drink one's own urine, seeing one's child dangled outside an upper-story window with the threat to let go.

"Our people broke down the denunciations in all sorts of ways. By sex: 1,461 male; 382 female. By age: 495 between the ages of twenty-two and twenty-five; 442 between twenty-six and thirty; 27 denunciations by individuals over sixty. We've got a chart of the types of torture broken down by age and by sex. We've compiled a list of the sites where torture took place—we were able to identify 242 such places in all—broken down by state and by security organization in charge. Sometimes I wonder how our team was able to do all this in just a few years. We've got incidence of torture by year. As you can see, 1969 and 1970 were by far the worst: over a thousand in each year." (There were denunciations that involved tortures taking place in several years, and also some that testified to the tortures of others besides the defendant.) "But there were already 203 as early as 1964, and there were 585 as late as 1975, when the liberalization was supposed to have been well under way. Also, you get some strange statistical bulges. Here you can see that disappearances actually went *up* once the *abertura* started—probably partly because the security services despaired of having their victims handled in the old-fashioned way by the courts, with outright repression waning, but also because there were incriminating witnesses who now had to be eliminated. And then we've got an extraordinary sequence of charts that take particular torture centers—for instance, this chart here, on the notorious Rio headquarters of the DOI-CODI—and break up the denunciations of torture by year, vertically, and type, horizontally. So you can see that at that location electric shocks, for example, were at their peak in 1970 but sexual violations didn't reach their peak until 1977."

Wright paused for a moment, gazing at the stack of volumes he'd piled up. "It's as if the team members wrung every last piece of information out of the material"—his hands squeezed an imaginary sponge—"so that there wouldn't be any possibility of an original angle for future researchers."

Yes, that was how it was. But something else about the Brasil: Nunca Mais project's thoroughness struck me—or, rather, not so much about the thoroughness as about the manner of presentation. It was almost as if through the pristine elegance of the way they marshalled their exhaustive data the team members had imagined they might somehow be able to overmaster the horror.

As Project A ballooned to its 6,946 pages and twelve volumes, the coordinators of the enterprise realized that a more succinct summary volume would have to be prepared—a Project B, as they took to calling it—and that it would have to be drafted by experienced writers, which none of them were. Late in 1983, therefore, they decided to approach two practicing journalists for assistance on this phase of the operation. I got a chance to speak with one of the journalists.

We met in the newsroom of a major São Paulo paper, where he works, and sat huddled over to one side throughout the interview, just out of earshot of his busy colleagues. "It's hard for me to remember a lot of this," he said, "because the stories you remember are the ones you tell over and over, and I never tell any of these."

I asked him how he'd joined the project.

"One day, late in 1983, I was invited to a private meeting with the Cardinal at his home," he recalled. "I'd covered church activities, so I was known to him. He explained the situation to me—how this material had been collected, and how he especially wanted to find a way of conveying its significance to the young. He described what he and his colleagues were looking for, and he arranged for me to be taken to the storehouse and shown the material—which I was, a few days later. A second journalist was approached and, following similar interviews, invited to participate. We were given a month to review the material, at the end of which we were to present a proposed chapter outline and a schedule for completing the writing. And, of course, we were told to keep everything an absolute secret."

I asked the journalist about his initial reaction.

"I was utterly astonished at the existence of the archives and amazed that the team members had been able to keep the project a secret thus far; I was overwhelmed by the sheer amount of the material; I was frightened, as a human being; and, as a journalist, I was exhilarated."

The two journalists developed an initial outline consisting of twelve chapters and then divided up the work, each taking on the writing of six. "We had agreed that we would keep our old jobs, so as not to arouse suspicion," the journalist explained. "This meant that I was able to work on the book only at home, after ten at night. The year 1984 was an extraordinarily interesting one for a political reporter—perhaps the most exciting in Brazil since the imposition of the dictatorship, what with all the maneuvering leading toward an electoral college's selection of the first civilian President, set for January, 1985. As a journalist, I was covering all that. Reporter friends would come over after work to jabber and gossip about all the excitement, but, come ten o'clock, I'd plead drowsiness and push them out. 'How can you be sleepy at a time like this?' they'd want to know.

"I immersed myself in the material. It was a very strange time. The country was opening up, and there was a sense of buoyancy and optimism. But I was still back there in the period of darkest, most claustrophobic gloom. Friends couldn't understand why I was always so anguished. As a journalist, I had known that some of this was going on, but I'd had no idea of the depth and the systematic nature of the violence. I was constantly haunted, as I went through the material, by that sense of 'What if I'd been in this person's situation?' I'd been a student during the sixties, I'd been politically concerned. A few minor changes in my life and it could well have been me making those denunciations. In fact, it's just a fluke that it wasn't. I was eaten up by

the testimony of people whose children had been tortured as a way of getting at them, and by the stories of people who had just happened to get in the way, to be in the wrong place at the wrong time. I started having nightmares every night. My whole personality changed, partly because of the morbidity of everything I was studying, but also because of my having to keep it all a secret. I'm ordinarily a fairly open, outgoing person, so the secrecy was especially warping. The Cardinal was paying me a standard reporter's wage, but I ended up plowing it all back into psychotherapy."

I asked him whether he had discussed the project with his wife, and he said no.

"I have several kids and they were all pre-teen-age at the time," he said. "They'd ask me what was I doing, and I'd say, 'Writing a book,' and they'd ask, 'About what?' I'd say, 'Oh, it's related to the Church,' and they'd change the subject. I kept the manuscript extremely well hidden—sometimes too well. I'd occasionally be sent off on reporting assignments. Once, I came back and I'd hidden the manuscript so well I couldn't find it for two days. I became convinced that it had been confiscated."

The two journalists turned each chapter in as they went along. Jaime Wright later told me how, as each chapter arrived, the project's leaders would convene a meeting and read the chapter aloud to each other. "My specific assignment was to de-adjectivize the text—to take out any words that might indicate an ideological position or betray a lapse in balance," Wright recalled. "I subsequently reported to the Cardinal that some of the adjectives had nevertheless slipped through, and he smiled, and said, 'Well, we have to show our feelings, too.' "

My interview with the journalist was coming to its end. He told me that they had completed the manuscript during the early fall of 1984 but had held off even showing it to a publisher until after January of 1985, when the electoral college had in fact met—there had been considerable question up the the very end whether the military would allow it to—and nominated the united opposition's candidate, Tancredo Neves. "I wouldn't like to work on a project like that again," he said. "I hope I never have to." The tone of his voice, however, left little doubt that if the situation ever presented itself again he would.

We talked a bit more about the secret—how well it had held since the book's release. "I've met with the Cardinal on several occasions since then, and he's never so much as broached the subject. I don't even know if he liked the job we did." We looked out over the bustling newsroom, and I asked him whether any of his colleagues now knew of his involvement. He smiled and said no.

The way Project B was composed, chapters consisting of excerpted testimony were interleaved with chapters providing background and context. (This structure was retained in *Brasil: Nunca Mais* and its American edition.) "What happened in Brazil to produce so many acts of grim cruelty?" the report's authors thus ask after forty pages of horrifying instances. "Were these acts of inhuman hate simply the handiwork of a few insane individuals who by chance worked in official agencies?"

To answer those questions, the authors begin with a historical overview. They acknowledge that torture itself has especially deep roots in Brazilian history, going back to the time of slavery; that the Brazilian military displayed a propensity for intervening in civilian affairs well before 1964; and that even during such past interventions, torture was routinely practiced in interrogations of political dissidents. However, they maintain, what happened after 1964 was different in kind. "Torture was administered to members of the political opposition on a systematic basis. Moreover, the practice was an essential component of the semi-autonomous repressive system that eventually grew out of all proportion even to the authoritarian state itself. Torture became a daily fact of Brazilian life because those sectors within the military that justified all measures for the maintenance of internal security held sway within the state apparatus."

In trying to explain how this could have come to pass, the authors put great stress on the birth, care, and feeding of the doctrine of national security—a process of intellectual breeding and nurturing which occurred at the Escola Superior de Guerra, the Higher War College, in Rio, in the decades after its founding in 1949. The ESG was launched by veterans of the FEB, the Brazilian Expeditionary Force, which had fought during the Second World War, under American command, in Italy. The authors quote one of the doctrine's foremost theorists, General Golbery do Couto e Silva: "The FEB was not only important because of our going to Italy. Possibly more important still was the FEB's visit to the United States [on the way back]. . . . I went and my stay had a great impact on me." The report's authors further suggest that "when these officers returned to Brazil, they had been profoundly influenced by a new concept of national defense. They had learned in American war colleges that strengthening the national system against possible external attack was in fact less important than shoring up institutions against an 'internal enemy' that might be trying to undermine them."

Through the fifties, the report argues, the staff members at the ESG took some of these American notions and refined and extended them with specific application to the Brazilian situation—that of an underdeveloped nation with the potential, given the proper direction, of becoming a major world power. Against a geopolitical world view that framed all internal questions in terms of the East-West rivalry—a Third World War that the ESG staff believed was already well under way—they not only elaborated theories of why the military might someday have to intervene to protect the country from such Communist-front subterfuges as overweening labor unions and overactive land-reform movements[3] but also speculated in detail about how such interventions might be accomplished, and what sorts of policies a scientifically rigorous regime would want to pursue following such an intervention. The members of the ESG staff were quintessential technocrats—indeed, the most intellectually sophisticated proponents of this kind of doctrine anywhere in the Americas during that decade.

Their ideas gradually spread throughout the Brazilian military establishment, particularly by way of the top-level training school for the Brazilian army's high command, the Escola de Comando do Estado Maior do Exército, ECEME, where the ESG theorists had great influence and Golbery's main textbook, *Strategic Planning,* was a virtual Bible. (Any officers aspiring to higher command in the Brazilian army had to graduate from ECEME. In addition, ECEME offered frequent residencies to top officers from the military services of other South American countries, such as Uruguay.) Thus, while in 1956 ECEME's curriculum still made no mention of lectures on counterinsurgency or internal security, by 1961 such classes were proliferating, and by 1968, 222 class hours were being devoted exclusively to internal-security doctrine and another 129 to nonclassical forms of warfare, as against only 21 hours devoted to such traditional military topics as territorial defense against external aggression.

All of this was in gestation, during the early fifties, at the ESG, and in fact, it occurred to me while I was reading the *Brasil: Nunca Mais* account and others that at the very moment when a "consciousness-raising" ethos was coming into being in northeastern Brazil, as part of the incipient phase of what would become "liberation theology," its antithesis, the "doctrine of national security," was being perfected in Rio; and that many of the debates and much of the history of the ensuing thirty years throughout the Americas—in Guatemala, Chile, Argentina, Uruguay, Nicaragua, El Salvador, and so forth—could be seen in embryo during this period in Brazil.

The Brazilian military flirted with the possibility of a coup several times during the fifties and the early sixties but pulled back on each occasion. However, the ascension to the Presidency in 1961 of João Goulart, a progressive nationalist intent on various schemes for land, education, and labor reform, quickened the pace of events.[4] Goulart's intentions were resoundingly affirmed when, early in 1963, he won a landslide victory in a national plebiscite, by a margin of four to one, but the political situation continued to deteriorate, as did the economy. The *Brasil: Nunca Mais* authors suggest that (partly in response to a growing clamor from conservative elements in the Catholic hierarchy) high military officers, leading financial and industrial figures, the upper class in general, and, presently, the middle class as well were all radicalizing quite precipitately on their own, but that "the readiness of the United States to collaborate in the planned coup was the final signal that spurred to action those generals interested in overthrowing President Goulart." (Alfred Stepan has shown that of the core group of senior officers who went on to form the first military government after the coup, 100 percent had received training abroad, with 80 percent receiving such training in the United States—this as against a figure of only 24 percent foreign training for senior officers who were not in the core group.) The report's authors cite various secret American initiatives designed to further destabilize the already precarious political and economic situation (this story has been traced in compelling detail in A. J. Langguth's remarkable book *Hidden Terrors*), and they particularly highlight the clandestine activities of the American Embassy's military attaché at the time, who had been the United States Army liaison officer to the FEB back in Italy—Lieutenant Colonel Vernon Walters.

In his memoirs, *Silent Missions,* Walters, for his part, acknowledges having paid frequent calls on his close wartime buddy (and Golbery ally) General Humberto Castello Branco in the months preceding the coup that culminated in Castello Branco's being named the first President of the new military order. Walters also tells of being invited to a private luncheon with Castello Branco the day after his inauguration, and describes how, three years later, he and Castello Branco shared a "last supper" the night before Castello Branco ceded Presidential authority to a new general. But he insists that during this time he never gave Castello Branco any advice on Brazilian internal affairs, and, indeed, that the subject never came up.

Langguth paints a markedly different picture, documenting in considerable detail the intense and varied activities of both Walters and his boss, United States Ambassador Lincoln Gordon, aimed initially at undermining Goulart's authority and then at coordinating military opposition to his regime. On the night of March 27, for example—half a week before the April 1 coup—Walters was cabling assurances to the State Department that General Castello Branco had "finally accepted leadership of forces determined to resist Goulart coup or Communist takeover." (The insurgent generals and their American allies would contort themselves into all sorts of linguistic knots—speaking of "superversion," rather than "subversion," and "overmining," instead of "undermining"—in attempts to account for how a constitutionally empowered and overwhelmingly reaffirmed President needed to be prevented from undertaking a coup against himself.) A few days later, top CIA, State Department, and Defense Department officials in Washington were cabling back with highly detailed questions regarding the impending coup: "What plans are there for interdicting possible 'breakout' of First Army from Rio? We assume interdiction should occur in the escarpment area on road between Rio and São Paulo and also on road between Rio and Belo Horizonte . . . Would it be necessary for U.S. to mount large matériel program to assure success of takeover?" Just in case, a 110-ton package of arms and ammunition was massed at McGuire Air Force Base, in New Jersey, ready for immediate airlift to Brazil should Gordon deem such assistance necessary. A United States carrier task force was also dispatched toward the South Atlantic. Meanwhile, back in the American Embassy in Rio, on March 31 officials received a prearranged coded signal from the insurgent officers: "The balloon is up!" Early the next day, Ambassador Gordon gathered Walters and a few other members of his "executive action group" together in his heavily secured eighth-floor office to wait out the impending carnage. That carnage, however, never occurred, because President Goulart declined to fight: "I don't want to be responsible for bloodshed among Brazilians," he declared. By April 2, the coup had triumphed entirely, and Goulart soon went into exile in Montevideo, Uruguay.

Ambassador Gordon was quoted as saying, "This is a great moment in the history of civilization." Walters, for his part, stayed on in Brazil for another three years, and his career flourished. In 1972, President Nixon appointed him Deputy Director of the CIA, a position he held throughout the time, as was subsequently shown in congressional hearings, that U.S. intelligence services were deeply involved in covert efforts to undermine and topple President Salvador Allende in Chile. Following a hiatus during the Carter Administration, General Walters went on to serve Ronald Reagan in various capacities, initially as ambassador-at-large (travelling, for example, to Buenos Aires as early as February, 1981, to enlist the Argentine junta's assistance in providing training for the covert army the CIA was beginning to cobble together from the scattered remnants of the deposed Nicaraguan dictator Anastasio Somoza's National Guard) and then later as ambassador to the United Nations (from which pulpit he regularly excoriated the Nicaraguan Sandinistas for the way *they* were supposedly trying to destabilize *their* neighbors).

The *Brasil: Nunca Mais* authors hold the United States co-responsible to a significant degree for the doctrine of national security, its imposition on Brazil in the 1964 coup, and the growing use and increasingly effective organization of torture in Brazil thereafter. However, they also allow for specifically Brazilian contributions to the terror. "Tortures continued systematically," they quote one victim, Haroldo Borges Rodrigues Lima, a thirty-seven-year-old engineer, as testifying in 1977. "They were accompanied by threats to subject me to new and harsher torments, which were described to me in detail. They said with great pride that in this matter they owed nothing to any foreign organizations. On the contrary, they told me they were already exporting know-how on the subject."

Amplifying this theme in conversation, several of the team members told me that they felt that the Brazilians had themselves devised all sorts of tricks, such as the proper use of the parrot's perch, and the very idea of death squads (plainclothes police assassinating their foes in secret), a tactic that originated in Rio in the fifties as a means of dealing with organized petty criminals who had been managing to slip through the notoriously corrupt criminal-justice system. (This was another instance of the Brazilian fifties' incubating the rest of the century for the rest of the continent.) According to these team members, the Brazilians and the Americans together standardized these techniques and facilitated their dissemination elsewhere—to Argentina, El Salvador, Chile and so forth.

"The April 1964 takeover resulted in the shelving of nationalist proposals of development," the *Brasil: Nunca Mais* authors note, in an understatement. "Despite periodic minor adjustments, the economic policy imposed by the military depended on two major strategies: the concentration of income and the denationalization of the economy." They go on to explain that "denationalization of the economy in particular meant opening up all doors to foreign capital through measures such as easy credit and fiscal incentives for the establishment of multinational corporations in Brazil and the removal of obstacles to the repatriation of profits." The *Brasil: Nunca Mais* thesis in regard to the institutional need for systematic torture during the successive military regimes after 1964 is simple. The authors suggest that the "free market" (Chicago School type) economic model favored by the military's technocratic advisers required the creation of an "inviting" economic environment—reduced wages; subdued unions; a quiescent peasantry; lower taxes, which inevitably led to cuts in social services; and so forth. The military and their advisers had decided that such a model was not only good for the nation but essential to its destiny; indeed, they decreed as much.[5] However, the model evoked substantial opposition from the great masses of people whose livelihoods were going to suffer as a result of its imposition. The doctrine of national security—the whole body of teachings that had been promulgated for decades at the ESG—allowed the military to dismiss such opposition as fundamentally antithetical to the "national interest," and to move actively toward its suppression.

The *Brasil: Nunca Mais* authors acknowledge that during "the early years of the regime, from 1964 to 1968, some semblance of democratic normality was maintained," but point out that from the start formerly legitimate avenues for the expression of opposition—legislatures, the press, unions, peasant leagues—were increasingly constricted through a succession of Institutional Acts, which forced such opposition into more and more marginal venues. By 1968, the authorities in Brazil (like those in many places around the world) were facing an increasingly angry and active opposition movement, which began to turn to factionalized but still fairly dynamic urban-guerrilla strategies. Alongside this development, by 1968 in Brazil (as elsewhere in the world) students were becoming increasingly restive. Through the 1964–1968 period, the military had been relying more and more on its security services to identify and suppress the opposition, but in 1968 the "vicious cycle" of repression provoking armed resistance in turn provoking harsher repression culminated in the promulgation of Institutional Act No. 5—an act that introduced a period of what the *Brasil: Nunca Mais* authors describe as "barefaced dictatorship." In effect, what was happening was a slow-motion "coup within the coup," with the hard-liners affiliated with General Artur da Costa e Silva and (after his stroke) his successor, General Emílio Médici, wresting the Presidency and the direction of "the revolution" away from those who had surrounded the first President, Castello Branco. "When Médici took office on 30 October 1969 with the motto 'Security and Development,' he ushered in the most repressive and violent period since Brazil had become a republic," the report's authors assert. "A number of totally independent 'security organs' were created to carry out the suppression of civil liberties. In the following years, thousands of Brazilians were sent to torture, and killings by the state became routine."

Brazil did experience phenomenal growth once the generals had dampened resistance to their technocrats' policies (according to the World Bank, for example, between 1968 and 1973 Brazil registered successive annual industrial growth rates of 13.3 percent, 12.1 percent, 10.4 percent, 14.3 percent, 13.4 percent, and 15.8 percent), but the Brazilian Miracle, as it came to be called, benefitted only the richest 10 percent of the population. Everyone else got much poorer. According to the Brazilian government's own statistics, the richest 10 percent, who in 1960 controlled almost 40 percent of the country's wealth, had by 1976 increased their share to almost 60 percent. The share of the poorest 50 percent went from 17.4 percent to 13.5 percent during the same period—a decline of almost a quarter in their already meager share of the pie. (In 1980, the bottom 25 percent of the population registered no income at all, and the next 25 percent earned below the minimum wage.)

And, indeed, that was the plan. The "free market" technocrats were deliberately seeking to concentrate wealth in such a way as to generate a certain kind of growth surge, which would propel Brazil into the front ranks of World Players in the East-West rivalry. Poverty, the technocrats surmised, might be resolved later on, through some sort of trickle-down. But if so, it hasn't happened yet.[6] Paulo Sérgio Pinheiro, a noted São Paulo newspaper columnist, summarized the situation for me by saying that according to various indicators of such things as education, housing, health care, and mortality rates, the country that Brazil most resembles in the world today is the Republic of South Africa.

As *Brasil: Nunca Mais* makes clear, the extensive, systematic use of torture in Brazil began to subside after 1974, when the hard-liner Médici was replaced by General Ernesto Geisel, who now launched a very gradual process of liberalization, initially known as the *distensão,* or relaxation. The report's authors emphasize the role of growing pressure from civil society in forcing the generals into that process. But others have suggested that the emphasis may belong elsewhere. Alfred Stepan of Columbia University commented to me that "to understand the coup, and what happened afterward, you have to look at the internal dynamics of the Brazilian military as an institution—why various groups of officers at various points behaved in certain ways and how that behavior changed." (Stepan undertook precisely that sort of investigation in his 1971 book, *The Military in Politics*—which he wrote while affiliated with the Rand Corporation—and in its 1988 sequel, *Rethinking Military Politics: Brazil and the Southern Cone.*) Elio Gaspari, the deputy director of the newsweekly *Veja,* made much the same point when I spoke with him in his offices in São Paulo.

Both Stepan and Gaspari portray the events in Brazil from 1964 through 1986 as a military revolution that escaped the control of the generals who launched it and was only subsequently recaptured by them. They point out, for example, that General Golbery, perhaps the foremost proponent and expounder of the doctrine of national security and a close ally of and adviser to General Castello Branco, the first

President, was frozen out by Castello Branco's successors, the hard-liners Costa e Silva and Médici, during whose terms the security services' terror reached its highest levels; and that Golbery resurfaced only in 1973, as a close adviser to *their* successor, General Geisel, one of whose main goals was to rein in their excesses.

Gaspari argues that torture came to a stop in Brazil in the years between 1975 and 1986 not so much because of the protests and resistance of civil society, as personified in Cardinal Arns, as because the military itself decided to put an end to it, for its own reasons. Stepan offers a variation on this theme, suggesting that Geisel and Golbery, and later General Figuereido, entered into a sort of tactical alliance with civil society against the torturers and their sponsors in the security hierarchy—opening up the press, for example, so as to further discredit and isolate the hard-liners—but that this tactical alliance got away from them, and the civilian opposition grew and consolidated itself much more quickly than they had imagined it would. Hence the surprising and, from their point of view, by no means welcome Presidential ascendancy of Tancredo Neves already in 1985. (Ralph Della Cava agrees up to a point with this interpretation, but he's not so sure about the extent to which the military has in fact lost control of the state, even with the recent victories of the opposition. He feels that a sort of military-industrial complex in effect still runs the country from its bases in the five key "cutting edge" economic sectors of arms manufacture, computers, nuclear energy, aerospace, and telecommunications, in all of which the military still commands a dominant position, no matter what the civilian façade.)

"There are all kinds of things wrong with torture," Gaspari told me, "but one of the main ones is that it poisons the system. For one thing, a sort of gangrene sets in, an accumulation of peripheral debts contracted in clandestinity which can only be rewarded illegally. The agencies working extralegally inevitably start behaving illegally as well: the torturers become smugglers and blackmailers and extortionists, and no one dares to stop them. Beyond that, unless everyone in the army participates in the torture you quickly develop two kinds of soldiers in your army—combatants, who are fighting the terrorists, and bureaucrats, who see to the army's everyday functioning and continuity. A day will come when the combatant will not accept the orders of the bureaucrat. If two majors are vying for the same promotion and the bureaucrat wins, the combatant may withhold his allegiance. This leads to terrible indiscipline and institutional instability. The military traditionally launch the coup in the first place because of the institutional instability of the civilian politicians, but one of the great paradoxes is that there is never so much military indiscipline and institutional instability as during a military dictatorship, especially when part of the dictatorship is engaging in torture. Here in Brazil, we were seeing rebellions of one sort or another almost every six months.

"There were people in the military—notably Golbery and his associates—who realized that the torturers were going to have to be isolated, marginalized, and eliminated, *so as to save the Army.* Those people grew in authority—especially after 1972, when two cases in particular galvanized a change in military opinion. One was the case of a battalion commander who ended up killing two soldiers while torturing them in connection with an investigation of allegations that they had been smoking marijuana. My God, the officers began to think, we're killing our own. The other case involved an incident in which a security agent was taking sexual advantage of members of a prisoner's family who were coming in to plead on the prisoner's behalf. The agent was having sex with a female relative of the prisoner after leading her to believe that he'd intercede in some fashion on his behalf—that sort of thing. And this horrified them. It's very strange. Rape as a part of torture was perfectly OK: that was an effective method of investigation, a way of sparking fear which would provoke confession and elicit information—all very professional. But rape for pleasure—the very thought that the torturer could be doing anything for his own pleasure—that really shook them up. After that, the tide began to turn."

I tried some of these notions out on some of the Brasil: Nunca Mais people with whom I spoke, and while they agreed that there were complexities to the military's internal dynamic which their survey had barely touched, they also felt that the importance of those internal differences could be overstated. "Look," one of them told me. "Some people want to make this distinction between the good technocrats and the bad torturers. Castello Branco and Golbery were good; they briefly lost out to Costa e Silva and Médici who made the mess, but then Golbery and company resurfaced with Geisel and his successor Figueiredo, and they cleaned up their own shop. The trouble with that kind of account is that, one, Golbery was one of the foremost theorists of the doctrine of national security in the first place. Two, although torture peaked in the late sixties and early seventies under Médici, there was already a lot of it as early as 1964 under the technocrats. Three, it was in 1964 already that the technocrats established the SNI"—Service of National Information—"as a sort of Brazilian combination FBI/CIA, with Golbery as its first head. Now, even Golbery subsequently despaired of having created a monster in the SNI, this massive security pyramid with the interrogation chambers as its base. But the most important point is that that evolution was inevitable. The technocrats endorsed and enforced a particular economic plan at the outset; and they were only too happy to take credit for the economic successes of that policy in the Brazilian Miracle. Golbery, for his part, spent his sabbatical years as the president of Dow Chemical–Brazil. But they cannot then disclaim responsibility for the subsequent upsurge of the torture network that proved necessary in keeping that plan on track. So yes, there were internal distinctions to the dynamic, but, finally, the doctrine of national security that justified the coup subsequently mandated the torture."[7]

Summing up the legacy of the doctrine of national security, the *Brasil: Nunca Mais* authors wrote: "It exposed Brazilian citizens to the arbitrary exercise of power, foisting upon the nation an imported ideology which, when applied to Brazil, produced a prolonged period of unjust social policies. In the final analysis, these policies sought to perpetuate longstanding social inequalities." One can't help but savor the bitterly intended irony of the phrase "an imported ideology" in that formulation.[8]

Late in the fall of 1984, Cardinal Arns invited Frei Ludovico Gomes de Castro, the director of Vozes, the foremost Catholic publishing house in Brazil, to a confidential meeting. Arns told him that the manuscript he was about to hand him needed to be treated with the utmost discretion, that he would permit him to read it on condition that he discussed neither its contents nor its very existence with anyone else, and that if he then was interested in publishing it he would permit him to do so only on three conditions: that he maintain absolute secrecy in the production of the book right through the date of publication, that there be no advance publicity for the book as the date approached, and that there be no announcement whatever on the date itself and no publicity of any kind thereafter. The book was simply to start surfacing in bookstores all around the country and then take on its own life.

Frei Ludovico, who, like Arns, is a Franciscan, asked for and was granted permission to show the manuscript to just one colleague at the publishing house, another Franciscan—indeed, a former student of Arns's. This was Frei Leonardo Boff, the great theorist of liberation theology and the people's church—who, incidentally, during that very period was coming under increasingly stern scrutiny by conservatives at the Vatican. Frei Leonardo quickly reviewed the manuscript and reported to Frei Ludovico that not only would it prove to be one of the most important books in Brazilian history but henceforth there would be Brazilian history before and Brazilian history after its publication.

Frei Ludovico agreed to publish Project B under the conditions stipulated. The book still did not have a name. In fact, up to that point the entire secret enterprise had gone under the mysterious acronym TPP—short, in the minds of its coordinators, for *Testemunhos Para a Paz* (Testimonies for Peace). All the computer questionnaires and the archival forms, for example, bore those initials. At the last minute, the project coordinators decided to change the name to *Brasil: Nunca Mais,* drawing their inspiration from the recent publication of the Argentine volume *Nunca Más.* In doing so, they hoped to further guarantee the project's retrospective security.

The team decided to delay publication until after the inauguration of the civilian President-elect, Tancredo Neves, which was slated for March 15, 1985. They did not want to chance provoking the cancellation, by a suddenly spooked military, of that inauguration. They also resolved to hold off publication of the list of 444 torturers a while longer than publication of the book—until the renascent democracy could take somewhat firmer root. The tragic lingering illness and subsequent death of Tancredo Neves before he could assume the Presidency, and his replacement by his running mate, José Sarney, a considerably more conservative politician—in fact, one who had been a longtime ally of the military and had been selected as the united opposition's Vice-Presidential candidate only in order to widen the front's appeal—did not deter the team members from their resolve. If anything, the newly complicated historical circumstances heightened their eagerness not to let the record of the prior period fall by the wayside. They continued moving toward publication, which they now scheduled for July 15.

Meanwhile, Cardinal Arns sent Wright to New York City on an important mission. The team members were planning to let word leak out soon after publication that the entire archives, in microfilm form, had already been transported out of the country and were safely stashed away somewhere in Europe, thereby rendering futile any efforts at confiscation. They also felt that they needed to be able to leak news, at the time of the Brazilian edition's publication, that an American edition was already under contract and in preparation, in order to forestall any peremptory efforts at censorship or outright banning of the book in Brazil.

Wright called on Robert Bernstein, a prominent New York human-rights activist, affiliated with both Helsinki Watch and Americas Watch, who also happened to be chairman of the board of Random House. Bernstein requested that Alfred Stepan give an advisory opinion, whereupon Wright delivered the manuscript in person to Stepan.

"As it happened, I was laid up in bed that week with a slipped disk," Stepan told me. "Wright came over to my home. He seemed incredibly nervous as he described the project to me—perhaps more than he needed to be, but then again, perhaps not. He struck me as 100 percent dedicated, 90 percent sure that they had indeed pulled things off, but still 10 percent worried. You can imagine—he'd been living with that tremendous anxiety for over five years. Anyhow, he left the Portuguese manuscript with me overnight, I started reading, and I found myself progressively more absorbed and, indeed, flabbergasted. I mean, I'd certainly known something of the existence of political torture in Brazil. But this was astonishing—both in terms of the nature of the evidence gathered and the fact of who had done the gathering. And the scale—this had clearly been an enormous project, and somehow they'd managed to keep it a secret. As a scholar, I'd had my thoughts, but I never expected to have them confirmed. These people had proved the systematic nature and extent of torture in Brazil. Without this book, it would have been possible to go on denying such allegations, as many had been trying to do, but after this book the facts were undeniable. Beyond all that, as you can imagine, it was an extraordinary experience for me personally to be reading such a text amidst all that druggy pain."

Stepan, of course, conveyed an enthusiastic recommendation to Bernstein, and Random House quietly fell in line with the developing project.

Wright himself did the translation for the American edition, accomplishing much of the task in a single month of seclusion in Geneva. On one of his last days there, he called on his colleague Philip Potter, the recently retired general secretary of the World Council of Churches, who had known Wright's murdered brother Paulo in his own days as a Christian youth activist, and who had in effect been the principal financial backer of the entire Brasil: Nunca Mais project, in his capacity as leader of the WCC. In a significant gesture of ecumenical solidarity, Potter had readily agreed to write a foreword for both the American and the Brazilian editions, to accompany Cardinal Arns's preface. Handing the foreword's typescript over to Wright, Potter now said, "You know what has been moving me so much in all this, Jaime? That finally, with this volume, we will be doing justice to your brother Paulo and the others like him."

Wright returned to São Paulo and delivered Potter's foreword to the printers. The book rolled silently on toward publication.

On July 15, 1985, without any fanfare, copies of *Brasil: Nunca Mais* started appearing in bookstores all over Brazil. Apparently, distribution to Brasília itself was lagging behind, for on July 16 the justices of the Supreme Military Court dispatched a staff person by plane to Rio to pick up a copy. On his return, they closeted themselves, launched an extensive (and eventually fruitless) investigation into the monumental security foul-up, briefly considered invoking the dormant but still valid National Security Law in order to ban the book altogether, received word of both the upcoming American edition and the safely hidden microfilm, and decided instead to just do nothing and hope that the book's publication would pass unnoticed.

The following week, Elio Gaspari's *Veja* devoted a three-page spread to news of the mysterious book's publication. The week after that, on July 31, 1985, *Brasil: Nunca Mais* made its first appearance on the national best-seller list—at No. 1, a position it retained for the next twenty-five weeks. It has since gone through twenty printings, and as recently as April, 1987, it was still on the best-seller list. With more than 200,000 copies in circulation, it has become the single best-selling book of nonfiction in Brazilian literary history.

The Cardinal's personal staff, I was told, were torn in the days immediately following the book's release—astonished and admiring at their boss's extraordinary ability to keep a secret, hurt that he'd kept it from them.

The newspapers were scrambling for fresh angles on the story. "One afternoon," the journalist who had been a co-author of Project B told me, "the reporters and the editors here at the paper were having one of our weekly story meetings, to plot new assignments. This big new sensation *Brasil: Nunca Mais* came up in the conversation, and somebody said, 'You know what I really wish is that somebody would try to find out who put that book together and how they did it.' Someone else chimed in, 'Yeah, why don't you take a crack at it?'—speaking to me. 'You're in real tight with the Cardinal.' It was an excruciating moment for me as a journalist—to be sitting on such a scoop and to have to keep sitting on it. In fact, I ended up slouching, and slouching further—so far that I almost slid right out of my chair. But, thank goodness, the conversation soon moved on to other topics."

I asked the man who had coordinated the photocopying part of the operation in Brasília how he felt on the day of the book's publication.

"Relieved."

I asked him how he felt the first time he came upon a copy in a store.

"Emotional."

Did he buy it?

"No. An unsuspecting friend had already given me a copy as a gift. Afterward, several other friends gave me several other copies."

One day, the journalist's kids asked him what had become of the book he'd been working on. He took them aside, swore them to secrecy, and then whispered to them that the manuscript had become this *Brasil: Nunca Mais* they'd been seeing at all the bookstores. "And they've kept their promise," he told me. "They haven't told anyone, even their school friends. Every week, though, they hand me that week's copy of the newspaper, with the book's position on the best-seller list circled in red."

"The book had less of an impact than one might have expected," Elio Gaspari commented when I interviewed him at his *Veja* offices.

I asked him whether he thought that *Brasil: Nunca Mais* was a book more bought than read.

"No," he said. "It is a book both bought and read—avidly read. No, that's not my point. Rather, it's a question of who has been reading it. People in this country over age forty bought few copies. Either they already knew all about the torture and didn't want or need to hear more, or they didn't know and didn't want to know. Furthermore—and this is fundamental—the book came out after the compromise of the elites had been sealed. The transition from military rule in 1985 was consummated only because the civilian elites in this country—personified by the politicians—had in effect already signalled to the generals that they would not delve into the past and would honor the amnesty. There was to be, in effect, a giant coverup—for the sake of the future, they all assured themselves. The appearance of the book was a definite snag in that coverup, but it didn't fundamentally alter the spirit of the politics which had initially sustained it. I think, however, that the compromise was possible for many reasons besides its obvious expediency. For one thing, here in Brazil, although there had been much torture, there hadn't been nearly as many disappearances or outright murders as there were in Argentina, for example. For another, what torture there had been was, for the most part, over a decade past—unlike the situation in Uruguay, for instance, where the military were torturing people right up to their abdication, in 1985. The per-capita extent of torture, for that matter, was much, much lower in Brazil than it was in Uruguay. And, perhaps most important, here in Brazil, as opposed to both Uruguay and Argentina, the military itself had played a substantial role in gradually reining in the torturers over the years since 1975—admittedly, more out of concern over the breakdown in internal discipline than out of concern for the human rights of the regime's opponents. Beyond that, large sectors of the civilian elite had at least tacitly supported the military during much of its tenure, and these people were only too happy to move on beyond such a past. At any rate, the compromise was achieved, and it now held, despite the book's publication."

"Where the book truly had an impact," Alfred Stepan told me, "was with the young, the generation that came of age in the early seventies, for whom a whole swath of history had been suppressed as part of the repression. It seems that those were the people who bought the book in such huge numbers and made it such a cultural presence. Brazil, for all its inequalities, is in many ways a consensual society—there's a great tendency to let things pass. *Brasil: Nunca Mais* worked against that tendency, so that even if its immediate political impact was relatively limited, it had a deep impact on how people, and especially the young, came to think about the recent past."

Cardinal Arns has commented that frequently on his pastoral tours through the country strangers come up to him, beaming with pride, and report, "I'm in your book—that's me on page such-and-such." They seem in some small but important way mended by the mention.

Around the time I was in São Paulo, in late 1986, one of the main characters on the country's most popular prime-time television soap opera, "Roda de Fogo" (Wheel of Fire), began carrying a copy of *Brasil: Nunca Mais* tucked prominently under her arm. Everyone I spoke with was eagerly anticipating the episode that was going to air shortly before Christmas, when—or so the tabloids were all proclaiming—this character was actually going to confront her former torturer.

Throughout the country, the compromise of the elites notwithstanding, grassroots organizations calling themselves Tortura Nunca Mais began to form, addressing themselves not only to the bedevilling legacy of past political torture but also to the scandalous problem of continuing torture and mistreatment of common criminals. I was told that most precinct houses in Brazil still have electric-shock machines and that many have parrot's perches that can be set up or struck down virtually at a moment's notice. The wildly disproportionate distribution of wealth in Brazilian society, a perennial reality aggravated by twenty years of military repression, has recently led to a sharp increase in petty crime, such as theft and pickpocketing, which, in turn, has led an anxious upper middle class to range itself increasingly behind the arbitrary and often brutal authority of the police forces. The year 1985 saw more than 550 killings by police in metropolitan São Paulo alone—an astonishing rate of well over one per day. Some victims died as they were being arrested, others from beatings routinely administered in the vans on the way to the precinct houses, others from torture administered there. In almost every instance, death was publicly attributed to the prisoner's resistance or effort at escape—just as the occasional deaths of political prisoners under military rule had been. In recent months, perhaps partly as a result of the sensation caused by *Brasil: Nunca Mais,* the Brazilian press has shown growing interest in such stories, although the middle class remains much less perturbed by arbitrary violence directed against poor people than by political violence directed against middle-class students and professionals. Cardinal Arns, for his part, has been one of the leaders trying to prick the public conscience in regard to the poor.[9]

Nor was *Brasil: Nunca Mais* wholly without tangible political impact. Partly as a result of the ground swell of public awareness and revulsion which its revelations engendered, President Sarney felt compelled, on September 23, 1985, to sign the United Nations Convention Against Torture. Only fifty-seven nations have thus far signed the Convention, and only nineteen have ratified it as well. (The United States has done neither.)

The archdiocese team waited until November 21, 1985, a few days after the first municipal elections held under the new civilian regime, to release to interested journalists its list of 444 torturers. The next morning, papers all over the country published the list in full, under headlines trumpeting some of the more surprising names. Many of the onetime torturers had in the meantime risen to high positions. Brazil's Ambassador to Paraguay, General Mário de Mello Mattos, was on the list, as was Carlos Alberto Brilhante Ustra, who was pulling down $6,000 a month as the military attaché to the Brazilian Embassy in Montevideo. Colonel Francisco Antônio Coutinho e Silva, until recently the military adviser to Jânio Quadros, the mayor of São Paulo (and, twenty-five years earlier, the Brazilian president whose tenure immediately preceded Goulart's), also made a prominent appearance on the list—a fact that provoked a sharp polemical outburst by the mayor of Brazil's largest city aimed at its archbishop. ("This is none of the Church's business," Quadros said. "I don't name priests; the Cardinal shouldn't interfere with my appointments.") Coutinho e Silva was subsequently promoted to the post of transportation director for the city of São Paulo.

In some places—notably the state of Rio, where the leftist Leonel Brizola (former President Goulart's brother-in-law) had been elected governor—some men whose names appeared on the list were summarily fired. In other places, during the months ahead, some men found their careers blocked: the list was occasionally consulted as promotions came under consideration. But for the most part those whose names appeared on the list retained their positions and, thanks to the amnesty, had little more to endure than the public's contempt.

Of all the names that appeared on the list, perhaps the most remarkable was that of General Octávio de Aguiar Medeiros. General Medeiros had come a long way since his days as a colonel with the 12th Infantry Regiment stationed in Belo Horizonte, where in 1969, according to Denunciation No. 1422 in the *Brasil: Nunca Mais* archives (that of a twenty-four-year-old student named Nilo Sérgio Menezes de Macedo), he had headed a torture team that tormented its victims with beatings, electric shocks, denial of sleep, denial of sun, denial of medical attention, and all kinds of "*selvageria animalesca,*" "animal-like savagery"—administered, it seemed, in a spirit of "pure sadism." In fact, in the years since then Medeiros had risen all the way to the directorship of the SNI, the military's combination FBI/CIA. It had been his job—if it had been anyone's—to make sure that something like the Brasil: Nunca Mais project never happened. From very early in the history of the project, its coordinators had known that the head of the SNI himself would have had a compelling personal interest in cracking their secret.

How, finally, had they managed to keep their project a secret all that time? It was a question I asked everyone I spoke with during my visit to Brazil. "That," the newspaper columnist Paulo Sérgio Pinheiro asserted, "was the *true* Brazilian Miracle."

"Yes," Elio Gaspari concurred. "In a country with no secrets, this they managed to keep a secret. It is absolutely remarkable. I think, though, that it had a lot to do with the seriousness of the people involved and the seriousness of the work. It's a little bit like the difference between the Manhattan Project and the Pentagon Papers in your United States. The people who were involved in producing the Pentagon Papers couldn't take its need for secrecy seriously, and so the story inevitably broke. But with the Manhattan Project secrecy was *of the essence.* It didn't make sense to have the project at all unless you were going to keep it a secret. I think these people were involved in a sort of Brazilian version of the Manhattan Project."

"They were able to keep it a secret because they were openly bold," Philip Potter surmised. "And because they had courage. You know the origin of the word 'courage'? It means to have heart. These people were able to hold their tongues because their hearts were full."

"Was it because the security police were stupid and inept?" Jaime Wright asked himself when I asked him my question. "Was it because they were overly confident? Perhaps, perhaps. But I think the more likely reason was that after so many years of successful repression they could not *imagine* that anyone would still have the gall to be attempting anything on such a scale. The possibility never entered their minds. It didn't—it *couldn't*—occur to them."

On my last day in São Paulo, I talked again with the man who had run the photocopying part of the operation. He joked with me about the personal costs of continuing to keep the secret. He had run as an underdog candidate in the recent district elections for a seat in the constituent assembly and lost by a relatively narrow margin. "If I had been able to mention my participation in the Brasil: Nunca Mais project, I would probably have won by a landslide," he said. "Ah, well."

I asked him, too, why he thought the secret had held.

"Efficiency," he said emphatically. "Efficiency and luck." He paused for a moment, smiling. "And divine protection."[10]

Cardinal Arns was unavailable during my visit to Brazil, but Jaime Wright agreed to pass on certain written questions to him for written reply. I asked the Cardinal about some of the religious and theological issues raised by torture. In a thoughtful and scholarly answer, he quoted one of the first Popes to condemn the medieval practice of torture, Pope Nicholas I, who, in 866 A.D., in his *Reply to the Bulgars,* wrote,

> If a thief or a footpad is arrested and denies what he is accused of, you say that the judge should have his head beaten and his chest pierced with iron pins till he confesses the crime. But neither human nor divine law permits such a thing. A confession should not be extorted but voluntarily made. If it turns out too that, after inflicting such punishment on him, you find no proof for the alleged crime, won't you be forced to recognize how wicked your action was, and be smitten with shame? In the same way, if the accused, unable to stand tortures, confesses crimes that he didn't commit, who, I ask, is responsible for that foul deed but the one who forced him into that desperate but fictitious confession? What is more, everyone knows that if a man says what isn't in his mind, he isn't confessing, he's simply uttering words. So give up such procedures. And detest, from the bottom of your hearts, what you were so demented to do.

Cardinal Arns also noted "the very simple and clear mandate against torture in the New Testament," from Luke 3:14: "Do not mistreat anyone." He quoted the Second Vatican Council's *Gaudium et Spes,* of 1965, which amplified this theme by declaring that "whatever violates the integrity of the human person—such as mutilations, physical or moral tortures and attempts at psychological domination—is effectively worthy of censure, for it greatly contradicts the honor of the Creator."

Cardinal Arns went on to explain, "The Church's condemnation of torture goes back to the Creation story, in the Old Testament: 'So God created man in his own image, in the image of God He created him; male and female He created them' (Genesis 1:27). If man was created in the image of God, the torturing of a human being violates God Himself who created him."

Jaime Wright made a similar point in a conversation I had with him. "Look," he said. "According to the Book of Genesis, a person is made in the image of God. When you're torturing someone, you're mangling and destroying the image of the Creator."

And Marshall Meyer, the former rabbi of Buenos Aires and a veteran of Argentine President Raúl Alfonsín's National Commission on the Disappeared, made reference to the same biblical passage from a Jewish perspective when I spoke with him. He quoted a passage from Sanhedrin 4:5 of the Mishnah, the codification of ancient rabbinical commentaries on the Torah: "Therefore was one single man created first, Adam, to teach you that if anyone destroys a single soul from the children of Man, Scripture charges him as though he had destroyed a whole Universe—and whoever rescues a single soul from the children of Man, Scripture credits him as if he had saved a whole Universe."

II

THE REALITY OF THE WORLD

1

Liberty

The passenger ferry out of Buenos Aires had been chugging huskily through the night, heading due east toward Montevideo, Uruguay. (Buenos Aires and Montevideo are virtually aligned along the same parallel, the thirty-fourth South, the same one, for that matter, that bisects Santiago, Chile, and Capetown, South Africa—a doleful parallel, indeed. The thirty-fourth parallel North, for its part, cuts through Beirut, Nagasaki, and Los Angeles.) After spending the first few hours above deck, gazing into the ink-black, prodigiously spangled southern sky, I'd retreated below for a few hours sleep in a cramped, windowless cabin. I'd awoken around six-thirty, gotten dressed, and clambered back up to the ship's prow. The sky was dawn-gray now, the sea gray-green, and off in the distance, where they met, the darkly silhouetted skyline of Montevideo shimmered, like a mirage. The sun, newly risen, beckoned us on, a sheet of glare spread across the waters, and uncannily, I suddenly found myself experiencing the strongest, most poignant sense of *homecoming*—an almost palpable pang. I was seeing Montevideo as if I were one of her long-exiled sons, coming home, coming home at last, recognizing each of her spires and cupolas, savoring that familiar horizon (and even gauging the way in which certain things had inexorably changed in the years of my absence), reexperiencing the whole world of memories each and every one of those spires evoked. . . . Actually, the sensation lasted only a few moments, but if I characterize that momentary feeling as uncanny, it's because in fact I'd never been near Montevideo before.

"There's our mountain," Marcelo Vignar, a burly fellow passenger with whom I'd shared a draught of beer and stars the night before, now proclaimed, coming up behind me and energetically clapping me on the shoulder with immense, friendly good vigor. " 'Monte video': 'I see the mountain!' Or else, 'Monte VI d.e.o.' " He traced the formulation with his finger along the dewy railing. "The sixth mountain you'd spot coming along the coast from the other side, *de est ouest,* from east to west." Of course, the joke was that this mountain, looming over the western flank of the rapidly approaching harbor, barely qualified as a hill. Uruguay is notoriously flat: mile after mile after mile of scrabbly, unrippled pastureland. "You remember how last night we spoke about the good old days when Uruguay was known as the Switzerland of Latin America. Well, *that* was our Alp."

We'd spoken about a lot of things the night before. Vignar was a psychoanalyst who had lived in exile from 1975 till just recently, holed up in Paris, though aching every day to return. (I suddenly realized that my uncanny surge of *déjà vu* probably derived from the fact that I'd subliminally been experiencing the oncoming vista through *his* eyes.) Yes, we'd spoken about the days when Uruguay had enjoyed a reputation as one of the most democratic, socially progressive nations *anywhere in the world*—an oasis of stability and social concord on a particularly troubled and turbulent continent. We'd spoken of the gradual disintegration, during the late fifties and sixties, of the prosperity which undergirded that stability, and of the resultant polarization of Uruguayan life—how an increasingly reactionary political establishment, confronted with a dynamic, tactically sophisticated urban guerrilla movement, the Tupamaros, came increasingly to rely on a once laughably inconsequential military apparatus for the suppression of that movement and subsequently of virtually all the country's progressive sectors (which, in Uruguay, was arguably virtually all of the country): the unions and professional associations and universities and newspapers and then the political parties themselves. We spoke of the sequence, from 1968 on, of increasingly constrictive states of emergency which culminated, in 1973, in a coup in which the military swept away even the façade of civic normalcy, launching over a decade of brazen dictatorship. From having been the freest nation in Latin America, Uruguay had transmogrified itself into the country with the highest per-capita rate of political incarceration anywhere on earth.

We spoke of his own personal experience of those years. He described how he'd been roused from his bed at three one morning in 1972, trussed up, blindfolded, hooded, and dragged to some sort of incarceration cell, accused of having given medical assistance to a Tupamaro. How long, I asked, had they kept him in prison? "An eternity," he replied emphatically, and then, sighing, softening, "Well, actually, just two months—but they didn't tell you anything, you had no idea how long they'd be holding you or what they'd be doing next. If I'd known in advance that they'd be keeping me just those two months, well, that would have been easier to endure. But instead it seemed like forever, with every second permeated by fear, by dread anticipation. *L'état de menace:* that's what makes you crazy—it's not just what they do to you but the terror of what they might do to you next, at any moment, at *every* moment." Had he himself been badly tortured? "Not nearly as badly as many of those I encountered there, or later," he assured me. "But to be torn from the everyday comfort of your home, blindfolded, hooded and dragged away for twenty-four or seventy-two hours, that's a torture in and of itself, an absolute torture—no less so for all the other horrible things they can do on top of that."

Following an urgent international campaign mounted on his behalf by loyal colleagues, he'd been released, and he and his wife, also a psychoanalyst, stayed on for another three years. "But our situation was becoming untenable," he explained. "It was becoming impossible to do psychoanalysis anymore, to listen to people in confidence, in secure privacy. Furthermore, they'd made another big sweep. Things were momentarily calm, but I was convinced they were just torturing those people, breaking them, extracting their 'confessions' and preparing to go on to the next rung in their supposed conspiracy. So we decided to flee. My first great relief, that first night in Paris, was just in going to bed. To go to bed knowing you'll be waking up, come morning, right in the same bed you've gone to sleep in—you have no idea how voluptuous a pleasure that can be."

Vignar and his wife both established new practices in Paris, often treating fellow exiles or victims of torture from the Southern Cone. His wife Maren had been the first to report the story of one small child, a patient of hers, whose tale went on to achieve an almost legendary renown among the repressed populations of the region. This five-year-old girl had been going every few weeks to visit her imprisoned father; each time she'd bring along a new crayon drawing, and each time, seemingly, the guard would forbid her delivery of the gift. "No pictures of people!" he shouted one time, confiscating the incriminating document. "No pictures of animals!" he declared the next, as he tore up her rendering of the family dog. And then the next: "No pictures of birds—birds are animals, I already told you about animals." The time after that, though, the little girl arrived with a drawing of a forest, and the guard grudgingly let it and her through. "Oh," said her father, "look at the wonderful gift you've brought me, I'll be able to put it on my wall and it will be like a window for me. Look here at these wonderful trees, the big trunks, the branches, how well you drew in the leaves, and here, what are these little circles in the foliage, are they fruit . . . ?" "Shhh," the little girl commanded her father. "Quiet, Daddy. They're the eyes of the birds. *They're hiding.*"[11]

Vignar had recalled that story for me the night before, beneath the canopy of stars, in part as a way of explaining why he'd begun returning to Montevideo now, in the wake of Uruguay's tentative return to democracy after March, 1985. He'd been going back and forth between France and Uruguay, participating in conferences with titles like The Consequences of Repression in the Southern Cone, advising former colleagues at the Colegio Médico on how to resuscitate medical education programs—basically struggling with the problem of how to help coax his severely traumatized country out of its hiding. He and his wife were wrapping up their Parisian practices and would soon be returning to Uruguay for good. He was by no means sanguine about the prospects for any quick recovery of his beleaguered homeland—the social fabric had been devastated and the economy laid waste. Even now—this was in late November, 1986, late spring in the southern hemisphere—Uruguay's reconstituted civilian parliament seemed on the verge of acceding to what he saw as the extortionate demand of an unrepentant military that a complete and unconditional amnesty be extended to any security personnel accused of human-rights abuses. Such a concession, which would foreclose not only the possibility of legal prosecution but even that of systematic documentary investigation, Vignar felt, would only further hobble the country's chances for reintegration.

This morning, though, as he stood there beside me at the ferry's prow, his legs firmly planted, his arms spread along the railing, the wind blowing through his grey-flecked beard, the sun glinting off his wide forehead, his face was exultant. "Montevideo," he kept repeating, in a kind of rapture. "Montevideo, Monte . . . video!"

The ferry docked at its regular berth in the fairly empty harbor—a harbor which seemed like it might once have enjoyed a more flourishing trade. The passengers were ushered into a clapboard hanger where a small battalion of uniformed customs officials waited to inspect our luggage. The one I drew was a sloppy, rotund, semi-comical character —a personage utterly pithed of any authority, let alone dread. He rummaged about in my bags, then splashed liberal dollops of some gooey substance on their flanks and slapped on a sequence of numbered labels: REVISADO no. 062314, 062315, 062316, etc. It all seemed an exercise in bureaucratic officiousness, an example of the sort of civil service job-padding and patronage make-work which had probably contributed to Uruguay's economic crisis in the first place. On the other hand, not that many months ago, such bureaucratic gestures would have provided a first introduction to an utterly controlling, almost strangulating structure of surveillance.

Indeed, during the decade of their hegemony, the Uruguayan military managed to run one of the most effective and pervasive totalitarian systems anywhere in the world. It wasn't just a matter of per-capita incarceration statistics, though those were astonishing. Of Uruguay's entire 1970 population of somewhat less than 3 million (half of whom lived in the capital, Montevideo), somewhere between 300,000 and 400,000 went into exile during the next decade and a half. Of those remaining, according to Amnesty International, one in every fifty was detained at one time or another for interrogation; and one in every five hundred received a long prison sentence for political offenses. (Comparable figures in the United States would have involved the emigration of nearly 30 million individuals, the detention of 5 million, and extended incarcerations for over 500,000.) The sheer scope of this emigration, detention, and incarceration, however, only begins to suggest the extent of the military's absolute mastery of Uruguayan daily life during this period.

I myself began to get a sense of what life in Montevideo must have been like during those years later that very evening when I joined Vignar for dinner at the home he had only just recently begun reclaiming. He'd invited several friends, some of whom had stayed on in Uruguay the entire time. One couple, a psychoanalyst named Ricardo and his wife Beatriz, neither of whom had been imprisoned or exiled, described how nevertheless they'd cowered the entire time. "A few years into the *dictadura,*" Beatriz recalled, "we found ourselves one evening looking over our wedding pictures—now, this was only a few years after the wedding itself—and we suddenly realized that hardly anyone in those pictures was still around: this one was in prison, that one had been disappeared, this other one was in Sweden, his former girlfriend was in Cuba, that one was dead. . . ."

"Meanwhile," Ricardo elaborated, "our own lives became increasingly constricted. The process of self-censorship was incredibly insidious: it wasn't just that you stopped talking about certain things with other people—you stopped *thinking* them yourself. Your internal dialogue just dried up. And meanwhile your circle of relationships narrowed."

"Yes, exactly!" another dinner guest concurred. "In all those years, over a decade, my husband and I made only one new set of friends."

"One was simply too scared," Ricardo continued. "You kept to yourself, you stayed home, you kept your work contacts to a minimum. The suspicion of everyone else, the sense that they were monitoring everything—or else just that reflex of self-protection, how it was perhaps better not to extend one's affections to people who might at any moment be picked up and taken away: all of that served further to famish the social fabric."

I noticed (here and elsewhere in the days ahead) how, even now, in the wake of the country's return to democracy, the language of indirection continued to hold sway: everything was "you" or "one," hardly ever "I" or "me." Cautious, elliptical, hypothetical . . . deniable. Denied already in the saying.

"It's so hard to describe, or even to remember, what our minds and mindsets were like then," Ricardo continued. "That was then and this is now—and the two seem utterly divided one from the other. Today I cannot even remember what it was like then. Then I could not even dare to fantasize what it might be like now."

"Marcelo," another guest interjected, addressing himself to our newly returned host. "The cafés—can you imagine?—cafés all over town closed down for lack of customers." (I recalled how the remarkable Uruguayan writer Eduardo Galeano had evoked the 1716 founding of Montevideo in the second volume of his *Memory of Fire* trilogy, the masterpiece he composed during his own years of homesick exile. He'd described the few shacks on the windswept cove, the general store, and then: "Out of the general store, the café will be born. Montevideo will be the city of cafés. No corner will be a corner without a café as an accessory for secrets and noise, a little temple where all loneliness can take refuge, all encounters be celebrated, with cigarette smoke serving as incense." I subsequently read the following account of the years of the dictatorship by a fine young Uruguayan sociologist named Carina Perelli: "Fear exterminated all social life in the public realm. Nobody spoke in the streets for fear of being heard. Nobody protested in the lines for fear of being reported to the police. One tried not to make new friends, for fear of being held responsible for their unknown pasts. One suspected immediately those who were more open or were less afraid, of being 'agents provocateurs' of the intelligence service. Rumors about tortures, arrests, mistreatments were so magnified by our terror as to take on epic proportions. Many cafés closed their doors for lack of patrons; the rest vegetated in the dullness of a clientele rendered morose by its self-imposed mutism. The fear of accountability loomed, larger than life, over every single activity in the public realm.")

"They seemed to know everything about everyone," another guest now put in. "It turned out that already for several years before the coup the military had been compiling archives—their *archivos*—with detailed information about people's lives and work and opinions. If you'd signed some petition years earlier on behalf of civil liberties, or in support of a strike, or against the American invasion of the Dominican Republic, it didn't matter what, it turned out they had it in their archive. They'd divided up responsibility, so that, for instance, the Navy was in charge of monitoring the employees of the state petroleum monopoly, students were the responsibility of the police, the medical profession came under the authority of the artillery."

"Yes," Vignar interjected at this point. "Remember how I told you last night about my two-month imprisonment back in 1972—now this was still before the final coup. But as I say, my colleagues at the Colegio Médico rallied on my behalf and I was released. A few days after my release, there was to be this big demonstration in support of what was by that time a rapidly expiring democracy. I anguished as to whether I should attend or not, but finally I decided to go over for just a few moments to visit with the medical contingent, who I knew would all be massed together in this one particular corner of the square, to thank them for their solidarity. Which is what I did. I wasn't there for more than five minutes. A few days later, I had to go back to the military barracks where I'd been held to sign a few papers. The commanding officer spotted me, called me over and said, ever so paternalistically, 'Do you think it's wise, Doctor, just a few days after your release, for you to be seen like that at a demonstration?' "

"They had informants everywhere," another guest explained, "or anyway made you think they did. All the phones were bugged, or might as well have been."

"And then on top of that, there was that incredible system of the A-B-C!"

The dinner guests proceeded to describe for me the way the military authorities assigned each and every Uruguayan citizen one of three classifications, the designation being stamped into his or her files at the central archives. "A" citizens were politically trustworthy and hence could be employed by the state (the country's principal employer), could travel freely, and were extended certain minimal freedoms. "B" citizens were deemed ideologically suspect and hence could be employed privately but not by the state (tens of thousands were sacked); their travel privileges were severely limited and they faced continuous petty (and sometimes not so petty) harassment by the security services. "C" citizens weren't citizens: they were pariahs, pure and simple; they'd been utterly stripped of their rights and even the possibility of employment (any private company that endeavored to hire a "C" citizen invited, for starters, a crippling series of government audits). And the point was that anyone at any time could suddenly find himself reclassified as "C"—because, after all, they knew everything.

One guest recounted the story of a friend, a systems engineer who'd been branded "C," couldn't find any work, and so went to the military authorities to appeal the designation. The officer who at length received him reviewed his file and then said, "Ah, you see, you're a sandwich man." *A sandwich man?* "Yes, son of a former Congressman and brother of a Tupamaro. You see: son-of, brother-of—the sandwich combination. I mean, you have to understand our position. If you had a house and you'd rented it and the people you'd rented it to had destroyed it and the next year their son came by wanting to rent it all over again, you wouldn't very well want to rent it to him, now, would you? It's what the Marxists call historical materialism." At which point the fellow quipped, "Gee, maybe I'd better read up on my Marx." The officer was not amused. "No," he said sternly. "No, I wouldn't recommend that at all." End of interview.

One of the couples at this dinner had brought along their daughter, now a freshman at the university but back in the early days of the *dictadura,* a young schoolgirl. "They used to have us memorize all these lessons in class," she now commented, "about the absolute evil of communism, how people in Communist societies had no freedoms, how everything down to the slightest detail was absolutely controlled, how everybody lived in total fear, and so forth, but it was hard to tell the difference with how we were actually living. Of course, you never so much as whispered this. There was incredible regimentation. They were completely maniacal on the subject of proper dress: everyone had to wear blue stockings, polished black shoes—for heaven's sake not brown, God forbid you should come in with brown shoes—no jewelry, girls had to wear their hair tied back, boys' hair had to be short-cropped. You were checked everyday, and if anything was wrong you were sent home—and if you had an exam that day, for example: tough luck. Each school was assigned a retired military officer, or else some associate or relative of a military officer, as its new director. In every class, in addition to the teacher there was a teacher's aide, someone who in the old days was supposed to facilitate interactions between teachers and students, only now he was there mainly to take notes on the behavior of both the teachers and the students."

Everything required state approval. You couldn't hold a birthday party without obtaining permission from the security officials in charge of your neighborhood precinct. Elections for team captains of amateur soccer teams were supervised by military commanders in charge of such things, who retained a veto power over the results. Between 1973 and 1982, twenty-eight newspapers, including *Marcha,* arguably the most prestigious literary-political journal in Latin America during the sixties, were shut down by the authorities. As late as 1983, another nine newspapers were closed, along with a radio station. Uruguay's once vibrant cultural life became utterly attenuated. Most writers, painters, and musicians who hadn't been arrested had fled the country. A young pianist who stayed was one day forbidden to perform Ravel's Piano Concerto for Left Hand Alone, because, naturally, it *was* for the left hand. Censorship was absolutely ironclad. Unions were gutted and quiescent; universities purged and revamped.

"The whole country was run like a prison," one of the dinner guests said, summing up. "The actual prisons were merely the punishment cells."

What in hell's name had happened here? What had become of Uruguay, "the model country," the Switzerland of Latin America, "the paradise of fat cows," the Great Exception, the Sweden of the South? I, too, remembered it that way from the report I'd largely cribbed back in elementary school from the pages of *National Geographic.* "Those who study Uruguay and Chile," Professor Charles Gillespie of the University of Wisconsin recently wrote, "traditionally dispute which country was the 'most democratic' prior to their similar fates in 1973. However, the absence of militarism made Uruguay the more politically envied nation by Latin Americans during this century." In New York, prior to my trip, I'd had occasion to talk with former ambassador George Landau, now the director of the Americas Society—and he, too, recalled Montevideo fondly from his days there as a commercial attaché on his first diplomatic posting in the early fifties. "In my time," he said wistfully, "the Uruguayan military were so marginal, so inconsequential, that they took care to change out of their uniforms each evening, before they went home, so that they wouldn't be mistaken for bus drivers." Carlos Etchegoyen, a psychotherapist I met in Montevideo and who currently specializes in the rehabilitation of victims of the recent political repression, recalled how, when he was growing up, "the military were mainly in charge of street parades and cutting the grass in the plazas and clearing the litter off the beaches."

Carlos Etchegoyen grew up, during the fifties, in a country where schooling, through the university level, was free to all citizens. The literacy rate crested above 95 percent. Full health coverage was a universal right, even if at times the standard of care was rudimentary. Special laws encouraged home ownership among a vast middle class (social scientists estimated this class at over 40 percent of the population) and protected most workers—at any rate, most urban workers—through a system of continually renewed rent freezes and subsidies. Senior citizens were equally protected through a generous web of guaranteed pensions.

This remarkable—and, at least in the Latin American context, virtually unparalleled—welfare state apparatus had its origins at the turn of this century. The independent entity known as Uruguay, for its part, had its origins during the first quarter of the last century, though European colonization of the region dates back to the first quarter of the sixteenth century. The first white man ever to make landfall on what was to become Uruguay, Juan Díaz de Solís, in 1516, was killed, along with his entire shore party, by a band of native Charruas Indians. In the years thereafter, however, the native Indian population was itself virtually wiped out by parties of Spaniards venturing east from their bases in Argentina, and Portuguese moving south from encampments in Brazil. (Uruguay today has very little mestizo presence or influence, and though there are some blacks, mostly in the rural northern areas of the country, the overwhelming majority of Uruguay's population is homogenously white European—another difference from most of the rest of the continent.) Around 1810, in a skirmish somewhat peripheral to the main Napoleonic wars consuming Europe, the Argentines declared their independence from Spain, hoping that the eastern province, the Banda Oriental, would secede with them. But an Orientalist caudillo, José Gervasio Artigas, the father of Uruguayan nationhood, thereupon declared the province's own independence, fighting both the Argentines and the Spanish loyalists garrisoned in Montevideo, and presently Brazilian troops who once again came pouring down from the north as well. In the final analysis, though, it was the British who, in 1828, in the person of diplomatic envoy Lord Ponsonby, imposed a mediated solution on the chaotic dispute, constituting the República Oriental del Uruguay, with its population of 80,000, as an independent buffer state between Argentina and Brazil.

The choas, however, hardly ended. The historian Eduardo Rodríguez Fabregat once compiled an inventory of the ensuing seventy years of Uruguayan history, through the end of the nineteenth century, tallying "four or perhaps more visible foreign interventions, thirty-seven revolutions, three mutinies, two international wars, two tyrannies and two dictatorships. In those seventy years," he continued, "there were eighteen presidents, four dictators, one triumvirate, one Council of State and your half-dozen small, indefinable interregnums. Of those eighteen presidents only eight completed their mandate. The other ten either fell to revolution or rose through it or through insurrection."

Martin Weinstein, chairman of the political science department at William Paterson State College in New Jersey, who is one of the foremost authorities on Uruguay in the United States, recently observed that "The sophisticated two-party system that would become one of the dominant features of Uruguayan political life in the twentieth century began as little more than warring bands of gauchos." In fact, those factional loyalties *predated* Uruguay's nationhood, and Uruguayans often point with pride to the fact that their two principal parties share the longest continuous histories of any two such parties in the world. In the jumble of nineteenth-century Uruguayan politics and civil warfare, one faction distinguished itself by wearing red hatbands and was hence known as the Colorados, while another wore white and was therefore labelled Blancos. Increasingly, the Colorados came to represent the interests of the capital, Montevideo, against the more rural and conservative interests championed by the Blancos. This phase of Uruguayan history came to a head in 1903 with the presidential election of a dynamic young Colorado journalist (himself the son of a Colorado general and president) named José Batlle y Ordóñez, known to his contemporaries as Don Pepe, and to posterity simply as Batlle (pronounced BAH-jay).

Batlle's election provoked one last spasm of insurrection, put down in a final military campaign during 1904. Thereafter, Batlle systematically set himself the task of nation-building. "Our republic," he proclaimed, with typically visionary fervor, "should take the advantage currently available to it of this period of formation, in which it is as easy to correct vices and incipient defects as it is to implant new institutions. . . . Our condition as a new people enables us to realize ideals of government and social organization that older countries cannot effectively implement without overcoming enormous and tenacious resistance." When opponents, like the patrician Blanco leader Luis Alberto de Herrera, would criticize the scale of his reformist ambitions, complaining that Uruguay was too small a venue for such sweeping experiments, Batlle countered, "We may be a poor and obscure minirepublic, but we will have advanced minilaws!"

The vigorously pro-labor tone of much of what came to be known as the Batllista legacy had already been foreshadowed in some of Batlle's newspaper polemics back in the 1890s. (Batlle himself had been heavily influenced by his student days on the Left Bank in Paris.) Thus, for example, in 1896 he had affirmed that "Strikes are a protest against the invariably precarious general situation of the worker, against modern slavery which converts the owner into the master. They say, 'We want the salary of a working man to be measured not by what is absolutely indispensable for his subsistence, but by the value of his labor; we desire that if he produces at a rate of fifty pesos a month, he earns fifty pesos, which is what he produced, and not thirty, which is what he needs to survive; we wish to take this difference of twenty pesos out of the hands of the owner in order to return it to the hands of the worker to whom it rightfully belongs.' " Once president, Batlle translated such notions into practice with trailblazing minimum wage laws and other state interventions on behalf of social justice, such as the consolidation of various essential services and commercial or industrial sectors into public monopolies.

According to Weinstein, "Batlle's political genius rested on his recognition of the importance of the new immigrants and their children as an urban mass that could be made the backbone of the electoral strength of the Colorado party." Indeed, according to the 1908 census (which pegged Uruguay's total population at just over 1 million), 42 percent of Montevideo's population was foreign-born, the overwhelming majority consisting of workers from Italy and Spain themselves imbued with the spirit of Mediterranean labor radicalism. Meanwhile, Batlle also managed to make peace with his Blanco opposition, in part through a complex apportionment of perks and patronage slots known as "coparticipation" (the state bureaucracies and industries were proportionally staffed with clients from both parties), and in part by pretty much leaving the rural sectors of the country out of his reformist schemes. Thus, for example, as late as the 1950s, the distribution of land in this seemingly modern welfare state was distinctly feudal, with the top 1 percent of landowners controlling 34 percent of the ranchland, while the bottom 42 percent of owners laid claim to barely 2 percent of the country's total acreage. The rural underclass, consisting of 10 percent of the country's population, lived in slums so squalid that they were commonly referred to as *pueblos de ratas,* rat towns—and the sunny beneficence of Uruguay's advanced social legislation barely reached them at all.

Batlle remained the towering figure in Uruguay to his death in 1929, on the eve of the Great Depression. (His Blanco counterpart Herrera survived him by a full thirty years!) He imparted his own somewhat quirky anticlericalist passions to the Uruguayan polity, insisting that the word "God" be lowercased every time it appeared in his newspaper, and stipulating that no public buildings bear the names of saints. Although present-day Uruguay is nominally 80 percent Catholic, fewer than 5 percent regularly attend church, and Batlle's public secularism is still religiously observed. Notwithstanding the military roots of his own triumph, Batlle likewise imparted his profoundly antimilitarist convictions to the country. The peaceable democracy he forged lasted into the sixties, with only one interruption, during the thirties, when the sitting president summarily dissolved Congress and holed himself up not in some garrison, not in a police station, but in the local firehouse. The ensuing regime boasted no authoritarian features and has been memorialized as the *dictablanda,* the soft dictatorship. By the forties, in any case, Uruguayan democracy had been completely restored, along with Uruguayan prosperity.

Uruguayans today sometimes blame the subsequent debacle on Vietnam. Uruguay's welfare state thrived, in large part, owing to the success of its argicultural exports—beef, leather, and wool—and those exports boomed during the first and second world wars and on through the Korean conflict. Bucolic Uruguay supplied meat to war-ravaged populations, and clothes (or anyway the wool and leather with which to make clothes) to the ravaging armies. Commodity prices were high and life was easy. If only the United States had drawn the line against world communism in some less tropical locale than the Mekong Delta, Uruguayans sometimes speculate wistfully, if only it had drawn the line in some cold and wool-needy climate like, say, Finland, then the game might still be on.

As it was, both prices and exports began sliding precipitously during the fifties, a decline which coincided with the growing continentwide crisis in the "import-substitution industrialization" model which had characterized economic planning throughout Latin America since the 1930s. One afternoon, back in New York, Professor Weinstein sought to explain the dynamic to me: "Sometime during the thirties, during the Depression, economic planners all over South America began to chafe at their countries' dependency on the industrialized countries of the North; at the way, for instance, that they exported food only then to have to import canned food, or raw minerals only then to have to import manufactured goods. Their annoyance at this pattern grew as the prices they were getting for their own raw materials continually seemed to be falling. In response, they decided to try to generate a certain degree of independence by fostering and protecting young industries of their own geared to domestic consumption. Why don't we can our own production, they'd say, make sweaters instead of exporting wool—that is, substitute for our imports through our own industrialization, hence the term 'import-substitution industrialization,' or ISI, as it's called. The strategy called for high protective tariffs and extensive state involvement in entrepreneurial activities—semi-public monopolies, favorable loans, targeted tax breaks, and so forth. ISI usually contributed to an upsurge in the power of labor unions, since an urban industrial proletariat now rose to the fore. And it often coincided with charismatic populist movements, such as Perón's in Argentina or Vargas's in Brazil. This last characteristic wasn't so much the case in Uruguay, where labor power and state intervention in the economy already had strong precedents going back to Batlle's time, and in any case there hadn't been any such commanding leaders since him. But Uruguay likewise threw itself into the model—for instance, raising high tariff barriers to protect its young industries—and for a while ISI worked there, as it did elsewhere. The living standards for much of the population did go up.

"But by the late fifties and increasingly into the sixties, the model began to fail all over Latin America. One of the problems with ISI, especially in a small country like Uruguay, was that you quickly saturated your internal market—only so many Uruguayans, for instance, needed shoes—and, what with everybody else having their trade barriers up as well, where were Uruguayans supposed to export any extra shoes? Furthermore, in a small country like Uruguay, you weren't able to generate any economies of scale. Beyond that, the more you industrialized, the more you required specialized equipment of the sort which could only be imported from the more industrialized North; so you still had to import from outside and hence still had to rely on your exports of undervalued commodities—you weren't importing sweaters any more, but you still had to export wool at disadvantageous prices so as to be able to import industrial looms. You were back at square one: the dependency was still there. And, of course, the more commodities you had to export, as before, the more their prices fell.

"One after another, these countries hit the wall with ISI, only now they had a considerably more mobilized working class which was understandably weary of making concessions. Tensions rose, the economies buckled, and in one country after another, the military ended up seizing power, with more violence or less depending on how mobilized the working class had become. Because one of the essential challenges facing these military regimes in the Southern Cone—or anyway, the challenge as they saw it—was how to *de*politicize all these assertive workers, so as to be able to reinsert your country into the worldwide capitalist system. That's why, during the seventies, you got the fiercest repression in the three most politically advanced societies in the region —Chile, Argentina, and Uruguay. The repression in Uruguay was so brutal precisely *because,* prior to that, the society had been so civil."

Now, Uruguayan politics during the fifties was characterized by the dying-out of the last members of the generation of great leaders (such as the Blanco Hererra) and a decided failure to replenish the political space with politicians of anywhere near their caliber. Furthermore, the system of "coparticipation" and the pervasiveness of patronage-style politics mitigated for the longest time against any honest confrontation with the looming economic crisis. Productivity was plummeting, with inflation rising—and presently roaring. During the first half of the fifties, the only countries *in the world* with poorer growth rates than Uruguay were Malawi and the Dominican Republic. In 1967, Uruguay's GDP fell 5.4 percent, while inflation rampaged at 89.3 percent (the following year it even topped that, at 125.3 percent). Meanwhile, people were fiercely defending the education, health, and pension benefits which they'd grown to think of as their just prerogatives; rich people were spiriting their savings out of the country; speculation and corruption were rampant; the feudalist agricultural baronies in the interior were proving less and less efficient; strikes were becoming both more frequent and more bitter—and all the while, the politicians seemed paralyzed. Worse, they and their constituents were steeped in denial: everyone insisted on believing that, after all, this was still Uruguay, the Great Exception, paradise of the fat cows. . . .

One afternoon in Montevideo I visited with Lucia Sala, a distinguished historian affiliated with the Humanities Faculty at the National University in Montevideo, at her home. She, too, had only recently returned from thirteen years in exile, in her case in Mexico. In fact, she'd only recently been reunited with her husband, who'd spent those same thirteen years in a Uruguayan military prison. (Almost the entire time of our visit he lay napping in the cool darkened bedroom off the kitchen where we sat talking.) I asked Professor Sala the question I'd taken to asking everyone, how she felt it was possible that a country with as rich and deep a democratic and nonmilitarist tradition as Uruguays's could have plunged itself into such nightmarish repression. She looked at me intently and then answered carefully, precisely, measuring out each word. "I think that any country that undergoes a crisis as deep as that of Uruguay could end up with a military dictatorship." She paused. "Any country," she repeated emphatically.

A few weeks later, back in New York, Martin Weinstein gave me his answer: "By the late fifties, none of the politicians had the courage or maybe even the power to do anything but fake it. The Uruguayans were living better than they had any right to live, time was catching up with them, and nobody had the guts to tell them. It's just like the United States today, how we're obviously living beyond our means, and yet. . . ." His voice trailed off.[12]

One of the main entrances to the National University in Montevideo is flanked on either side by statues—one of Cervantes and the other of Dante—an arrangement no doubt originally intended to celebrate the twin national heritages claimed by the overwhelming majority of contemporary Uruguayans, the Spanish and the Italian. Nowadays, however, those statues tend to summon a darker association as well, for they recall the trajectory of the Tupamaros, the band of young urban guerrillas whose careers, during the lates sixties and early seventies, did indeed arc inexorably from the quixotic toward the infernal.

From Cervantes to Dante, yes, but the image they preferred to project in their earliest days—the one which survives to this day at the rallies of the regrouped, though decidedly chastened, veterans of those early struggles—was that of the marriage of Chaplin and Che. The late sixties, of course, saw an upsurge of student and young people's radicalism all over the world—in Paris and Warsaw and Berkeley and Tokyo and Mexico City. But student radicals all over the world looked upon their Uruguayan counterparts with undisguised admiration. Nowhere else did young radicals seem to bring to their activism quite the brio, quite the panache, that the Tupamaros of Montevideo managed to —or so, anyway, did things seem at one time, at the outset.

While traditional Uruguayan politics had become deadlocked, paralyzed, and obliviously complacent, Uruguayan young people, at least—and especially the college-educated young people of whom Uruguay could claim the highest proportion on the continent—could see their own futures foreshortening precipitously in tandem with the national economy's. And beyond that, they could see the rampant corruption and persistent injustices which no one in the Uruguayan establishment any longer seemed willing to confront.

The Tupamaros actually began, in the early sixties, as a splinter from Uruguay's fairly peripheral Socialist Party. Raúl Sendic, a young party activist, had abandoned his Montevideo law school studies one exam short of completion to go off and organize the abject sugarcane workers of the interior. He'd proved extraordinarily effective at this task, orchestrating a huge march on the capital that drew favorable comments and calls for reform from the establishment media and even some politicians. But then the months passed and nothing more happened. Sendic grew disgusted: Uruguayan politics seemed immune to traditional methods of intervention. Like many members of his generation, Sendic had been captivated by the example of Castro's revolution in Cuba (Castro had himself paid a triumphant call on Montevideo shortly after his victory in 1959). With the subsequent 1964 right-wing military coup in Brazil (whence the deposed president João Goulart and his brother-in-law, the populist firebrand Leonel Brizola, fled to Montevideo for exile) and then the American invasion of the Dominican Republic the following year, Sendic and many of his friends became convinced that the Crisis of Latin American History was at hand.

Sendic and his friends also became convinced that the traditional structures of the left in Uruguay—for example, the Communist Party and other such groupings still basically committed to the Uruguayan constitutional system—were as mired in the morass as all the other institutions in the country. Times were desperate, however: something new was needed, and quickly—not just more talk about a someday transformation, nor vacuous factional disputes about the contours of proper radical alignments, but immediate revolutionary action.

Armed action. *Now.* "Words divide us," proclaimed one of their favorite slogans. "Actions unite us." They continually studied the Cuban model (Castro and just a few followers landing on a beach, going into the mountains, establishing a focal point and through a series of carefully calibrated actions eventually provoking a wider rebellion). Though they realized that, given Uruguay's particular indigenous conditions, theirs would have to be largely an urban rather than a rural struggle, they wanted to be—as Fidel Castro's brother Raúl had phrased it—"the small motor that starts the big motor of the Revolution." They were convinced that the Big Revolution was latent and indeed imminent —in Uruguay as in all Latin America. (They were also intent on sparking but one of the "many Vietnams" of Che Guevara's prophecy). In such a context, they reasoned, armed action (even though virtually without precedent in modern Uruguayan history) would serve three vital functions—technical training for the larger battle ahead; self-defense of a still-fragile movement in the face of inevitably growing repression; and, perhaps most important, "radicalizing the struggle and creating consciousness." As one of them put it, "Revolutionary actions precipitate revolutionary situations." The way to make a revolution, finally, was to *start* making it. They worked hard to develop the kinds of tactics—particular sorts of armed actions, combining a minimum of bloodshed with a maximum of embarrassment for authorities—that would most effectively radicalize the already deeply troubled Uruguayan polity. They painstakingly organized their secret underground structures. They fully expected repression, though they were convinced that such repression (given their own heightened preparedness and the notoriously hapless reputation of the regime's armed forces) would prove largely ineffectual and would in any case only serve to further radicalize the situation. The more polarized Uruguay became, they were certain, the closer they would get to that moment when the Big Motor of Revolution would kick in—and then they would be Ready. They were quite sure of themselves.

And they were nothing if not imbued. "We have placed ourselves outside the law," they declared in an early manifesto. "This is the only honest action when the law is not equal for all; when the law exists to defend the spurious interests of a minority to the detriment of the majority; when the law works against the country's progress; when even those who have created it place themselves outside it, with impunity, whenever it is convenient for them. . . . We should not be worthy Uruguayans, nor worthy Americans, nor worthy of ourselves if we did not listen to the dictates of conscience that day after day call us to fight. Today . . . no one can take the sacred right of rebellion away from us, and no one is going to stop us from dying, if necessary, in order to be of consequence."

Officially, they called themselves the Movement for National Liberation, the MLN, but they preferred to go by a more dashing sobriquet, Tupamaros, a name they derived from the example of a forlorn Inca Indian chief, Tupac Amaru, who in 1780 led a heroic though doomed insurrection against the Spanish conquistadors and ended up hanged, drawn, and quartered in a Cuzco public square. No, no one was going to stop them.

At the outset, for example, they raided an empty hunting lodge and made off with rifles and ammunition. From there they graduated to raids on claptrap rural military outposts—they seldom even had to fire a shot, so preposterously unexpected and inconsequential did their enterprise initially appear. Their tactics infuriated the Uruguayan police charged with herding them in, who considered them cowards because they never seemed to stand up and fight. As the American journalist A. J. Langguth noted in his chronicle of this era, *Hidden Terrors,* "Half a world away, General William Westmoreland was making the same complaint about the National Liberation Front.

"When the Tupamaros did appear in public," Langguth continues, "they took the guise of public benefactors. One December, ten young people stole a food truck, drove it into a rundown quarter of Montevideo, and passed out turkeys and wine to the poor. Breaking into armories, the Tupamaros stole police uniforms and wore them to hold up banks around the city. If customers were waiting in line, the Tupamaros insisted that the clerk enter each deposit so that the bank, and not the customer, would be liable for the losses. On one occasion, they burst into a gambling casino and scooped up the profits. The next day, when the croupiers complained that the haul had included their tips, the Tupamaros mailed back a percentage of the money."

Through such "armed propaganda" and guerrilla theater, the Tupamaros generated a growing public following. They'd break into illicit money-laundering operations in the middle of the night and soon thereafter publish the organization's extraordinarily incriminating records, often embarrassing mainstream politicians and business leaders. They bombed a number of subsidiaries of American corporations, but again, always late at night, never intending to maim or kill, and usually with explosive charges far more noisy than destructive. They'd leave behind a spray of pamphlets. The posh Montevideo Country Club was spread atop a lovely hill, overlooking the gleaming blue sea and surrounded by a lazily undulating green golf course—all on public land, though land arbitrarily closed to virtually everyone in Montevideo, except club members, every day of the week except Sunday. Late one weeknight, the Tupamaros blew the clubhouse to smithereens, and the next morning virtually everyone in Montevideo, except club members, had trouble restraining a smile. Once, in the wee hours of another morning, they ransacked an exclusive high-class nightclub, scrawling the walls with perhaps their most memorable slogan: *O Bailan Todos o No Bailan Nadie* —Either everybody dances or nobody dances.

While the Tupamaros persisted in this antic insurrection, wider Uruguayan politics were taking a turn toward the decidedly more ominous. In the Presidential election of 1966, with the economic crisis worsening by the day, the electorate turned to a retired general, the Colorado candidate Oscar Gestido, who was widely hailed as an honest and capable administrator. Unfortunately, he died of natural causes before completing the first year of his term. He was replaced by his relatively unknown vice-president, a former newspaperman (and one-time boxer) named Jorge Pacheco Areco, who was both decidedly more conservative and decidedly more authoritarian. Within a week of taking office, Pacheco issued a decree outlawing the Socialist Party and several other marginal leftist and anarchist groups. Soon thereafter he shut down a couple of objectionable newspapers. "We elected Eisenhower," went the Montevideo joke, "and look, we ended up with Nixon."

With the economic situation continuing to deteriorate, bank workers went out on strike in June, 1968. Pacheco responded by declaring the first of several limited states of emergency (Congress could have overridden his initiatives at any moment but at each juncture chose to demur), appropriating emergency powers to himself and, in this case, militarizing the striking workers. When students began demonstrating later that summer (Uruguay's winter), Pacheco ordered the demonstrations put down with force: several students died, the first political deaths in Uruguay since 1904.

On August 7, 1968, the Tupamaros tried a new tack. According to Langguth, "They kidnapped the closest friend of President Pacheco, Ulises Pereira Reverbel, and held him captive in what they called a people's prison. From a public relations standpoint, the Tupamaros could hardly have chosen better. Pereira, who once killed a newsboy for selling a paper attacking him, had been denounced as the most hated man in Uruguay. The Tupamaros held Pereira a mere four days. But it was long enough to set the Uruguayans laughing at him, at their police department, at the President. When Pereira was released, not only unharmed but apparently a few pounds heavier, the poor in Montevideo took to joking, 'Hey, Tupamaros! Kidnap Me!' "

Around the same time, the Tupamaros began breaking into the homes of American business and consular officials, photographing their private rooms, and then sending snapshots to the invaded parties the next morning: "A memento of our most recent visit." In one daring raid, they took over an entire town—Pando, with a population of over 30,000—without firing a shot, seizing the banks, casinos, and even the military headquarters for several hours. (This particular time they badly botched their retreat, and the aftermath of the raid became quite shockingly bloody.) They were beginning to drive people crazy.[13] The police in particular, under extraordinary pressure from their superiors, were responding with growing desperation. For the first time in modern Uruguayan history, they began having systematic recourse to torture as a means of cracking underground Tupamaro structures. In addition, off-duty police elements began acting as renegade death squads.

In June, 1969, Daniel Mitrione, an American AID official, arrived with his wife and six of their nine children for a new posting in Montevideo. Mitrione, the one-time police chief of Richmond, Indiana, had joined the AID's Office of Public Safety in 1960. His most recent prior foreign postings had been in Brazil, in Belo Horizonte and Rio, where he'd worked with the police between 1960 and 1967 as that country drifted from democratic governance through a military coup and into the single most repressive period in its modern history. Between 1967 and 1969, he'd served on the faculty of the International Police Academy in Washington, D.C. Officially, he was now in Montevideo to help professionalize the Uruguayan police. ("Professionalizing the police" was a frequently stated goal of American foreign assistance during those years, in the spirit of President Kennedy's Alliance for Progress.) What Mitrione was actually doing in Montevideo remains a matter of considerable controversy, although more so outside Uruguay nowadays than within. American State Department officials and officers in the U.S. Embassy in Montevideo to this day insist that Mitrione was in fact merely trying "to encourage responsible and humane police administration to enable police forces to become better integrated in the community," as they told the *New York Times* in 1970. The filmmaker Costa-Gavras, who based his 1972 film *State of Siege* on the Mitrione case, paints a decidedly different picture. More to the point, not a single Uruguayan I spoke with during my stay, from anywhere along the current political spectrum, demurred from what has in the meantime become the virtually universal Uruguayan consensus on Mitrione: he was in Montevideo training police in more scientifically effective methods of interrogation. In lieu of the sloppy and haphazard brutality which they'd been wont to display before his arrival, Mitrione was offering them almost surgically precise techniques of torture. Langguth, whose carefully documented book *Hidden Terrors* begins as a sympathetic portrait of Mitrione, likewise reluctantly came to the same conclusion, though only at the end of thorough research and only definitively in the revised second edition of his book.

In August, 1969, faced with another round of strikes, Pacheco for the first time ordered the military to intervene. The army commander of Zone 1 (the Montevideo region), a constitutionalist general named Liber Seregni, refused to do so and resigned in protest. During the next several years, the army itself was rent by a growing conflict between authoritarians and constitutionalists, with the latter becoming progressively more isolated.

In April, 1970, a parliamentary commission concluded that during the previous several months

> . . . the system of mistreatment, brutality and torture used against prisoners by the police of Montevideo has become habitual and, so to speak, normal. [This] includes everything from simple personal mistreatment with word or deed, blows, brutalities, deprivation of water and food, prohibition to take care of physiological needs in the usual places, wrenching of limbs, use of handcuffs and other painful and unnecessary bonds, to the use of electrical needles, burning genital organs and anus, etc., with cigarettes. . . . The tortures and brutalities described have been practiced on innocent persons who had not yet been tried in court, innocent persons who were judged on the basis of statements torn from them by these methods. . . . Particularly noxious methods have been used against women.

On July 31, 1970, a group of Tupamaros kidnapped Dan Mitrione as he was leaving his home and spirited him off to a secluded hiding place where, during the next several days, they interrogated him at length (although apparently without resort to physical torture). They released a dossier documenting their contention that their captive was a torture instructor and announced that they would continue to hold him hostage pending the release of several of their own comrades currently held in Montevideo prisons. Pacheco, for his part, responded by absolutely refusing to capitulate to Tupamaro demands; instead, he declared a state of siege and launched massive house-by-house searches throughout the capital. Dozens, hundreds of people were herded in and tortured. Someone apparently broke, for in one particularly portentous development, the Montevideo police did manage to bag not only Sendic but most of the rest of the top Tupamaro leadership as they gathered to discuss strategy at a secret meeting house. There are many historians and commentators in Montevideo today who feel that those arrests ironically sealed Mitrione's fate, for the decision as to what to do with him in the face of Pacheco's intransigence now fell to a band of inexperienced Tupamaro footsoldiers, suddenly deprived of their more experienced and politically savvy leadership. Early on the morning of August 10, 1970, Mitrione's bound and gagged body was found in the back seat of a 1948 Buick convertible; he had been shot twice in the back of the head.

For all the uniformity of opinion one finds today in Montevideo regarding Mitrione's role as a torture instructor, there's an almost equally strong consensus decrying the Tupamaros' decision to murder this father of nine children that way, in cold blood. The Tupamaros now quickly began to lose their image as idealistic rascals. Indeed, the entire political scene began to sour with a vengeance. Responding to the spiralling repression, the Tupamaros were becoming both more overtly revolutionary in their program and more violent in their tactics. Bank guards were now getting shot during Tupamaro holdups. Increasingly desperate Tupamaros and police officers were facing off against one another in bloody confrontations (battles that would, in the end, claim the lives of fifty security officers and sixty-five Tupamaros). Popular support for the Tupamaros—or, at any rate, popular indulgence—began to waver. Even though they still had one last, extraordinarily theatrical stunt up their sleeve—the September, 1971 tunneling escape of all 106 of the political prisoners being held in Montevideo's main Punta Carretas prison—the end was drawing near.[14]

Following that September escape, the Tupamaros declared a truce pending the November presidential and legislative elections. Pacheco handpicked a successor as reactionary as himself, a political dynast named Juan María Bordaberry, who became the leading contender among the Colorados. The front-running candidate among the Blancos, once the more conservative of the two parties, was the comparatively progressive constitutionalist caudillo Wilson Ferreira Aldunate. In addition, a new third party, the Frente Amplio, a broad front of various leftist and labor groupings, united under the banner of the recently retired constitutionalist general, Liber Seregni. The campaign was unusually intense, and in order to understand its outcome, one has to understand Uruguay's unique (and uniquely perverse) electoral law, another legacy of the Batlle era. Every five years Uruguayans indulge in a "double-simultaneous election," one in which the primary and the general election are hooped together and take place on the same day. Any number of presidential lists—reflecting every conceivable range of political shading—may run, say, under the Colorado banner; similarly with the Blancos (the Frente Amplio have tended to remain united under one list). In the end, the candidate who receives the most votes from among the party which received the most total votes is declared the winner. In 1971, Wilson Ferreira received far and away the most votes of any single candidate; and, indeed, the constitutionalist candidates among all the parties received an undeniable majority (58 percent). But with the Frente Amplio taking 18 percent of the vote in its first outing, the Colorados' six candidates and the Blancos' three candidates virtually split the remainder, with the two parties each garnering just over 40 percent. It appears in retrospect that the Blancos, in fact, did outscore the Colorados and that Wilson Ferreira should have been declared the winner (oh, how history might have differed!). But Pacheco engaged in a series of fairly blatant electoral feints and sleights-of-hand —which conservative Blancos, for their part, declined to protest—so that in the end Bordaberry was able to steal the election. (The Brazilian military government—in 1971 in the midst of its own most repressive phase, under the command of the extreme hard-liner General Médici —had been preparing to invade Uruguay should the election not turn out to its liking.) Buoyed by the electoral result, Pacheco took advantage of the interregnum before Bordaberry's March, 1972, inauguration to transfer responsibility for the war against the Tupamaros from the police to the military, which in turn formed a united command in preparation for a new offensive.

During Pacheco's final months and Bordaberry's first several weeks, the two presidents moved ever more aggressively to curtail traditional Uruguayan constitutional rights and socioeconomic entitlements. In response, on April 13, 1972, the unions launched a massive general strike. The next day the Tupamaros reemerged from their electoral hiatus, coordinating the assassination of several alleged death squad members. Bordaberry, for his part, reacted by declaring a "state of internal war," promulgating a "law of internal security," and ordering the military into an all-out assault on the Tupamaros.

The military accomplished this task with overwhelming and brutal efficiency. During the next half year (particularly between July and August, 1972), the military incarcerated thousands of individuals (torturing the great majority) and systematically dismantled the Tupamaro structures, plucking them apart one member at a time (plucking each member apart, one member at a time), until by early 1973, the Tupamaros had been effectively destroyed as a coherent organization. The Tupamaros insist on this and even the military today admits as much: six months before the final coup which was to bring them to the undisputed fore, the military had *already* triumphed in the battle which they would subsequently use as their pretext for seizing and maintaining absolute power.

Vigorous protests continued to be heard in Congress and throughout the larger polity, however, well into 1973. The military felt that though the Tupamaros had been destroyed, their supporters, and indeed their progenitors in the unions, the civilian politicians, the university, and the professions remained to be disciplined. In the next several months, it became increasingly difficult to tell whether it was Bordaberry who was using the military for his own repressive purposes, or the other way around. On June 1, without congressional approval, Bordaberry summarily suspended most remaining constitutional rights. On June 27, 1973, in the final culmination of a five-year-long slow-motion coup, the military suspended Congress itself, instituting a Supreme Military Council as the entire executive and legislative authority of the country and subordinating Bordaberry to the role of ineffectual figurehead.

Nowadays, when Uruguayans look back on this period, the Tupamaros come in for a lot of blame. They are retrospectively viewed as immaturely foolhardy at best, and recklessly nihilistic at worst. Back in the United States, Martin Weinstein takes a somewhat more judicious view: "I don't believe the Tupamaros were the reason Uruguay became a dictatorship, though they contributed to the process. With or without them the system was not going to hold—but they speeded up its breakdown. I mean, civil liberties in general were still protected under Pacheco at a point when the Tupas went into their armed revolutionary mode. They were acting on the basis of a view of society that then quickly became the case, partly because of their actions. In the early sixties, they might have been absolutely correct in their analysis of the situation, but in the early sixties, Uruguay had one of the lowest violent death rates anywhere in the world! They took that society and through a dangerous game of chicken, they speeded it up. I mean, if you're going to rob banks with guns, banks have guards, and eventually somebody's going to get killed. Still, finally, the Tupamaros were pawns—

they were way out of their depth, and they became the excuse for a massive working class repression which was coming anyway."

In Montevideo, I had occasion to speak with Mauricio Rosencof, a noted playwright who had been a leading Tupamaro activist and then spent well over a decade in prison. I asked him whether as a Tupamaro he felt some responsibility for the advent of the Uruguayan dictatorship. "And in Brazil?" he cut me short. "In Argentina? In Chile? In Guatemala? In Salvador? There were no Tupamaros in any of those places and the same thing happened in all of them."

In its recent twentieth-anniversary issue, *Report on the Americas,* the journal of the North American Congress on Latin America, featured an interview with Eleuterio Fernández Huidobro, another of the Tupamaro founders (and subsequent prisoners of the military). What, he was asked, have you done well in your life? "I think the best thing I have done in my life," he replied, "is to try and make thought and action, word and deed, one and the same thing. I believe this, at the risk of appearing ridiculous and in spite of the mistakes that might have been made in the past. The best thing I and the Tupamaros have done is to live by our ethics by acting in concert with what we believe."

And what, he was asked, is the worst thing you've done? "Perhaps the worst thing we did is to have been defeated."

Political paralysis in the face of a widening economic collapse, the rise of an urban guerrilla movement provoked by and in turn accelerating an increasingly reactionary drift in establishment politics—all these no doubt played their roles in the process that finally overwhelmed the Great Uruguayan Exception. But one more component was necessary: a transformed military. A military, that is, transformed not only in terms of its size, its heft, but also in terms of its own sense of its role and mission. For while it is true that, as Juan Perón observed regarding all coups in Latin America, "The military never comes in uninvited"—and it can certainly be argued that it was invited in, in the Uruguayan case—still, it is also true that prior to the late sixties in Uruguay, there would have been no effective military force to have been "invited in" in the first place.

Back in the days of the country's relaxed prosperity, Uruguay's military was both peripheral and overwhelmingly democratic. Several of its leading officers had at one time fought for Republican Spain! There were always some ultrarightist elements—these even had their own newspaper—but they were largely marginal. As late as 1967, when the ultrarightists demanded that the faculty of the military academy publicly endorse an antiguerrilla offensive then under way in Bolivia, the majority of officers refused to go along, insisting that in a constitutional system, the military was not even supposed to have an opinion regarding foreign affairs.

During the fifties, Uruguay's military consisted of under 15,000 men. There was no draft, but neither was the military a caste unto itself (as was largely the case, say, in Argentina). The military schools drew primarily from the lower middle classes, particularly from the interior (for though education was free, most schools were located in Montevideo, where poor rural youths couldn't afford to live, while at military school, room and board were provided). The officers, as a group, came out of the middle class, and in some cases out of military families. But promotion was based on a bureaucratic system of merit-testing.

That, and much else, now began to change. As the political situation intensified, the security forces steadily grew in size and in budgetary allotment—the military ballooning from 15,000 men in 1968 to 21,000 in 1970 to 33,000 in 1975 to 43,000 in 1985, with the Ministry of the Interior adding another 25,000 men to that total.[15] In 1973 for the first time Uruguay spent more on its military than on education, a situation that persists to this day, despite the return to democracy. While in the sixties the Uruguayan military could claim only 14 percent of the total national budget, by 1985 the amount had climbed to over 40 percent. In the early phases of this process, the external political conflict was mirrored inside the military itself, as rightists began battling constitutionalists for hegemony (and for control of that rapidly swelling budget). The rightist President Pacheco tended to back the rightist generals, and when, for instance, they now suspended merit-testing as the basis for promotion, he in no way objected. During the ensuing period, over 600 constitutionalist officers were purged from military ranks, an astonishingly high number in such a relatively small army (one fellow was cashiered in 1973 simply for having named his baby son Liber).

But none of this was happening in a vacuum—similar sorts of transformations were occurring all over Latin America. This was particularly true of the gradual metamorphosis in military doctrine; in the rationale, that is, which Latin American military establishments advanced for their own existences. Latin American military groups had long been vaguely anti-Communist, and they'd regularly interposed themselves against particular uprisings of their own people (although, again, this had not regularly been the case in Uruguay). But it was only during the late fifties and sixties, as we have seen in the case of Brazil, that a doctrine began to emerge in which militaries throughout the hemisphere defined themselves as their respective countries' principal bulwarks against an all-consuming, pervasive Communist challenge. While their colleagues in NATO, for example, based their planning on the requirements of a Third World War that just might break out one day in some hypothetical future, for the new Latin American military theorists, that war was already well under way.

And in at least one regard, it was a good thing that it was, because otherwise these militaries might have been hard-pressed to find any reason at all to go on existing at such levels. "During the fifties," as the Uruguayan sociologist Carina Perelli has noted, "the collaboration between Latin American armies and the U.S. military had rested on the perception of the threat [being one of] Soviet aggression through conventional war operations. . . . However, as of 1960, the idea of conventional war in South America—either in the form of direct aggression by an extracontinental power, or of a possible conflict among countries in the area—began to be perceived as highly improbable." This provoked a sort of identity crisis, "a certain draining of the sense of mission." Indeed, there was a period in the late fifties when it might have been possible to imagine most of the other Latin American militaries becoming more like Uruguay's (instead of what then actually happened, which, of course, was the precise opposite).

The decisive factor which came along to arrest any such incipient identity crisis, however, was Castro's stunning victory in Cuba in 1959. We've already considered the bracing impact that victory had on an entire generation of young leftists in Latin America, particularly the Tupamaros. In this context, however, the point is that Castro's example had an even more telling impact on the militaries in the region. In one sense, the whole grim history of the ensuing period in Latin America may be understood as the reverberations of the Cuban bell tolling across the decades.

Castro's victory, for its part, had such profound consequences only because it occurred within a particular context, or rather, two such contexts: first, the historic hegemony of the United States over other countries in the western hemisphere, and secondly, the heightened rivalry between the United States and the Soviet Union, between "capitalism" and "communism," during that particular period, the so-called Cold War.

Long before the Bolshevik revolution, the United States had been imposing its vision upon its neighbors. As early as 1829, Simón Bolívar noted that "the United States [seems] destined to plague and torment the continent in the name of freedom." Bolívar may well have had the recently enunciated (1823) Monroe Doctrine in mind. Historians of that doctrine, one of the cornerstones of American foreign policy, have long marvelled at the way (in the words of Dexter Perkins, summarizing his three-volume history) "a doctrine which was intended for the protection of Latin American states [evolved] into one that justified and even sanctified American interference in and control of the affairs of the independent republics of the continent." The humorist Dave Barry recently framed the matter succinctly when he boiled the whole Monroe Doctrine down to three simple precepts:

1. Other nations are *not allowed* to mess around with the internal affairs of nations in this hemisphere.
2. But we are.
3. Ha ha ha.

This was the doctrine which, of course, legitimized (to the extent any unilateral assertion of authority can legitimize anything) the repeated military forays by the United States into Mexico, the Caribbean, Central America, and Latin America well into the twentieth century.

But with the turn of the century (and the American occupation of the Philippines), the Monroe Doctrine came increasingly to constitute only a single aspect of a larger, more global policy. This was especially true after the Bolshevik revolution, and even more so after the Second World War. That policy had as its central focus the ongoing availability of raw materials for our own manufacturers and the ongoing openness of foreign markets to our finished products. Senior American policy planners were astonishingly frank about what was at stake and what would have to be sacrificed. Thus, for example, in a top-secret memo on the dramatic situation in the Far East in 1948, George F. Kennan (then Director of Policy Planning for the State Department) wrote:

> We have about 50% of the world's wealth, but only 6.3% of its population. . . . In this situation, we cannot fail to be the object of envy and resentment. Our real task in the coming period is to devise a pattern of relationships which will permit us to maintain this position of disparity without positive detriment to our national security. To do so, we will have to dispense with all sentimentality and day-dreaming; and our attention will have to be concentrated everywhere on our immediate national objectives. We need not deceive ourselves that we can afford today the luxury of altruism and world-benefaction. . . . We should cease to talk about vague and . . . unreal objectives such as human rights, the raising of the living standards, and democratization. The day is not far off when we are going to have to deal in straight power concepts. The less we are then hampered by idealistic slogans, the better.

It is interesting in this particular context that Kennan, the author of the famous containment policy, didn't even bother to refer to the threat or supposed evils of communism in this précis on the need to protect our vital interests. Elsewhere, of course, he would, as in a speech he delivered to American ambassadors stationed in Latin America and gathered together for a conference in Rio in 1950. Noting the spread throughout the region of a dangerous new heresy—"the wide acceptance of the idea that the government has direct responsibility for the welfare of people"—and the consequent imperative that we assert "the protection of our raw materials" (a curious use of the world "our") as a major element in our foreign policy, Kennan went on to acknowledge that

> The final answer might be an unpleasant one, but . . . we should not hesitate before police repression by the local government. This is not shameful since the Communists are essentially traitors. . . . It is better to have a strong regime in power than a liberal government if it is indulgent and relaxed and penetrated by Communists.

A few years later Kennan would be shunted out of the State Department, in part for being too moderate (perhaps because he was the sort of person who'd find that final answer "unpleasant" or who could even entertain such notions as "human rights, the raising of living standards, and democratization"), but the policies he articulated still held sway.

Throughout the forties and fifties, Latin American governments were trying, as we have seen, to institute various ISI development models. Repeatedly these efforts were seen as threatening to the vital national interests of the United States, and often they were decried as Communist. In 1954, the foreign minister in Guatemala's new reformist regime complained about a U.S. policy that amounted to

> . . . cataloguing as 'Communism' every manifestation of nationalism or economic independence, any desire for social progress, any intellectual curiosity, and any interest in progressive or liberal reforms. . . . Any Latin American government that exerts itself to bring about a truly national program which affects the interests of the powerful foreign companies, in whose hands the wealth and the basic resources in large part repose in Latin America, will be pointed out as Communist; it will be accused of being a threat to continental security and making a breach in continental solidarity, and so will be threatened with foreign intervention.

A few months later, this man and the government he represented were toppled in a CIA-engineered coup.

Michael McClintock, a historian specializing in Latin American affairs on the London staff of Amnesty International, has noted, "When not characterized by overt military intervention or long-term occupation, U.S. intervention in the security affairs of its neighbors before World War II was relatively insignificant." After the war, however, the United

States increasingly preferred to wield its various doctrines by proxy—though not, it should be added, by unilaterally imposing its foreign will on a series of uniformly prostrate nations. In each of these countries there were significant elements of the indigenous populations who feared the same sorts of things the United States feared. Indeed, Kennan's stark percentage formulations regarding the "disparity" between the relative population of the United States and its share of the world's wealth was repeatedly mirrored, in microcosm, *within* the borders of each of these countries; so that there were native businessmen and bankers and landowners as eager to see their national security services properly expanded and indoctrinated as the North Americans were. This was the case throughout Latin America (though, again, not at the outset as markedly so in Uruguay). It was especially the case after the traumatic shock of Castro's triumph in Cuba.

One notable response to that triumph was the new American President John F. Kennedy's Alliance for Progress, a dramatic initiative which combined signficant new infusions of financial aid with a stepped-up program to strengthen and integrate the various security forces of the Americas (as, for example, in the AID program which eventually brought Daniel Mitrione to Uruguay). Again, top American policymakers were remarkably candid about their intentions. Kennedy's Defense Secretary, Robert McNamara, as early as 1963 testified before Congress:

> The best return on our investment in military aid probably comes from the training of selected Army officers and key specialists in our military academies and training centers in the U.S. and abroad. These students are carefully selected by their countries so that they in turn become instructors when they go home. They are the leaders of the future, the men who have the skills and will instruct their own armed forces. I don't need to dwell on the value of having people in positions of power who have firsthand knowledge of how we think and act in the United States. For us having these friends is invaluable.

And shortly afterward, at the time of Lyndon Johnson's swearing in, McNamara addressed this theme again: "Our primary objective in Latin

America is to aid, wherever necessary, the continual growth of the military and paramilitary forces, so that together with the police and other security forces, they may provide the necessary internal security."

One of the ways in which the United States attempted to coordinate security operations in this hemisphere in the wake of Castro's victory was through the Conferences of American Armies, begun in 1961 and, according to McClintock, "held almost every year on U.S. initiative, bringing together the top officers of virtually every Latin American army. From 1961 to 1967 the conferences were largely organized and run by the counterinsurgency-oriented United States military. One American officer . . . described them as a 'powerful element' in the creation of an integrated security orientation in the region . . . since they 'permitted direct person-to-person contact at the highest levels of each service.' " Top Uruguayan officers were regular participants.

Lower-level officers from throughout the hemisphere were regular guests at the campus of the School of the Americas, at Fort Gulick in the Panama Canal Zone, at Fort Bragg in North Carolina, and at other U.S.-sponsored venues. (Close to a thousand Uruguayan officers trained at Fort Gulick alone!) Official American spokesmen regularly lauded these schools for the way they served to familiarize Latin American officers with the democratic and constitutionalist aspects of North American governance. That might have been so, but according to Selva Lopez, a historian I met in Montevideo who has been compiling statistics on the Uruguayan officers who trained in the United States and Panama, their favorite classes (in order of popularity) were: international security, counterinsurgency, intelligence, and ("for a select few," she cautions) interrogation.

The United States was nowhere near as deeply and directly involved in the final subversion of Uruguay's democracy as it had been in the case of Brazil's or would be, later that same year, in the case of Chile's. Nor did the United States provide the Uruguayan military with massive military assistance following the coup. (Then again, it didn't need to. As Martin Weinstein has observed, "The military didn't need much material assistance in order to repress the country. Once they'd eliminated the Tupas, nobody else had any guns. They didn't need helicopters or anything. There was no tradition of resistance: nobody in several generations had had to think in those terms. Uruguay was a tiny country, very easy to suppress.") What the U.S. State Department did lavish upon Uruguay all through the early seventies were excuses—public assurances that all the repression going on down there was merely a temporary response to an immediate emergency.[16] And before that, what the United States had equipped Uruguay's military with was doctrinal justification.

For many years, it was the fashion in progressive circles in the United States to insist that the doctrine of national security was an entirely American export—concocted by the CIA, exported by the AID, under the banner of the Alliance for Progress, or some such—at any event, definitely "Made in the USA." Curiously, though, most progressive analysts in Latin America today dismiss that characterization as a massive oversimplification. Some of them almost seem to take nationalist umbrage, as if the notion implies that their militaries weren't monstrous enough to come up with the doctrine without prompting. Others insist that though there was obviously considerable U.S. involvement in the doctrine's development, there were also many other foreign sources, and then on top of that there were the further interactions of the various Latin American militaries sharing and refining the doctrine among themselves. The main thing the guests at the School of the Americas and its brother institutions were exposed to, according to this line of reasoning, was *each other.* Proud graduates of the schools include Augusto Pinochet of Chile; Gustavo Álvarez of Honduras; Jorge Rafael Videla, Eduardo Viola, and Leopoldo Galtieri of Argentina; and Manuel Noriega of Panama—valiant coup-makers all, and in many cases each other's classmates. On top of that, these people would then send their underlings to each others' schools—places like ECEME in Brazil and similar institutions in Chile and Argentina.

As for the doctrine itself, Emilio Mignone, one of the foremost and most courageous critics of the military in Argentina, recently parsed the matter for me as follows: "The doctrine had three principal foreign sources which differed for each of the three major countries in which it took root. In Brazil, the main theorist was General Golbery, and yes, there you had a definite American influence, by way of the Brazilian Expeditionary Force, in which Golbery served, which operated in Italy during the Second World War, under American command, with Vernon Walters as liaison, and so forth.[17] In Chile, the main theorist was Pinochet himself, who originally taught at the Superior War College, and his main influences were German—that is, nineteenth-century Prussian theorists like Clausewitz or else early twentieth-century people like Ludendorff. The Chilean army modelled itself on the Prussian ideal. Though the Argentines began by modelling themselves on the Prussian ideal as well (around 1920, half of the top officers in the Argentine army had been trained in Germany), there, by contrast, the principal more recent influences turned out to be French—that is, the French veterans of Indochina and Algeria who'd evolved a doctrine of counterinsurgency warfare based on their own experiences. The influential Argentine General Rosas was himself influenced by such teachings during his studies at the French War College in Paris in the late fifties. He brought those lessons back with him, and they were further reinforced by the presence of French military attachés, many of whom spent periods of semi-exile in Buenos Aires during the early sixties. They received their most coherent elaboration in the subsequent writings of General Osiris Villegas, who was himself heavily influenced by the French."

In later years there were other influences as well in other parts of the hemisphere—Korean, Taiwanese, Israeli—but the point is that this was no simple American graft. (Indeed, some Latin American analysts take perverse pride in speculating on an obverse flow of influence, suggesting, for example, that it was the intensely virulent Latin American hybrid of the national security doctrine which subsequently got introjected, with a vengeance, back into U.S. politics, by way of such Latin-America-obsessed characters as Oliver North, "Chi Chi" Quintero, Felix Rodriguez, John Hull, and General John Singlaub.[18])

At any rate, while I was in Montevideo, several contemporary historians suggested to me that the predominant doctrinal influences on the Uruguayan military were, as with the Argentines, the French. When the Uruguayan military finally went after the Tupamaros in earnest, their models were the French commandos in Algiers, systematically dismantling underground cells one tortured member at a time. They had all read the books of Jacques Massu, commander of the French paratroopers in Algeria. Indeed, they had even studied Gillo Pontecorvo's extraordinary agitprop film *The Battle of Algiers* as a training exercise. The French were particularly helpful on questions of tactics—and justifications for those tactics. Thus, ironically, did the Great Uruguayan Exception, initially launched under Batlle's enthrallment to France's anticlerical and socialist example at the turn of the century, come crashing to earth, seventy years later, under an entirely different sort of French enthrallment.

In 1979, Latin American bishops, meeting in conference at Puebla, Mexico, published a paper, "Thoughts on Political Violence," in which they noted that "The last few years have seen the growing importance of the so-called doctrine of national security, which is in fact more ideology than doctrine. It is linked to a certain elitist, hierarchical, political and economic model which denies the vast majority of the population any part in political decision-making."

One wouldn't want to come upon the doctrine of national security alone in some dark alleyway. It is a fearsome piece of work. To begin with, there is the matter of the sheer breadth of the threat it feels justified in enjoining. The enemy—the International Communist Movement—is perceived as covertly operating everywhere, all the time, in all fields of human endeavor. The threat is no longer conceived as one of conventional war, nor even as one of sedition (the doctrine's word for armed insurrection), but rather as one of subversion. In 1981, at the Fourteenth Conference of American Armies, the Uruguayan Army offered a paper in which it defined subversion as "actions, violent or not, with ultimate purposes of a political nature, in all fields of human activity within the internal sphere of a state and whose aims are perceived as not convenient for the overall political system." A nice, tidy formula.

In a recent essay, the Uruguayan sociologist Carina Perelli pointed out that a war against subversion thus characterized must in essence be political and psychosocial: only as a final resort should specifically military action ever need to come into play. As Perelli paraphrases the doctrine, "The ultimate material employed by the enemy is human nature itself, which is weak, malleable, 'bad': the battlefield is, then, the everyday existence of mankind, with its vices and passions." She cites the Chief of Staff of the Brazilian Army, General Breno Borges Forte, who, at the Tenth Conference of American Armies in 1973 (the year of the final Uruguayan coup), declared, "The enemy is undefined . . . it adapts to any environment and uses every means, both licit and illicit, to achieve its aims. It disguises itself as a priest, a student or a campesino, as a defender of democracy or an advanced intellectual, as a pious soul or as an extremist protestor: it goes into the fields and the schools, the factories and the churches, the universities and the magistracy; if necessary, it will wear a uniform or civil garb; in sum, it will take on any role that it considers appropriate to deceive, to lie, and to take in the good faith of Western peoples."

As Perelli observes, "Within this framework, everything and everyone becomes suspect, given their potential subvertibility by International Communism. The apparent Messianism of the region's armed forces finds its root here: only a closed and total institution that resocializes and permanently controls its members, and that embodies those values, has sufficient degrees of purity to take charge of a fight of this sort. The rest of the social and political actors—even those who constitute temporary allies—are susceptible to subversive contamination, frequently without knowing it, since they bathe in the enemy's favorite cultural medium: liberal democracy and the open society that regime implies."

The doctrine thus enjoins a struggle that is permanent (one which allows "no room for distinction between periods of peace and periods of war") and one that is also total (one which allows "no room for negotiation or conciliation"). This is a war for Crusaders, for "the soul of the nation," and indeed, it is not surprising to come upon such declamations as this, in a 1981 edition of the Uruguayan military magazine *El Soldado:* "The incarnated, concrete, living expression of any sovereign nation is its armed forces, whose mission is the defense of unity, of integrity, and of honor, as well as of everything essential and permanent in the Country: the supreme interests of the Nation." Or this, from a 1979 issue of the same magazine: "Our Country will be strong and honorable through its army, and its army will be so through the force that derives from its spirit."

Not surprising, that is, until one remembers that a mere fifteen years earlier, these were the guys who collected the litter on the beaches and not much else. Not surprising, until one remembers that these are Uruguayans talking, citizens of what was once one of the most secular, sardonic, tolerant, "modern," least dogmatic countries in the world.

Indeed, when one comes upon some of the more high-strung religious perorations, such as this one from a 1985 issue of that same magazine, one can hardly believe one's eyes:

> Moreover, there is only one philosophical current that constitutes a coherent whole capable of condemning Marxism by opposing to it a doctrine which is positive and not merely negative or anti: it is Christianity, or more precisely the Catholic Church itself, unaffected by free inquiry. The True Church, that embodied in doctrine by the teachings of the Holy Fathers, that of St. Augustine, St. Thomas Aquinas.

This in a country where it is *still* virtually unheard of to capitalize the name of God in print.

This last passage, however, does manage to suggest some of what was really going on in Uruguay just below the surface as the doctrine of national security was being seared into the country's flank: this was a continuation of the Inquisition. Independent of the political and economic issues which were also being fought out—and I do not in any way mean to downplay those—this was additionally a strange and mysterious eruption of a set of passions and postures which might have been thought long dormant, especially in Uruguay.

Toward the end of her piece, Perelli notes mildly, "With its Manichean and conspiratorial vision of history, this doctrine has certain internal structuring mechanisms that make disconfirmation by empirical contrast impossible." There is a crazy mad howl welling up from the middle of that mild sentence, and it was into the core of that madness that Uruguay, in 1973, was about to descend.

They called their main prison Liberty. I'm not making that up. Libertad prison, located about thirty miles outside Montevideo, was the main holding center for male political prisoners sentenced to the sorts of long, long terms which came to constitute the conerstone of Uruguayan military justice. (Women were principally held at another center, Punta de Rieles.)

Initally, the preponderance of them were Tupamaros, but later they included student activists, professors, labor leaders, journalists, lawyers, doctors, social workers, onetime members of the Communist or the Socialist Party or other suddenly proscribed parties, constitutionalist soldiers, and many others. Comprehensive statistics are still hard to come by.

During the heyday of the *dictadura,* one demographer commented that it would be easier to estimate the population of some remote Guatemalan tribe than that of the Uruguayan military prisons, and official figures have not been compiled to this day, but thousands upon thousands of individuals served time—the majority, six years or more —in Libertad and its adjacent institutions. Relatively few Uruguayan oppositionists were liquidated outright (109 were killed, and 163 were "disappeared," according to the Servicio Paz y Justicia, or SERPAJ, the main human-rights-monitoring organization in Montevideo)—certainly nothing like as many as in Argentina or Chile. But, as the president of Uruguay's Supreme Military Court said in 1979, speaking of the political-prisoner population at that point, "Since we don't have sixteen hundred corpses, we have sixteen hundred problems." And the Uruguayan military-prison administrators addressed themselves to that sort of problem with particular zeal.

Members of a delegation from the International Committee of the Red Cross who had toured several prisons in the Southern Cone during the winter of 1980 observed in their final mission report, "Libertad is the place where [the] system is pushed beyond the usual limits, both in the area of security and in the search for every possible means of hurting the prisoners." Conditions at Libertad apparently so unnerved these Red Cross delegates that, for one of the very few times in the organization's history, a copy of their highly confidential mission report was leaked to the press.[19] The report noted that, bad as things were in Libertad, the systematic abuse of Uruguayan political prisoners routinely predated their arrival at the prison: "For all the prisoners, the tension and insecurity . . . did not start at the prison doors but, rather, earlier, at the time of the interrogation. They have all been tortured, kept in secret places of detention, questioned—all of them, without exception. . . . All of them have spent weeks, months, sometimes more than a year, in military units. In some units, prisoners are tortured with electrodes, in others they are suspended by their arms, which have been previously tied behind their backs, or kept with their heads under water until suffocation, not to mention similar refinements."

During my weeks in Uruguay, I spoke with several veterans of Libertad, and, indeed, all of them told tales of such preliminary "refinements." Dr. Líber Mandressi, a forty-eight-year-old plastic surgeon, said he spent "eight years and forty-five days" in Libertad. He was arrested on December 16, 1975, which was around the time the military began in earnest to turn its attentions to the Communist Party, of which he was a member. (The Uruguayan Communist Party had previously enjoyed a long history as a distinguished, if marginal, participant in the country's democratic politics.) Dr. Mandressi was initially taken to an abandoned factory, behind the barracks of a mechanized-cavalry regiment, that had been nicknamed El Infierno by its guests. "All of us were hooded all the time," he recalled. "And all of us were tortured for days on end, without even being interrogated at first. There must have been a hundred and fifty, two hundred people there; you could hear breathing, coughing, moaning—we weren't allowed to talk to each other. Occasionally your hood would slip a bit, but you could still see nothing. It was pitch-black. At one point, they kept us standing, our hands tied behind our backs, for four full days. One almost loses all sense of time in such situations, but four times I heard the birds outside chirping with the rising sun—that's how I know it was four days. Eventually, they'd take us in for their interrogations—beatings, shocks, *submarino* immersions. They weren't really after any information—they knew everything already, had everybody's name. It was all just part of the process. Once, I became aware that a seven-year-old boy had been brought in and was being forced to witness his parents' being tortured. I know I wasn't hallucinating—at the time, I thought I was—because I checked with others later, and they had all had the same hallucination."

One of the more appalling accounts of torture which I encountered during my stay in Uruguay came in the form of a written narrative, the testimony of Miguel Angel Estrella, the world-famous Argentine pianist, who was arrested as he was preparing to leave Uruguay, following a brief stay, in December, 1978. (An ardent Peronist back in Argentina, he had never engaged in any political violence and had undertaken no political activity whatsoever while in Uruguay.) During his first week of imprisonment, his torturers focused with particular relish on his hands. "They were like sadists," Estrella recalled in a subsequent book. "They applied electricity under my nails, without stopping, and later they hanged me from my arms. After two days of torture I hurt all over, and had no sensation whatsoever left in my hands. I touched things and didn't feel anything. They kept making like they were going to chop off my hands. The last time they even had an electric saw going. They'd pull on my finger and ask, 'Which is the finger you use most in playing the piano?' I didn't say anything, I was praying, and one of them says, 'Is it maybe the thumb?' They pulled on the fingers and made like they were going to slice them off with the electric saw. They said, 'We're going to cut off your hands, one finger at a time, and then we're going to kill you, just like with Victor Jara.' " (Jara, the great Chilean folk singer and guitarist, indeed had each of his fingers smashed, before he was killed, in Santiago in the days after Pinochet's coup in 1973.)

I asked Dr. Mandressi whether, being a plastic surgeon, he got many former torture victims as patients nowadays.

"No," he said. "You have to understand that these guys were specialists—the main torturers. They were highly trained in methods of exacting the maximum pain without leaving any significant physical traces—and, for that matter, without killing the victim in the process. There were relatively few deaths under torture in Uruguay. This was because there were usually doctors in attendance at the sessions."

This remarkable assertion—that doctors regularly supervised torture sessions in Uruguyan military prisons—was one I heard again and again in Montevideo, in the accounts of both victims and subsequent researchers. According to the most authoritative random survey so far made of former political prisoners, fully 70 percent claimed that doctors had attended their torture sessions.

In the wake of Uruguay's return to democracy, the country's revitalized Medical Association, under the directorship of Dr. Gregorio Martirena, has been the single most active professional organization seeking to document allegations of complicity by its members with the dictatorship and seeking professional sanctions against members whenever such allegations can be proved. Dr. Martirena informed me that as of September, 1986, cases were pending against eighty *médicos militares.* These were variously accused of direct participation in torture (monitoring vital signs of victims so as either to suspend or reinitiate the sessions, and in particular ferreting out those victims who they determined were exaggerating their physical distress), of sharing with the military authorities medical files which ought to have been kept confidential, of prescribing inappropriate psychotropic drugs at inappropriate dosages, of falsifying medical records in cases of problematic autopsies, and so forth.[20]

I asked Dr. Martirena how such systemic abuses could have developed. He explained that up through 1975, doctors working for the military had retained their civilian status, but that at that point they'd all been militarized. More than 100 doctors had refused to submit to such conscription, and many of those were themselves arrested and fed into the repressive apparatus. In fact, some of the worst cases currently bedeviling the Medical Association involve doctors' allegations of having been tortured by other doctors. In 1973, there had been only 300 doctors working with the military, but by 1985 there were between 800 and 1,000, out of a total of 6,000 in the entire country. Some of the behavior evinced by these doctors could be ascribed to the constraints of military discipline, some to true belief (many of the doctors who remained with the military after 1973 were devout acolytes of the doctrine of national security), but much of it involved considerations of professional ambition and financial reward (military doctors earned between twice and four times as much as their civilian counterparts).

I asked Dr. Martirena how the various cases against the military doctors were going, and he explained that most were still under way, that procedures were painstakingly designed to ensure due process, and that thus far only a few cases had resulted in determinations of guilt, which in turn entailed foreclosing the possibility of any future employment at institutions where the Medical Association held sway. However, in all of these cases, military officials had taken the guilty parties under their protection, assuring them of continued employment at inflated salaries in military hospitals; and the civilian officials who now presumably outranked these military "subordinates" in the newly reinstituted constitutional democratic order had either felt incapable of or uninterested in enforcing any further sanctions.

For his part, Dr. Mandressi went on to describe to me how after spending over a month at El Infierno, he'd been transferred, along with ninety others, to an abandoned garage, open to the elements including fiercely cold winter nights, hooded all the while, where, though general conditions were somewhat milder, the main terror consisted of an incredibly loud telephone, whose ringing invariably prefigured the return of one of the inmates to El Infierno for further questioning. Many of the sorts of torture centers described by Dr. Mandressi were located on remote military reservations, or else in the meantime have been destroyed. But a surprising number exist to this day—the buildings anyway—right in the middle of town in the midst of daily life, exhaling their horrendous memories like so many slowly decaying toxic dumps.

One afternoon, on that first trip of mine, I was given a tour of Montevideo by a young woman. The vernal warmth of the city—flowering trees, friends sitting around outdoor café tables—belied the horror of my guide's reports: how, for instance, everybody had known that torture was going on here, at the intersection of Maldonado and Paraguay, near downtown, in that apartment building right over there next to the police precinct house, because you could hear the screams, especially in the evenings, when the street noises had died away. We got in our car and headed toward the suburbs, coursing out of town on the Rambla, the beautiful boulevard that skirts the water's edge, one miniature scalloped bay after another, changing its name every few kilometers: Rambla Franklin Roosevelt, Rambla Francia, Rambla Gran Bretañia, Rambla Naciones Unidas, Rambla Presidente Wilson, Rambla Mahatma Gandhi, Rambla O'Higgins . . . Rambla República de México. Here we pulled over to the curb and looked across the beach, and all the other beaches, receding in the distance toward the glistening city of Montevideo. "This was one of the most notorious torture centers," my guide said, turning my attention to a gorgeous villa of brick, stone, and grillework on the landward side of the Rambla. "The victims were, of course, hooded, so they couldn't enjoy the view. But the torturers could, and I imagine they took many delicious breaks, lounging up there, sunning themselves on the balcony. Now the villa has been decommissioned, and bought by a private party." The car in the driveway bore military plates.

Some of the worst instances of Uruguayan torture took place not in Montevideo, and not even in Uruguay, but in neighboring Argentina. An ironic aspect of the doctrine of national security's descent upon the entire Southern Cone was the order in which it engulfed the various countries: Brazil, beginning in 1964; Uruguay, in June, 1973; Chile, in September, 1973; and Argentina not until 1976. Political refugees streamed from one country to the next. Many progressive Uruguayan students and activists fled first to a Chile still percolating with Salvador Allende's socialist experiments; after the coup there, they and many of their Chilean colleagues decided to settle in Buenos Aires. It was an understandable choice—these people wanted to be near their homes and their loved ones; they kept hoping their exile would be brief; they wanted, as one of them put it, "to at least stay in the same season"—but in many cases it proved a fatal one, for nowhere else in South America was the repression as physically savage as it soon became in Argentina, during the "dirty war." In keeping with the "doctrine of ideological frontiers," a corollary of the doctrine of national security by which neighboring militaries agreed to forswear considerations of local sovereignty—considerations that at one time constituted their very raison d'être—in order to pursue international communism across each other's borders, Argentina's military invited special commando units from the Uruguayan armed forces to Buenos Aires, to search for their nationals hiding there. (The same thing undoubtedly happened the other way around as well. Miguel Angel Estrella is certain that several of the men who tortured him in Montevideo had Argentine accents.) Many of the deaths and disappearances ascribed to the Uruguayan military in fact took place in Buenos Aires, where such techniques were more in fashion. If those victims had stayed in Montevideo, they would doubtless have been captured, tortured, and imprisoned, but they might still be alive.

Two of the Uruguayan military's most infamous murders were committed in Buenos Aires in May of 1976, when Héctor Gutiérrez Ruiz, the former president of the Uruguayan Congress's Chamber of Deputies, and Zelmar Michelini, the Frente Amplio's dynamic former senator (he was often referred to as Uruguay's Kennedy), were kidnapped and killed within hours of each other. The kidnappers bungled a simultaneous attempt to grab Wilson Ferreira, the Blanco senator who had been robbed of his Presidential victory several years earlier. He thereupon fled into exile in London. These actions were apparently part of a wider intermilitary offensive, in which the Southern Cone dictatorships made efforts to eliminate moderates who might try to rally "legitimate opposition" from their various safe havens around the world. Another such victim was Orlando Leteleier, Allende's former Foreign Minister, who, with his assistant, Ronni Moffitt, was assassinated, later that same year, by a car bomb planted by a Chilean hit squad in Washington, D.C.

Not all the Uruguayans captured in Argentina were disappeared—or, at any rate, permanently disappeared. One woman I met in Montevideo, a thirty-eight-year-old schoolteacher named Sara Méndez, told me that she had sought refuge in Buenos Aires and, in mid-1976, had been kidnapped. Her nineteen-day-old son was kidnapped along with her. That was the last she saw of the child, although she continues to search for him to this day. She was taken to Automotores Orletti, on Calle Venancio Flores, one of the worst torture centers in Buenos Aires, and was tortured continuously, under the direct supervision, she says, of a notorious Uruguayan colonel named José Nino Gavazzo. Several dozen other Uruguayans were also tortured there. (A further twist of irony is that only those Uruguayans who became victims in Argentina have had their cases fully and officially documented. *Nunca Más,* the report of Argentine President Raúl Alfonsín's National Commission on the Disappeared, includes a detailed survey of the fate of Uruguayans captured there. No similar effort has yet been undertaken by the reconstituted Uruguayan democracy to document the fate of Uruguayans captured in Uruguay.) During the first three months, the torturers tried to force Ms. Méndez and her compatriots to sign a document stating that they had been kidnapped not by the Uruguayan military, as their colleagues on the outside were frantically trying to tell anyone who would listen, but, rather, by those very colleagues, who, according to the document, were using such faked kidnappings as a way of sullying the honor of the Uruguayan military. Somewhere along the line, however, the torturers took a different tack: one day, the whole group of prisoners was secretly returned to Uruguay, where they were summarily "reappeared." Suddenly, their mug shots were being broadcast on Uruguayan television's evening news, and they were proclaimed to be a band of terrorists who had just been caught attempting to infiltrate the country from Argentina. (One of Michelini's daughters was part of this same group.) Following a mock trial, Ms. Méndez was sentenced to five years in Punta de Rieles.

Almost all the former political prisoners with whom I spoke in Montevideo described their initial reaction upon their arrival at Libertad or Punta de Rieles—whether from Argentina or from El Infierno or anywhere else—as one of relief. The reason was simple: the seemingly endless regimen of physical torture that had characterized their preliminary detention at last seemed to let up. Electroshock sessions, *submarino* immersions, and other such methods hardly ever occurred inside the prisons. Such torture had already served its purpose, and, besides, one could always be transferred back to El Infierno for a refresher course. The regime at Libertad and Punta de Rieles was more subtle. Major A. Maciel, who was a director of Libertad, observed at one point, regarding the prisoners under his charge, "We didn't get rid of them when we had the chance, and one day we'll have to let them go, so we'll have to take advantage of the time we have left to drive them mad."

Libertad, Punta de Rieles, and their associated institutions were methodically designed to demolish the mental, emotional, and moral integrity of their inmate populations. Furthermore, they were so designed by psychologists working closely with the military. "The war continued inside the prison," Dr. Martín Gutiérrez, Libertad's first psychiatrist and a subsequent senior adviser to the ruling junta, recently explained to Maxwell Gregg Bloche, an American physician who was investigating the behavior of military doctors in Uruguay. "Day after day, rule after rule—all was part of a grand design to make them suffer psychologically." It was precisely this drama—a prison conducted on behaviorist principles run amok—that so alarmed the visiting delegation from the International Red Cross.

Prior to the *dictadura,* behaviorist psychology had enjoyed relatively little currency in Uruguay. The psychology department of the university in Montevideo was overwhelmingly Freudian. One woman I spoke with, a psychology student who had been on the verge of completing her training the year of the coup, reported that, from one day to the next, most of her professors were fired, and more disconcerting yet, Freud himself was banished. New syllabuses were put together overnight, featuring behaviorist texts—especially American social psychology. She had to start again from scratch. She speculated that at one level Libertad was the behaviorists' revenge for past neglect.[21]

A Libertad veteran named Hugo recalled for me how, on the day of his arrival at the prison, he was immediately interviewed by a prison psychologist. "Now, I was arriving there after weeks of torture," Hugo said, "and here was this psychologist—very nice, expressing seemingly sincere concern about my well-being, wincing with apparent compassion at my descriptions of what had happened to me, assuring me that here everything would be safe, inquiring how he could be of help. The trouble was, everything was being taped, and every confidence was immediately betrayed. The same thing happened with everybody. If you told the guy you had this, that, or the other idiosyncrasy, he'd endeavor to find you precisely the sort of roommate who would most grate on you. If you mentioned that you were interested in historical books, he'd see to it that of the few books you ever did get, none were historical. If you said you just couldn't handle noise, he'd arrange for you to be placed in a cell right by the stairwell. If you said you desperately needed to be outside, he'd make sure that you got a cramped indoor job."

The regime at Libertad was based on a topsy-turvy system of negative and positive reinforcements. The reward end of the scale, for example, included the privilege of seeing visitors; the punishment, or sanction, end had various gradations, culminating in extended stints in *La Isla,* the dreaded block of isolation cells. (Of course, each category could be manipulated into its opposite: punishment might consist of the denial of visiting privileges, and it could get to the point where a reward was simply not being sent into solitary.)

The International Red Cross delegation noted in its report, "The implementation of every sanction is connected with a violation of the rules. The problem, however, is that such rules undergo daily changes, so that sanctions are never predictable. Every privilege may suddenly become a crime and therefore give rise to a sanction." Elsa Leone de Gil, a Uruguayan psychologist who has been specializing in the rehabilitation of former prisoners from places like Libertad, told me, "The environment was totally unstable and unpredictable. The prisoner inhabited a crazy world filled with perils. Orders were there to be followed absolutely, but they changed diametrically, arbitrarily, and without any notice, from one day to the next: Always keep this door open—always keep this door shut. Take a bath right now—at a moment when the water has been shut off—or else! Violations were recorded with mock-scientific thoroughness, so that you were made to see that—on paper, anyway—you had indeed now committed three violations, which had such-and-such a consequence. But it was all double binds piled on more double binds."

"Aquí Se Viene a Cumplir"—"Here One Comes to Obey"—declared a sign at Liberty. But it was precisely one of Liberty's horrors that within its walls to obey was almost impossible. Furthermore, even the rewards were spiked. For example, a family visit, when it did occur, took place by way of telephones, the inmate and his visitor separated by a double wall of glass, and at its conclusion the inmate still had to go through a full-body search. In addition, the conversation was continuously monitored, and the authorities eagerly exploited any chinks that became exposed in the process. Thus, as soon as one woman prisoner at Punta de Rieles, whose boyfriend had been faithfully visiting her for years, found out that he had fallen in love with another woman and intended to marry her, the authorities slapped the prisoner into solitary confinement, so that she could not be consoled by her friends on the inside.

Children's visits were particularly gruelling experiences, for both parent and child. A woman named Marta told me that whenever she took her four-year-old son to visit his father at the prison inside the Naval Artillery Barracks not only was she prevented from entering the prison at all, but the boy was required to walk the last block by himself.

He came to a huge door that opened and then closed with huge bolts. "There were three other kids in the room waiting, and eventually the four fathers were marched in, all wearing hoods, which they were not allowed to remove till the gate clicked shut behind the children," Marta said.

At Libertad, the International Red Cross noted, "the child who comes to visit (once a month) leaves his or her mother behind the barbed wire perimeter to meet his or her prisoner father in a pretty garden arranged specially for children's visits (sandboxes, slides, swings, etc.). The visit, which takes place on a bench, will be stopped as soon as the father makes an affectionate gesture. The punishment will be one or two months of disciplinary cell, with no visits. On the other hand, if the father makes no such gesture he will be able to meet his child during nine hours every year. In any event, following each visit the child is interrogated by a guard." In a further refinement, the authorities occasionally waited until a family had gone to the considerable trouble of travelling to the prison and standing in a long line before telling them that their loved one was being disciplined (which might or might not be the case) and hence was not being allowed visitors; the prisoner, for his part, was told that his family no longer cared and had stopped coming.

And all this was being painstakingly documented. Dr. Mandressi told me that at one point he was recruited to serve as an assistant to one of the prison's top psychologists, a doctor named Dolcey Britos, whom many former inmates have accused of being the mastermind behind the entire system. Whether or not Dr. Britos had conceived the whole thing, he clearly revelled in tracking it. Dr. Mandressi was shown reams of "statistical charts," ostensibly concerned with the classification of psychiatric disorders but in fact clearly intended to determine which sorts of sanctions proved most effective in aggravating which sorts of disorders.[22]

The prison psychologists also studied the effects of massive infusions of drugs. The International Red Cross report stated, "Tens of thousands of tranquillizers are handed out each month. Under prison conditions, the inmate's medical records are barely related to ordinary treatment, and are geared to a different purpose." Not surprisingly, under all these conditions many prisoners began to break; the prison psychiatrists did what they could to accelerate the process.

The Red Cross report documents a particularly tragic example in which "One prisoner, victim of a neurosis, spoke of having lived in his cell for several months with his father and his sister 'who had both been dead a long time,' until the prison doctor started to medicate him. Since that day, this prisoner cannot stand living anymore. He could live with his neurosis. He got used to the prison. With the added input of medicines, his condition has collapsed into psychosis." Once a prisoner had thus completely collapsed, the prison authorities made a point of finding him a new cellmate, one selected precisely on the basis of his particular vulnerability, at that moment, to the continuous presence of an insane roommate. According to the Red Cross report, one of the prison psychiatrists kept the following quotation, from the phenomenologist Ludwig Binswanger, framed above his desk: "I will pull out your eyes and put them in the place of mine; you will pull out my eyes and put them in the place of yours. Thus, you will look at me through my eyes, and I through yours."

No one had a name inside Libertad. Year after year, inmates were referred to by number alone: 612; 2228. . . . No one was allowed permanent possessions: whatever makeshift stash a prisoner might accumulate (a whittled keepsake, a daughter's drawing, a family photo) was subject to summary confiscation at any time. Late-night blitz searches were particularly frequent. Miguel Angel Estrella, who following his ordeal by chainsaw (in the end, his tormentors didn't actually cut off any of his fingers) was eventually remanded to Libertad (where he became #2314), recalled one such typical incident during his stay there:

> One time the guard barged into my cell. "So," he said, going over to a small photograph I had taped to the wall. "Who's that?"
>
> "It's my wife."
>
> "And who do you think she's fucking now?"
>
> "She's dead, Martha, my wife . . ."
>
> "Ah good! So she was a subversive just like you and they killed her."
>
> "No, she died of cancer."

> "So in other words she's no good for anything anymore."
>
> And with that he tore her photo off the wall, ripped it up and threw it at my feet. . . . Tears welled up in my eyes but I had to restrain myself. I couldn't even speak, I absolutely had to avoid registering any reaction. These sorts of provocations invariably led to thirty days in solitary—and often for your cellmate as well. The guy kept egging me on:
>
> "So, you subversives, when you talk about love, this is what you mean? You tear up your woman, you piss on her image, you stomp all over her. Doesn't it make you ashamed?"
>
> "I wouldn't be capable of doing such things." I began to pull my hands out of my pocket so as to gesture how I wouldn't be capable of doing that. . . . At which point he immediately slapped me with a sanction for "attempted assault."

No one had any privacy. According to Elsa Leone de Gil, Libertad's architecture was loosely modelled on that sinister eighteenth-century dystopia, the panopticon, a prison structure in which all the inmates could be observed without knowing when they were being observed. At Libertad, there were peepholes everywhere, and there were also bugging devices that would occasionally become conspicuously exposed, so that no one was ever permitted to imagine that he was *not* being observed at every moment. "Everything conspired to dehumanize the inmate," Gil explains. "When they were not being addressed by number, they were being called 'insect' or 'cockroach' or 'rat.' *'Apestoso'*—'diseased one'—was a frequent slur. The guards were trained to show revulsion at all times; they were never to touch an inmate's clothing or dishes, and were to act as if these really were infected." To vitiate against any possible softening in their attitudes, prison administrators saw to it that lower-level military guards never served stints of longer than two months. In this manner, as well, the generals contrived to assure the widest possible dispersion of complicity; no one in the army was permitted to imagine himself as some sort of innocent.

Hugo, the Libertad veteran, told me, "At first, things might have looked adequate, even better than adequate. Even the Red Cross people were initially fooled. For instance, they were told that we were shown movies all the time. That was true. Only, the movies were regularly shown out of focus. Or else the guards would take us to see a comedy and forbid us to laugh, on pain of sanction. And during one two-month stretch they forced us to watch a series of extremely violent movies, with extensive scenes of explicit torture—this at a time when the prison had just received a fresh batch of torture victims." "The authorities create tensions," noted the Red Cross monitors, "and then forbid the expression of those tensions."

Soon after word of Miguel Angel Estrella's incarceration at Libertad reached the outside world, an international support campaign was launched on his behalf. Hundreds of artists and musicians petitioned for his release. The Queen of England, by way of her cousin Lord Mountbatten, personally requested of General Álvarez, the then-head of the Uruguayan junta, that at the very least Estrella be provided with a piano, and in fact she sent him one. The authorities made an ostentatious display of their superior cultural breeding by announcing that, indeed, Estrella would be allowed to receive the Queen's piano. Only, what he actually received, there in his cell in Libertad, was the keyboard, ripped out and disengaged from the rest of the instrument. The prison authorities explained to Estrella (this world-class concert pianist, this prize pupil of the great Nadia Boulanger) that they didn't want his playing "disturbing the other inmates." Furthermore, he was even forbidden to receive any sheet music, since such pages would be peppered with terms in foreign languages *(fortissimo, pizzicato)* that could be concealing secret codes. All foreign words were forbidden at Libertad: saying "Thank you" in English would result in an immediate sanction.

"It was forbidden to sing," Estrella recalled in his testimony. "It was forbidden to smile or laugh. It was forbidden to draw—for instance the drawing of a woman was forbidden, especially a pregnant woman. Such a drawing would have been considered an act of subversion. Drawing a pregnant woman meant you longed to place in her belly the seeds of subversion. It was forbidden to draw a rose or a fish. Fish were symbols of resistance among the early Christians in Rome. If you drew a flower that even resembled a rose, that was a month in solitary, as 'ideological' punishment."[23]

The news was piped in, at full blast, over the PA system each day at noon—a recasting of the 6 A.M. national radio broadcast, which, already heavily censored, had meanwhile been further processed, staccato-cut, and static-jammed for prison consumption. (There would be a detailed account of a sports match, for instance, without the final score.) Every so often, the authorities staged nerve-jangling fake escapes—sirens wailing, floodlights sweeping, guns firing—just to keep everyone on his toes, and also to ferret out incipient leaders—people who might be caught trying to calm their fellows, for instance—for special attention.

An hour a day, inmates were allowed outside, to walk the grounds in circles, but never in groups larger than two; they were always subject to interruption by a guard, who would question each man separately about the topic of their discourse, under penalty of sanction. Most of the rest of the time, the inmates were kept locked in their narrow quarters, generally two to a cell, with a bunk bed wedged over to the side and one stool. Except during mandated sleeping hours, no one was allowed to lie on his bed, so one of the cellmates generally had to stand or pace.

This went on for years—six years, eight years, ten, twelve, more—until the prisoner's sentence had run its course. And then, when it was all over, the inmate or his family was expected to pick up the tab for room and board—a figure that could easily run into the thousands of dollars.

Shortly after democracy returned to Uruguay, in March of 1985, all of Libertad's inmates were released, and the prison itself was shut down—permanently, it was hoped. In November of 1986, however, following a riot of ordinary prisoners at a separate, somewhat overcrowded institution, the democratic authorities decided to reopen Libertad—temporarily, it was hoped, and this time under a civilian administration. I asked around Montevideo whether any former inmates might be willing to go there with me, and at length I was directed to a young man—I'll call him Alfredo Peña—who agreed to do so. Early one morning, we hired a taxi and headed west out of town.

Peña was thin and small-framed, and looked so young that when he informed me he'd put in twelve and a half years at Libertad, I could hardly believe him. He had been arrested at the age of twenty, he said, while he was a student activist at the university. A few years earlier, he explained, he had been romantically involved with a girl who was the daughter of an Army colonel. He had met her at an outing of his progressive parish—he'd been more religious in those days. On finding out about his daughter and Peña, the colonel had become obsessed. "At that time, this colonel's family lived in a modest apartment," Peña recalled. "Since then, believe me, he's moved up in the world. But he was already an extremely reactionary and authoritarian man; he treated his wife and his children the same as his men—life was war, and people were either subordinates or enemies. I refused to behave like a subordinate, so he hated me, and he continued to do so after his daughter and I broke up."

The countryside streamed by outside, generally flat, rolling hillocks, scrabbly ground, occasional stands of eucalyptus serving as windbreaks. "Anyway," Peña continued, "it turned out that there was a Tupamaro leader who happened to be named Alfredo *de la* Peña, and one day—this was shortly after the coup—the military apparently got hold of a document about some Tupa action with this guy's name on it. They published it, and three days later they suddenly hauled me in and began torturing me. One day, the colonel showed up at the torture center, yelling and screaming. He held me personally responsible for corrupting his daughter, both morally and politically, and now this proved everything—he was convinced that I'd seduced his daughter to spy on him, and he assured me that my continuing misery would be his ongoing personal project."

I asked Peña the colonel's name. He said he would prefer not to give it, and, for that matter, he'd prefer it if I didn't use his name, either. I asked if he was afraid the military might be coming back. "They don't have to come back," he assured me. "They're still here, only barely behind the curtain, totally unscathed."

Peña was tortured for weeks, and eventually he signed a confession —"I had to, I couldn't take it anymore"—on the basis of which he received a twenty-five-year sentence. He was released only when Libertad itself was shut down. Since then he had been able to track down a copy of his confession, and it turned out that the text was word for word identical—"right down to the spelling errors"—with the document about the Tupamaro action which the military had published three days before his arrest.

Peña went on to recall how a few months back, he'd been sitting with some friends at an outdoor cafe when he was introduced to a man who blanched at the very mention of his name. "I thought you'd been disappeared," the fellow stammered. It turned out that sometime after Peña's own jailing, the real Alfredo de la Peña had in fact been apprehended and that, indeed, he was on the sad, relatively short list of those the military actually did disappear.

We drove on, past occasional clumps of clapboard shacks, the homes of small-plot peasants (subsistence farming being the most the ground here seemed willing to grudge). Peña smiled: he was not past seeing the grim humor in his tale. In fact, he had a strong, tough, and probably saving sense of humor. "Everybody had his own story," he continued. "I had a friend who got married in 1972. He had a wedding reception, and then he and his bride went to a house in the country they'd rented for the night. They got there at three minutes to twelve. At twelve-fifteen, there was a knock at the door, and the guy went to the window to see who was there. It was a young kid with a bunch of flowers from a florist. So he opened the door and reached out to take the flowers, and suddenly, from behind this kid, the police came barging in. They bagged both him and his bride and dragged them away. The bride was later released, but the groom was tortured until he confessed to something or other; he ended up in Libertad, like me, and was released only at the end, like me. We always called him Billy the Kid—the fastest gun around—because his bride had a baby nine months after the wedding night."

A few moments later, Peña started in on another story, one from his own torture days. He told how a companion at the center was once thrown back into their cell, following a stint of *submarino,* incredibly battered. "I could see him through a crack in my hood, and I recognized him—he'd been a teacher of mine. He was moaning, spitting blood, saying he'd lost four teeth. I told him he should go back and look for them. A bit later he was was hauled out again, for some more battering. 'So,' we asked him when they brought him back, 'did you find them?' "

Peña laughed and then became quiet. "The guy committed suicide after his release." He sighed. "You know how they say there were only a couple hundred actual deaths under the dictatorship? That doesn't include all the people who couldn't hack it later, or who died of illnesses they contracted in prison. There have been hundreds of those, but nobody counts them."

The countryside kept streaming by. "I have no idea where we're going. I hope *you* do," Peña said to the driver, who did. "I mean, I was there for twelve and a half years, but I hardly ever *went* there—at any rate, not without a hood. You can see, though, what a terrible trek it was for people's families. Visitors had to be at the prison's gates by 8 A.M., and there were long lines, so visitors often had to arrive the day before and find someplace out there in the middle of nowhere to spend the night." This was going to be Peña's first time back.

And then there it was, looming on the horizon. "That's it," the taxidriver said. I don't know what I had expected—maybe the wretched, crumbling dungeon from the movie *Kiss of the Spider Woman*—but this was something altogether different. It was a sleek, white, rectangular, *modern* edifice. Basically, it looked like a Holiday Inn: five floors hovering in midair above massive steel pylons (the easier to prevent escapes, I suppose), two wings spreading out from a squat central tower (the panopticon's observatory). Road signs began to point the way to "RECUPERATION CENTER No. 2," which was what the prison was now called. We veered off the highway for the final approach.

More signs. A bleached billboard declaring, "Uruguay: the Task of Everyone" with, as backdrop, the silhouette of a large nesting bird stenciled over a map of Uruguay. A few moments later, another tattered billboard, the faces of smiling children and the legend "Nuestra Esperanza"—Our Hope. "The families were never allowed to drive these last two miles," Peña said. "They had to walk—old, broken parents, wives lugging infants and bundles. And then we had to walk, too, on the day of our release. Nobody was allowed to meet us at the gate. We had to walk the two miles out to the highway."

We drove on toward the entry, past a few preliminary checkpoints. "They're obviously trying to put on a better public face. In the old days, we would have been up against the wall by this point, rifles at our foreheads, soldiers screaming." When we presented ourselves at the main gate, unannounced—a foreign journalist and his guide—there was a certain amount of phoning back and forth, but presently we were ushered through several sets of gates. ("In the old days," Peña commented, "the Navy was in charge of the first gate, the Army of the second, and so forth—all part of this method of spreading complicity") and right into the office of the prison's new director, a dapper police commander named José Luis Pereyra Roldán. He apologized for the relative mess of his office, explaining that he and all the guards and janitors and inmates had arrived only a few weeks earlier. "We even had to figure out how to get the water and electricity turned back on," he said. Actually, the place was quite presentable. A little flag on his desk bore the spooky motto "Libertad o Muerte," and from the wall behind him peered the stern image of José Gervasio Artigas, Uruguay's George Washington (whose image has been appropriated, over the years, by everybody in Uruguay from the Army to the Tupamaros). The director assured us that the current prison regime had nothing in common with its predecessor. There were no soldiers here, he said, and he himself had been the civilian police commander in charge of a third of the precincts in Montevideo before he got his new assignment, which he didn't particularly like. "For that matter, none of us do. We do it to be of service." The director excused himself to attend to a phone call, and Peña nudged me, nodding toward the ashtray on the desk. At first, I didn't get what he was driving at, but then I noticed its insignia, "Brazilian Army," and the motto, in Portuguese, "Progress Through Order."

The director hung up and turned back to us. He wasn't going to be able to let us into the prison itself, he said—things were just too new and chaotic—but he could assure us that the prisoners were being well cared for; there were doctors, lawyers, psychologists, social workers, and teachers in abundance; visiting privileges were liberal; and the food in particular was excellent, plenty of meat. There were, of course, no political prisoners, only common criminals—muggers, pimps, murderers. The crime rate in Uruguay was low, and though it had initially risen with the return of democracy, it had now leveled off, to an average of only four felonies per day in all of Montevideo. "I mean," he said, "we're nothing like Fourteenth Street in Washington, D.C."—an odd reference, which he clarified by saying that back in 1972 he had received a fellowship to attend courses there at AID's International Police Academy.

After a while, he invited us to tour the grounds, exclusive of the prison itself, and assigned his lieutenant to show us around; this man unlocked the various gates but otherwise maintained a polite, deferential distance. "Well, obviously things have changed," Peña commented, *sotto voce.* "But a lot of things still remind me of the past. For instance, the whole manner of talking. They used to say exactly the same sorts of things in the old days. Take the business about the food, how fresh truckloads of meat arrived everyday—which was true, they did. Only, the guards carved off most of the good stuff to sell on the black market, and we inmates got mainly bones and gristle. There was incredible corruption. From our windows we could see trucks, overflowing with fruit, entering the compound, making a loop, and heading right back out, without even stopping."

We went into the building reserved for family visits. Peña had obviously never entered from this side; he'd never seen the large waiting room with its eerie Beckett-like label—*Sala de Espera* (the Spanish verb *esperar* means both "to wait" and "to hope"). Further inside we came to the room where the visits themselves were conducted, the long rows of facing tables no longer separated by the double panes of glass, which had been removed. The telephones over which prisoners and visitors had once had to commune had been removed, though their wires still dangled. Off to the side, through an open door, we could make out a dark warren of small cubicles: "The monitoring rooms," Peña whispered. Just before the exit, still in place though presumably no longer in use, stood a floor-to-ceiling wall divider with a face-size oval cut out of it, like one of those comic screens used by boardwalk photographers. "At the end of our visits," Peña explained, "we were allowed to kiss, but only through the hole, and never using our hands."

Outside again, Peña came to a sudden stop. "*La Isla,*" he whispered, nodding toward a particularly dilapidated white bungalow: the isolation chambers. "That was the worst sanction. They'd throw you in there for months at a time, into a tiny, windowless cell with nothing in it but a bare electric bulb, which was on twenty-four hours a day, and a spigot, whose water was controlled from the outside—you had to plead with the guards. A thin mattress was removed each morning and sometimes not returned in the evening. The meals gave you your only sense of time, but sometimes they skipped those, too, at random. You were hungry, but you couldn't tell whether you were supposed to be. You were on edge all the time, with no distraction whatever—no books, no pen, nothing. I used to keep track of time by killing one fly a day—dead flies wouldn't draw suspicion. One day, I was taken outside for a few minutes while they conducted a search—a search, for God's sake! What on earth did they think I could be hiding? But it was good, because when they let me back in I immediately noticed two new buzzing flies."

At Libertad prison, stints in the *Isla* could last up to ninety days at a stretch—a horrendous ordeal, but one that pales in comparison with the single most exquisite "refinement" in the Uruguayan military's arsenal, one the generals reserved for nine top Tupamaro leaders, who spent more than a decade each in absolutely solitary confinement.

Mauricio Rosencof was a thirty-eight-year-old, internationally renowned playwright when he was arrested on May 19, 1972, in an early stage of the final, all-out assault on the Tupamaros that coincided with the first months of the Bordaberry Administration. The son of Polish-Jewish immigrants (his father, a member of the Uruguayan Communist Party, had founded a tailors' union where meetings were initially conducted in Yiddish), Rosencof had himself founded a Communist youth group and traveled to the Soviet Union, around the time of Khrushchev's fall. "There," he says, "I realized the dreams of my father had not come true, and I began to adopt a more critical attitude"—one that, back home, proved no less critical of the pace of reform within the Uruguayan system. "One thing you have to understand about Latin America," he explains, "is that people watching their children dying of malnutrition can't be continually asked to wait for slow changes." He was one of the first to join Raúl Sendic (whom he'd met in 1956 when they were both young journalists covering a rice workers strike in the interior) in founding the Tupamaros. He was less an activist than a propagandist for the movement, but he proved particularly effective in that capacity and was therefore particularly despised by the authorities.

Following his arrest, he was tortured continously for nine months, so badly that he required four separate hospitalizations. He was then briefly remanded to Libertad prison. But one day in September, 1973, a few months after the military's final seizure of power and in the immediate wake of Pinochet's coup's in Chile, he and eight of his confederates were yanked out of their cells at nine o'clock in the morning and dispatched, in groups of three, to separate military reserves deep in the interior. The military declared that they were henceforth to be considered "hostages"—that was the word used, and that's how they became known—their immediate executions being the guaranteed price for any further acts of resistance by the shattered remnants of the Tupamaros.

"There wasn't a week that went by during those ten years," Rosencof told me, "when we weren't reminded that we could be dead at any moment. It would be simple, they told us—'shot in the back while attempting to escape.' We were kept in cells averaging two by one meters. They kept moving us around from one outpost to another, but the cells were consistent. No furniture. We could take three short steps on a diagonal, half turn, then back, like rats in a cage. That's if they even let us walk at all. Some years I spent, under orders, seated on a tiny bench facing the wall all day long. For a long time, Sendic was kept at the bottom of a dry well. We were beginning to think we were dead, that our cells weren't cells but rather graves, that the outside world didn't exist, that the sun was a myth. Seriously, in over eleven and a half years, I didn't see the sun for more than eight hours altogether. I forgot colors—there were no colors. The impact after all that of seeing green again for the first time was truly amazing.

"One of their games was denying us water. But once in a while they left a tin can there in the cell, which was a double relief. For starters, we didn't have to wait for the single time each day they allowed us to go to the bathroom, while we spent hours thinking about nothing but urinating, our vital organs trading places and our bladders supplanting our brains. But additionally, you can recycle your urine. If you let it stand until the salts sink to the bottom and the liquid settles to room temperature, it can be drunk at that precise moment. An hour later and it's nauseating."

I asked him how he survived at all.

"By dreaming," he replied. "Imagination. Taking long walks with my daughter. Sometimes, when the guards weren't looking, I'd stretch myself out for a sunbath on the beach. After a while I'd get hot and go off to get a nice, cold drink. Then the problem became hiding the bottle, because the cell was searched daily. You can imagine the trouble I'd have been in if the guards had suddenly uncovered a Coke bottle. Hiding objects acquired in my fantasies became quite a chore."

I'd read a memoir he'd composed where he spoke about how he made a confidante out of a rooster that wandered into his cell one day. I asked if the rooster had been real.

"I don't know," he said.

Some of the hostages survived by fantasy, others by brute rigor. I heard stories about Sendic down there in his narrow well. He was once asked how he survived. "I tried to grow," was his reply. The authorities allowed him an occasional Spanish edition of *Scientific American,* so he studied physics. (At the time of his arrest, his mouth and tongue had been shattered by a police bullet; he was denied proper medical treatment throughout the years of his incarceration, and it was only upon his release that surgeons began trying to salvage what they could. He'd never been a particularly dynamic speaker; now his voice, even after medical attention, was hardly more than a muddle, as no doubt had been the intention. He nevertheless began addressing rallies again, and the sheer effort his stigmata exacted conferred a certain fresh authority upon him.)

Others didn't survive at all, or at any rate, not whole. One died, of untreated cancer. And two went mad, one of whom was billeted alongside Rosencof the entire time. "I'd hear him screaming," Rosencof recalled. " 'Guard, get me water! Take me to the bathroom! I can't take it! I can't stand this anymore!'—more and more frantic, sinking deeper and deeper into madness by the week. We were all under continuous surveillance, soldiers peering at us through their peepholes day and night. But with him this fact seems to have provoked a psychotic breakdown. You see, he talked to himself all the time, and he became convinced that there was a tape recorder hidden somewhere in the room, recording all his words. And presently this tape recorder, which didn't exist, began to hum, to hum louder and louder, robbing him of sleep, and eventually robbing him of sanity itself. . . ."

What was the point of all this misery?

Obviously, one of its main functions, as the architects of the system declared outright, was to break the prisoners. But an even more important goal appears to have been to break the wider society. In Argentina, the repression affected a relatively circumscribed sector of the population; it would have been possible to live through the "dirty war" in Buenos Aires without personally encountering the family of even one of its victims. In Chile, similarly, the overwhelming brunt of ongoing repression, after the initial bloodbath and mass exiles, was borne by poor people, sequestered in their slums. Uruguay, however, was such a small country, and the repression there was so widespread, that everyone knew someone—knew several people, in fact—in prison or under torture. The military wanted it that way—relied on the fear that such knowledge engendered. Elsa Leone de Gil commented to me, "The panopticon at Libertad was merely a microcosm of the larger panopticon, which was the whole country. All Uruguay was under constant surveillance and subject to continual behaviorist conditioning."

And what, finally, was the purpose of that? What did the military want to do with a population that was so totally subdued? Eduardo Galeano, the noted Uruguayan writer, provided me with a characteristically terse, aphoristic reply: "In Uruguay, people were in prison so that prices could be free." Several other people I spoke with in Montevideo concurred, explaining that one of the main reasons for the military's repression was to enable the generals to hand the country's economy over to their "Chicago boys"—neoliberal economic technocrats, many of them trained at the University of Chicago under the monetarist influence of Milton Friedman, who prescribe an unfettered marketplace, with a minimum of government interference, as the cure for most of the world's economic ills (and in particular for those ills associated with the legacy of Import Substitution Industrialization). These economists generally oppose protective tariffs, social entitlements, minimum-wage standards, government safety-and-health regulations—the kind of things on behalf of which unions, for example, might be expected to struggle.

With the unions out of the way, the regime's economists might have thought they had been given a free hand. The Uruguayan military had a certain fondness for stark, proto-Fascist graphic imagery, and one particularly telling, and frequently reproduced, image was of a bold arrow labelled "Development," wrapped in a protective tube labelled "Security," hurtling toward a glowing star labelled "National Well-Being."

In Chile, that was pretty much the program. There the Chicago School held sway as completely and for about as long as it is ever likely to anywhere, and the considerable economic successes and failures of Pincochet's regime may provide the best extended case study for evaluating the merits of neoliberal free-market monetarism. In Uruguay, the situation was somewhat more convoluted. At the very beginning of the military period, in fact, it wasn't clear that the military wanted to take that route at all. One faction became so outraged by evidence of vast business and political corruption which it was uncovering during its interrogations of Tupamaros that it started to launch a reformist, almost progressive anticorruption offensive (something along the idiosyncratic lines of their colleagues in the Peruvian military back in 1968). By 1974, however, those zealots had been reined in. (One of their leaders, a Colonel Ramón Trabal, was mysteriously assassinated in Paris.) The free-marketers thereupon achieved ascendancy under the guidance of Finance Minister Alejandro Végh Villegas, a Harvard alumnus, actually, with prior practical experience advising military regimes in Argentina and Brazil. In the face of an occasionally wary military leadership (these soldiers, after all, had been reared in the Batllist welfare state), Végh and his successors were able to push through some, though by no means all, of the components of the classic package: a loosening of financial regulations, the cutting of social spending, the selling off of state-run corporations, the reduction of protective tariffs.

These actions at first produced many of the classic macroeconomic responses to Chicago-style planning. Between 1975 and 1979, industrial productivity soared by 17 percent, and the country's gross national product—stagnant or falling during the sixties and the early seventies —suddenly began surging at a historic high rate of 5 percent per year. "The social cost, however, was enormous, measured in emigration, falling real earnings, income concentration, and physical repression of all trade-union activists," according to Charles G. Gillespie, the political scientist at the University of Wisconsin. Real salaries, for example, fell 28 percent during that same period. But who among the workers was going to complain about such a calamitous decline, no less succeed in making such a complaint felt? Meanwhile, speculators made killings in real estate and finance, and multinational corporations encountered a friendlier environment. By the end of the military period, twenty of Uruguay's twenty-two private banks were owned by foreign conglomerates. Wealthy Argentines in particular, their own economy surging in similar fashion, poured into the vacation resorts of Punta del Este and Carrasco. The military decreed handsome pay raises for its officers, and even junior officers began moving into the wealthier suburbs, such as Montevideo's Pocitos district. A boom in luxury construction ensued.

By 1980, if one ignored the wider indications of general impoverishment (and the military-controlled press wasn't about to waste any ink bringing such figures to anyone's attention), one might almost have imagined the experiment to be a success. The generals, who were quite pleased with themselves, can perhaps be excused for assuming that almost everyone else was, too. Hadn't they put an end to the civil chaos of the sixties and the early seventies? (In 1976, for good measure, they had proscribed 15,000 former politicians, banning virtually the country's entire political class from any public activity for at least the next fifteen years.) Hadn't they brought prosperity?

It was against this backdrop—and, incidentally, under considerable pressure from the Carter Administration, with its vigorous human-rights agenda—that the Uruguayan generals now decided to set a plebiscite on a new draft constitution for November, 1980. They had noted Pinochet's success with a similar move in Chile in 1978. Just twenty-nine days before the scheduled vote, the military unveiled its new charter, consisting of 239 articles, compiled without the benefit of any public consultation. In his book, *Uruguay: Democracy at the Crossroads,*

Martin Weinstein writes: "In effect, the new charter would have ratified all the illegal acts of the regime and established a legal justification for the bans, political dismissals, and abuses committed by the dictatorship. In addition, 'national security,' as defined by the military and incorporated into the draft constitution, would have given the armed forces virtual veto power over all future government action."

Opposition to this constitution was furtive at first. Drivers took to running their windshield wipers with no cloud in the sky. Cafés posted signs with "NO" in huge letters and, underneath, in minuscule print, "*fumar*" (smoking). But for a very brief period shortly before the vote, the regime opened up the public space just a crack. For example, a new weekly entitled *Opinar,* edited by a lawyer and journalist named Enrique Tarigo, was allowed to publish, and to campaign against the proposed constitution. Tarigo himself was allowed to appear in a televised debate, and in it he expressed his objections vigorously. But such misgivings seemed to have been utterly drowned out by the regime's massive PR campaign, and polls of the still-cowed populace uniformly predicted a massive triumph for the constitution.

One evening over dinner, a group of Uruguayans endeavored to convey to me what the day of the vote was like.

"The results were a foregone conclusion," one woman said, prompting her companions. "Do you remember how we all stood in those sullen lines, no one so much as nodding at anyone else?"

"Nobody confided in anybody else how he was going to vote," another woman said. "Everyone assumed that everyone else was going to be voting with the military. And not only that—everyone was sure that if you so much as whispered to anyone else that you might not be, you'd quickly get yourself turned in."

"You voted, you left the precinct," a man commented. "Your eyes never left the ground, you just walked silently home."

"Back home that night," the first woman said, "we all sat glumly in front of our TV sets waiting for the inevitable. But it was the strangest thing: the early returns indicated that the constitution was going down to defeat."

"It turned out that everybody else had voted just like you!" the man exclaimed, becoming almost exultant at the recollection.

"The announcer kept breaking into this ironic smile as he continued reciting the incoming figures, remember?" the first woman said. "Remember how we all imitated him the next morning? And then the coverage blacked out altogether for a few minutes. It was as if the regime were hesitating, as if it were as surprised as the rest of us. Then coverage resumed, and the defeat continued."

Before the viewers went to bed that evening, the military's proposed constitution had lost, 57 percent to 43. I asked my dinner companions why they thought the regime had allowed the vote count to proceed.

"Uruguay has far too democratic a tradition for them to have faked the results," one man said. "It would have been obvious to everyone. Besides, it takes planning to fix an election, and they were certain that after the kind of decade that had preceded the vote, combined with the culture of repression, they couldn't lose."

"And besides," another dinner guest said, "they're Uruguayans. They longed for validation—for the legitimacy that such a vote would have retroactively afforded them."

"But after that," the first woman said, "already the next morning everything had clearly changed. People in the street regarded each other differently." Fifty-seven percent of Uruguay's population suddenly realized they were no longer alone.

The military's initial reaction to the results was stunned anger. The generals pointed out that in any case it was the constitution that had been rejected and not them. Furthermore, they maintained, the transition to any other sort of rule would have to be painstakingly gradual, with a limited national election impossible before November of 1984, and then only if everybody behaved. In the meantime, censorship, arrests, and torture continued. In fact, if anything, the military hardliners seemed to be in renewed ascendancy. (After all, look at the mess the "moderates" had wrought.) And then American pressure suddenly evaporated: in July, 1981, President Reagan, reversing a Carter ban, endorsed a fresh World Bank loan.

But now the regime's limited economic success began to sour. This was partly a result of the steep worldwide recession of the early eighties. In Uruguay, those international effects were aggravated by the regime's rigid adherence to monetarist strategies, aimed at stabilizing the country's currency, the peso, at any cost.

"The Chicago school technocrats advocated freedom in all prices," according to one of their critics, Alberto Couriel, a Uruguayan economist recently returned to Montevideo after having spent the years of the dictatorhsip in exile. "But they required that the government fix two sorts of prices, those of wages and those involving the projected exchange rate, in the latter case so that investors would have a secure environment for playing out their free speculations." Rather than letting the peso float vis-à-vis the dollar, the regime published a chart, a *tablita,* in which it announced the official exchange rate months into the future. As the peso's true value vis-à-vis the dollar moved further and further from that envisioned by the *tablita,* the regime quickly ran through its hard currency reserves and then began borrowing, at an exponential rate, in an attempt to back up the guaranteed rate. (This was the precise opposite of the usual Third World black market exchange situation: in Uruguay it was the central bank that was paying you more for your pesos than they were in fact worth anywhere else.) In 1976, Uruguay's foreign debt stood at about half a billion dollars; by April, 1981, it had climbed to $2.25 billion, and by December of that same year it had already reached $4 billion.

Meanwhile, speculators, convinced that this madness could not go on, were busy converting their pesos into dollars and spiriting them out of the country. In good Chicago School fashion, this process was unregulated. There was a period when almost as many dollars were leaving the country in capital flight as were being pumped in through desperately needed foreign loans. And Uruguay, of course, was being stuck with a legacy of interest payments on what were, in effect, transfers of dollars from one overseas account to another. By the end of their reign, the generals had saddled Uruguay with a debt of $5 billion, an extraordinary burden on a country with under 3 million citizens. (By contrast, an infamous basket case like Brazil, with its population of 140 million, faces a debt of $120 billion.)

Finally, in November of 1982, the regime suspended even the pretense of Chicago-style discipline, and the peso went into a free-fall, dropping from eleven pesos to the dollar to thirty-three in a matter of days. Those who had borrowed dollars on the basis of the government's assurances of a stable rate suddenly found themselves owing three times as much. A wave of bankruptcies naturally ensued. Economic growth stopped dead in its tracks, with the rise of 5 percent per year transformed into a 16 percent drop during the next two years. "A 16 percent decline in growth; an unemployment rate of 16 percent; a $5 billion debt; the exile or emigration of a fifth of the country's population, particularly its most technically skilled citizens; salaries losing half of their purchasing power between 1968 and 1984," Alberto Couriel summarizes. "This was the masterpiece of the Chicago boys."

In the midst of all this, at the end of November, 1982, the military allowed limited primary elections within the Colorado and Blanco parties (the Frente Amplio was still banned) to choose a group of delegates who might negotiate some sort of transition toward limited democracy and, under military tutelage, select a slate of acceptable candidates for the November, 1984, general election. Many individuals were proscribed from this vote, but the one whose specter most exercised the generals was the exiled Wilson Ferreira, the former Blanco Presidential candidate, who was spending his exile effectively lobbying against the regime in the capitals of Europe and North America. Not only was he barred from running in the 1982 campaign, but it was against the law even to mention his name. (When a prize bull from his ranch showed up at a county fair, with Wilson Ferreira's name displayed on the label dangling from its neck, the bull itself was arrested and carted away by grim MPs.) Notwithstanding such difficulties, the slate unofficially associated with Wilson Ferreira within the Blanco Party was the overwhelming winner in the 1982 primaries, receiving about 75 percent of the Blanco vote, while the Blancos received 53 percent of the total vote, compared with the Colorados' 45 percent. The anti-military candidates running in both parties garnered a total of 82 percent of all votes. The unmentionable Wilson Ferreira was thus clearly the front-runner in the early jockeying for the 1984 election.

Shocked and chagrined by the election results, the military returned to its hard line. Instances of arrest and maltreatment once again increased—most notably in June, 1983, when several dozen protesting university students were detained and tortured. A preliminary set of talks between the generals and some civilian delegates, at the Parque Hotel, on the Montevideo beachfront, broke off inconclusively in early July. A month later, the military issued a new decree, suspending all political activity. The Reagan Administration responded to this development by nearly doubling its request to Congress for military-training aid to the generals in Montevideo.

At this dark moment, a remarkable new figure arose: a young Jesuit priest—in this notoriously anti-clerical country—named Luis Pérez Aguirre. He was the extraordinarily handsome scion of one of Uruguay's wealthiest and politically most conservative landed dynasties. (His mother's family was very close to the Bordaberrys.) "With my family's wealth, I really could have had anything I wanted in a material sense," Pérez Aguirre told me one morning. "For instance, I loved flying planes. But gradually I came to a crisis in my life. When I flew, for instance, I was always looking for plenitude, wholeness, felicity. But, especially faced with all the suffering around me, I came to realize that you reach that plenitude only when you give, not when you take, pleasure—when you die to yourself so as to give life." Pérez Aguirre entered a Jesuit seminary in Argentina and subsequently studied in Canada as well.

In 1970, he returned to Montevideo and was ordained. He worked first with university students and then, for six years, among prostitutes. In 1979, he became more directly concerned with human rights. "I became preoccupied with the paralysis, the demoralization, and I felt it was my responsibility to do something." The first thing he did was to found a journal, *La Plaza*—in effect, "The Public Place." "*La Plaza* was the only place where people could talk freely, if initially only in a general manner, about what was going on," he recalls. "We focussed on the human rights situation, and required that our contributors sign their own names. The military, which was prepared to disrupt any clandestine activity, didn't know what to do with people who were organizing openly."

In 1981, following the award of the Nobel Peace Prize to the Argentine Adolfo Pérez Esquivel, for his work on behalf of the Buenos Aires branch of the human-rights organization SERPAJ—an event he covered in the pages of *La Plaza,* Pérez Aguirre decided to found a SERPAJ branch in Montevideo. It was the first organization devoted to work on behalf of the victims of repression and poverty to be established in Uruguay since the advent of the dictatorship. Pérez Aguirre was repeatedly arrested and incarcerated. But a growing movement of international support led to his eventual releases. "Once," he told me, "the Canadian government refused to go ahead with a big trade agreement until I'd been set free." He smiled, and added, "I was traded for beef."

I asked him if he was ever tortured. "Oh, yes," he said. "Of course. Repeatedly. That was the system here." He rolled up his shirtsleeves to show me a line of cigarette-burn scars running up each arm. "Physical, but especially psychological. They were very sophisticated in how they tried to break each person, through isolation and humiliation, and so forth. Once, in a Montevideo prison, I was brought into a public office and kept under the table, like a dog, with my legs cramping up, for hours on end, all day long, all the passersby seeing me like that. But religious people are trained for such situations. Once, in a military barracks, a cellmate of mine was thrown back into the cell after a session of torture, and he told me I was lucky, because I knew how to pray. All he could do, he said, was count up to a thousand and back. Still, the torture sessions could be quite arduous. Once, in the midst of everything, I started hearing someone speaking in English, giving instructions. At the time I thought I was hallucinating, but in retrospect I'm sure I wasn't."

SERPAJ took the lead in denouncing the tortures of the university students in June, 1983, and for the first time in the history of the dictatorship graphic and detailed testimony was provided on a human-rights violation as it was happening. Some of the opposition press, including Tarigo's *Opinar,* followed by extensively publicizing SERPAJ's charges. The regime became more and more annoyed. Pérez Aguirre started being taken in once a week for fifteen-hour interrogations.

When the Parque Hotel talks collapsed, one of his interrogators warned him that within days SERPAJ and all other political institutions were going to be delegalized. "We decided to raise the ante," he recalled. "Three of us decided to embark on a hunger strike. People were very skeptical. They told us that there was no tradition of Gandhi-style resistance in Uruguay, and that it wouldn't work. But we decided to go ahead. We established ourselves in the rooms in the convent that SERPAJ had been using as its offices." Uruguay's relatively pliant Catholic hierarchy had not supported Pérez Aguirre in any of his actions, but he had forged an association with a community of elderly nuns, and they had agreed, despite considerable pressure, to shelter his good works. "As soon as we started, there was a big commotion. People would come to visit us—especially the politicians—expressing solidarity. We didn't declare any particular terms for ending our fast. We just asked the population to reflect and to organize itself and to put pressure on the military and to inspire the political leaders, who were all depressed by the collapse of the talks and the new ban on political activity. It was hard to get word out, of course, since all the press was again being rigorously controlled. But we had a network, and people began coming to our office each day to talk and organize. After the second day, the convent was surrounded by the Army, and after the fourth day the phone line was cut. But people kept coming—hundreds of supporters. They would be repressed. The MPs were arresting two hundred at a time. But then more would show up. Everybody knew.

"And on the night of August 25, our old national holiday, the people reacted in a very impressive way. At eight o'clock, the lights all over the city went out. And then, at eight-fifteen, there began a great banging of pots. A huge noise, all over town. We gave up our fast the next morning. A group of diplomats from France and Holland came to help escort us out.

"The military didn't know what to do with us. They decided not to arrest us, but they delegalized SERPAJ. We reorganized under a new name, and some high-up untouchables lent us their support. But the important thing was that the politicians had been revitalized. And a few years later the new civilian government, as one of its first acts, relegalized SERPAJ."

The August 25 *caceroleo,* as it was called (*"Hola! Hola! Esta noche, hay caceroleo!"* the housewives of Montevideo chanted in their darkened back-yards as they smashed their pots together), was the first of several public demonstrations. On November 27, which had formerly been an election day, a huge demonstration, of over three hundred thousand citizens, converged on a central Montevideo square demanding a return to democracy. On January 18, 1984, resurgent unions managed to pull off a one-day general strike. Meanwhile, things were changing all over. The Argentine junta, thoroughly discredited by the fiasco of its 1982 war with Britain over the Falklands, was in fast retreat; a civilian

President, Raúl Alfonsín, had been elected in October of 1983 and took office in December. (Four months later, Wilson Ferreira returned from Europe and established himself in Buenos Aires, so as to be close to the developing action in Uruguay.) In Brazil, the *apertura,* the liberalization of its military regime, was in full swing.

Confronted with these trends, with the growing public opposition at home, and with the calamitous economy, the Uruguayan generals once again reassessed their situation. Back in 1976, the last elected president, the reactionary Bordaberry, who was still trying to use the military rather than simply be used by them, had written a memo warning them that if they assumed the tasks of administration, they would inevitably be judged by the successes or failures they produced in that administration, and that furthermore such a role would eventually threaten the institutional cohesion and integrity of the armed forces themselves. Bordaberry's warnings were ignored, but they were remarkably prescient.

Over and over, in country after country throughout Latin America, the doctrine of national security kept running up against the same wall: the doctrine required the military, as the one cohesive, unified, purposeful entity in the country, to take charge of administering both the war against subversion and the development of the country itself; but precisely through the vicissitudes of such administration the military's own cohesion, unity, and sense of purpose would come under threat. Corruption would eat away at discipline. Factionalism would sap morale. More than anything else, it was these sorts of concerns that in 1984 were animating the Uruguayan generals, and particularly the new head of the Army, the influential Hugo Medina.

The military wanted to get out, but on its own terms. And not all the way. It wanted to retain as much control as possible behind the scenes; in particular, it wanted to prevent a Wilson Ferreira Presidency, which at that moment still seemed the most likely outcome of an open 1984 election. With this in mind, the military now launched a campaign to assure a Colorado victory. To begin with, astonishingly, the generals relegalized the left, freeing the Frente Amplio's leader, General Seregni, from prison in March, 1984, and presently even reinstating the party itself. Somewhat alarmed at these developments, Wilson Ferreira boarded a boat in Buenos Aires on the night of June 15 and arrived in Montevideo, to great public fanfare, the next morning. He was immediately arrested and flown to incarceration in a barracks deep in the interior. Following another general strike, on June 27, the generals and the civilian politicians started a new round of talks, this time in the grounds of the Club Naval, in Montevideo. The Blancos boycotted these talks, in protest over the imprisonment of their leader. The Frente Amplio, however, participated (Seregni himself did not; though freed, he was still technically forbidden to pursue political activities), at least in part as a way of reestablishing their institutional legitimacy and beginning to efface the stain of the left's perceived role in the events that originally led to the dictatorship.

The Club Naval talks proceeded throughout July. The civilian negotiators were headed by the new Colorado Party leader, a widely respected center-right lawyer named Julio María Sanguinetti, who had been one of Bordaberry's last education ministers, though he resigned when his faction of the party left the government. Many felt he had largely sat out the dictatorship, neither collaborating with the military nor particularly distinguishing himself in opposition—though, in fairness, his supporters insisted he'd worked quietly behind the scenes, and he had, for example, resigned his post as one of the editors at *El Dia,* back in 1980, when the paper's owner refused to campaign against the military's constitution. Clearly, he and Medina had been involved in delicate behind-the-scenes talks for some time. (Clearly, too, he had become the Presidential candidate most favored by the American Embassy.) During the month, the military promulgated a series of Institutional Acts sequentially dismantling much of the repressive apparatus it had established in previous Institutional Acts. On August 3, the Club Naval talks concluded successfully, though without any formal signed agreements. Whether or not there were any secret protocols was later to become a subject of intense controversy.

The way was now cleared for the Presidential and legislative elections to be held on November 25. Sanguinetti would be allowed to head the main Colorado slate. Tarigo was enlisted as Sanguinetti's running mate, in order to help gain the support of the Colorado's more reformist wing. Neither Wilson Ferreira, still in prison, nor Seregni, still politically banned, was allowed to run. The Frente Amplio drained support from the Blancos, as the military intended, and Sanguinetti in any case ran a masterful campaign, portraying himself as a capable, steady, moderate, responsible administrator, with his eye on the future of the country. In the end, the Colorados claimed 41 percent of the vote (identical with their 1971 showing), the Blancos 35 percent, and the Frente 21 percent. The Frente only narrowly failed to win the Montevideo mayorality, probably owing to a last-minute decision by the military to have all the votes of its soldiers, no matter where they were stationed, counted as if they were residents of the capital. A few days later, Wilson Ferreira, who now had a fair claim to consider himself robbed of the Presidency for a second time, was released.

Sanguinetti took office, on schedule, on March 1, 1985. On March 8, he signed a bill that constituted, in effect, an amnesty for all remaining political prisoners. (The torturers and other military violators of human rights were explicitly excluded from this amnesty.) On March 10, Libertad was shut down, and its remaining inmates walked the two miles from the gate to the main highway, to be met by their families. On March 14, Raúl Sendic, the last of the eight surviving Tupamaro "hostages," was released.

Sanguinetti, for his part, decided to establish his executive offices in an imposing modern building on the edge of town, near the junction of several major highways, which the generals had originally built to house their Defense Ministry. (They were transferred to more modest quarters.) The building was named Libertad.

The released prisoners and the returning exiles now encountered a country that was, in the words of the writer Eduardo Galeano, "as if bombed by economic crisis." Alberto Couriel told me that in his absence his once proud Montevideo had been "Latin-Americanized." The city looked almost the same as it had when he left, eleven years earlier, but the houses were shabbier, the apartment buildings less well maintained, the cars more conspicuously out of date. "Like Havana," he said, with a smile. Everyone I spoke with commented on the nightly apparitions of decrepit horse-drawn carts carrying ragpickers on their midnight rounds, scavenging downtown garbage to bundle back to their hovels on the outskirts. And there were the children begging. According to SERPAJ, 240,000 Uruguayans—nearly a tenth of the country's population—are now children living below the poverty line. Mauricio Rosencof said, "Kids used to come up and ask you for money in the old days, too, but now they come in clusters, like grapes." Marcelo Vignar, the returning psychoanalyst, couldn't get over the proliferation of street vendors—onetime skilled professionals, people he'd worked with in the hospital, who had been forced out of their jobs and now lined the sidewalks, hawking maté gourds, old clothes, and lottery tickets.

The bleached-out store windows featured things like sneakers—or even books—available on the installment plan. Galeano commented, "In the old days, Uruguayans bought five or six times as many books as they do today. Then came censorship, and now what the police forbade is forbidden by price." Louise Popkin, an American translator and a frequent visitor, told me, "It's true that this place is not as poor as El Salvador or Mexico, but poverty here is much more conflictive because of the fall from a nostalgically imagined paradise. People here are *ashamed* of their current poverty—of having become so threadbare. They don't know *how* to be poor."

Sanguinetti, though, was turning out to be a responsible administrator, a man with a flair for the job, and he'd surrounded himself with capable public officials, most notably Enrique Iglesias, his Foreign Minister, who had served from 1972 to 1985 as the Executive Secretary of the United Nations Economic Commission for Latin America and the Caribbean. Sanguinetti and Iglesias and their colleagues were attempting to fashion an export-led recovery, and the exports for 1986 were indeed up 30 percent over those for 1985. Growth, which had stood near zero in 1985, was back at 6 percent in 1986. (Sanguinetti had been helped here by a steady worldwide decline in both oil prices and interest rates.) Unemployment was down from its high of 16 percent, late in the dictatorship, to just over 10 percent.

If the previous decades had shown anything, it was that neither the ISI nor the Chicago School model was going to work in Uruguay, and Sanguinetti and his men were now trying to cobble together some new approach, though one closer to the Chicago School model than the earlier one. For one thing, they were hoping to turn Uruguay, so strategically situated between the potential Argentine and Brazilian powerhouses, into a financial center or platform, a future Hong Kong or Singapore. With this in mind, they placed a very high priority on maintaining good relations with the country's creditor banks, and their record in keeping up the interest payments, of over $400 million per year, on the enormous debt was exemplary. The banks were once again holding Uruguay up as "a model country," although many Uruguayans grumbled that the banks were holding Uruguay up, plain and simple.

Yet, despite the rosy economic indicators that Sanguinetti's team was beginning to display, many Uruguayans harbored persistent doubts. In part, the surge in exports reflected the effects of an explosive consuming binge that Brazil had embarked upon during the heyday of its first inflation-fighting "Cruzado plan," which had now gone bust. And the decline in unemployment in part reflected continuing large-scale emigration, particularly among young people, many of whom were no longer even trying to enter Uruguay's cratered economy. The number of those leaving, in fact, still vastly exceeded the number of exiles returning.

One day, an elderly woman who was showing me around her neighborhood boasted about the local high school. "This is a great high school," she said. "Over half the graduating class has left the country." The young leave, and the great majority of the young who left a generation ago do not return. Back in New York, after my 1986 visit, I asked a forty-six-year-old Uruguayan journalist who works for a European press agency at the United Nations whether he had considered going back. "How could I?" he replied. "To what job? Besides, several members of my family down there rely on the small checks I'm able to send them. They couldn't afford to have me come back." The median age in Uruguay is forty-seven. In the United States, it's thirty-two.

The country's economy staggers along, and meanwhile the victims of the repression try to fit back in. Sanguinetti's government offered help by way of a decree stipulating that all former public employees who had been unjustly stripped of their jobs by the military regime, whether through imprisonment, blacklist, or exile, could return to them. This was, of course, a blessing for many (so far, more than 9,000 have taken the government up on its offer), but many others were in the position of my traveling companion Alfredo Peña. "I'm having a terrible time finding a job," he told me as we drove back from Libertad. "After all, my life was cut off at the age of twenty, and now, twelve years later, I'm just thrown back in. The people who were already established can resume their lives, perhaps, but I hadn't even started mine. Most jobs require experience, and I don't have any. The jobs that don't require experience are for young people—and the employers of young people don't want to waste their time with someone like me. And, anyway, I *am* awkward. I have had none of the experiences of my peers on the outside. In many ways, I feel I'm still twenty: I live with my family—I couldn't possibly afford an apartment of my own. I identify with twenty-year-olds, but they're different, too. It's a kind of limbo. In Argentina, the authorities disappeared people. In Uruguay, they disappeared people's lives."

"Once we got out, we were suddenly confronted with all these problems," Mauricio Rosencof commented. "Ridiculous problems—doorknobs, for instance. I had no reflex any longer to reach for the knobs of doors. I hadn't had to—hadn't been *allowed* to—for over thirteen years. I'd come to a closed door and find myself momentarily stymied—I couldn't remember what to do next. Or how to make a dark room light. How to work, pay bills, shop, visit friends, answer questions. My daughter tells me to do this or that, and one problem I can handle, two I can handle, but when the third request comes I can hear her voice but my head is lost in the clouds. I feel like an athlete who has stopped exercising and is suddenly required to run in a five-kilometer race—and that's just walking down the block. And walking down the block I'm in a perpetual cringe. I'm constantly stopping to let whoever is behind me pass: my body keeps expecting a blow from every side."

"You get different sorts of response from different people," Louise Popkin told me, speaking of her many conversations with released prisoners. "Some tell you, 'I'm a total mess, God do I need therapy.' Some say, 'You can't go through an experience like that and not be marked, I was marked, but I take responsibility for it and I try to go on.' Some say, 'What a marvelous experience prison turned out to be'

—they launch into some long political speech and end up insisting that they're fine, they're just fine. Of course, they're in the worst trouble of all."

"The prison experience is a bit like an ironworks," Marcelo Vignar, the psychoanalyst, told me, drawing on his experiences in treating victims of repression. "With a human being, as with iron, beating can either strengthen or break. Some people are deepened by the experience, others . . ." He shook his head, and mentioned a man I'd met a few days earlier. "He, for instance, has been made lesser, narrower. You should have known him before. He was expansive, delightable, brilliant. Now he's foreshortened, brittle."

Some returning prisoners were having children—and in a hurry. One of the ways they'd tormented the women at Punta de Rieles was with the prospect of ending up childless. Prison psychiatrists kept assuring their young prisoners that they wouldn't be released till well past menopause. In some cases they proved right, but other prisoners just made it. One evening I went to a rally of the reconstituting Tupamaro movement (the Tupas still retain their radical political agenda, though they have foresworn the use of violence, promising instead to pursue more traditional tactics, at least for the time being).[24] Several thousand individuals jammed into a small soccer stadium, the leaders orating fiercely from a stage framed by a "wall of martyrs" (blown-up photographs of dozens of felled comrades, draped with flowers). I was struck by all the gray hair in the audience—and then doubly struck by the relative youth of many of those with the gray hair. I was struck by that, and by all the babies. They'd cordoned off the back third of the soccer field as a large playground, and children were crawling and scampering about, oblivious to the fierce diatribes (even that of Sendic himself, with his commanding wreck of a voice), all taken up in a vast Breughelian swirl. I met a couple. They described to me how he'd been captured early on and sentenced to six years at Libertad. She could never come to visit him because she was hiding underground. Finally he'd been released, they'd met up and enjoyed a few days together, and then all of a sudden she'd been arrested and sentenced to ten years. She'd only been released as part of the amnesty. She was pregnant.

For all the hopes embodied by new children, many returning prisoners faced their biggest challenge in learning how to parent kids who'd grown up in their absence. "It takes thirteen years of preparation in the best of circumstances to learn how to be ready to parent a teenager," one therapist told me. "Here you have parents who've been away the entire time, who arrive on the scene confused, disoriented, and debilitated in all sorts of ways, and suddenly you expect them to deal with teenage kids! The situation is compounded by the years of idealization that have gone on on both sides—parents for whom the growing child on the outside was the thin, pure reed around which they organized their entire psychological survival; children who nurtured an almost fairytale conception of their absent parent's virtue and prowess and heroism. And now the parent is back, trying to regulate the volume on the record player. You see it over and over again, the kids finally shouting, 'Who are you to order me around? Where were you all those years when I needed you?' The parents crumpling when faced with the dissonance of this new reality in which *they're* being cast as the arbitrary disciplinarians. Families shattering under the strain. There are hundreds of divorces. You see these people who spent over a decade yearning to be with their families—and then they can't be with their families. You see them walking around the city, all alone."

You do see a lot of zombies walking along the streets of Montevideo. I asked Louise Popkin whether she assumed they were all veterans of Libertad. "Oh no," she said, "because I don't assume that prison was necessarily the worst experience. You had people in prison, you had people in exile, you had people in inxile—and all three of those experiences, in their different ways, created zombies."

Therapists who've been working with the survivors of Uruguay's repression often comment on the ways in which the three groups—those out of prison, those back from exile, and those who'd stayed and cowered—seemed to inhabit three different universes, each imagining they'd suffered more than the others, or that the others' suffering was somehow less real. They all talked past each other, further contributing to the general social fragmentation that was another legacy of the generals. "All of us were affected," a young therapist named Damian Schroeder commented. "That's why we try to avoid setting up therapy groups exclusively for torture victims, or relatives of disappeared persons, or returned exiles. That would just exacerbate the fragmentation, when what we desperately need are vehicles for reintegration." He explained that he preferred to work with groups that included, say, a veteran of Libertad, the grown child of a disappeared father, a returned exile, and a soul-wracked inxile. But, he went on, such groups were at best reaching only a minuscule proportion of the population; many were still too shell-shocked to seek help; and anyway, there were far too few resources and far too little money to help even those who were reaching out.

Marcelo Vignar, for his part, pointed out that therapy—individual or group—could only do so much, that finally the problems facing Uruguay in its reintegration were political. They'd been contracted as a community, and sooner or later they were going to have to be addressed as a community as well.

Perhaps the biggest problem that Uruguay faced in the latter half of 1986, and certainly the one most roiling the political waters, was the question of what to do with the former torturers. This problem has confounded each of the Latin-American countries in turn as one by one they have attempted to navigate the passage back from national-security dictatorship to some sort of constitutional democracy. And, as the participants at that Aspen Institute conference on the punishment or pardon of state crimes noted, the question here is not simply one of justice—what to do with particular individuals who can be shown to have participated to varying degrees in various sorts of tortures—but also one of truth, of how to document what really went on during the previous period and how to assimilate and honor that knowledge.

Such issues of truth and justice, meanwhile, have to be addressed within the context of the ongoing existence of social sectors that themselves participated, to varying degrees, in the repression. In Argentina, the process was somewhat facilitated by the fact that the military there abandoned power in abject defeat; for at least several months, the new civilian government in Buenos Aires found it possible to pursue both truth, through *Nunca Más,* and a modicum of justice, through public trials of leading members of the junta and other senior offenders. In time, the Argentine military regrouped and began to mount an increasingly stiff resistance to the civilian incursions, and the situation has grown more and more complex.

In Brazil, the process was finessed, in part owing to the fact that the military there managed to leave gradually, so that when the final transition to democracy occurred, the worst human-rights violations were a full fifteen years in the past. Besides, the worst violence had all along been aimed at a comparatively small sector of society. The transition was accomplished within the context of a consensus—subscribed to, for the most part, by both the ruling elites and the middle class (the only two groups with any real clout at the time)—that there would be no need for exhaustive trials or, for that matter, for any trials. The interests of truth were nevertheless fortuitously served by the remarkable efforts of the secret team that, working under the auspices of the archbishop of São Paulo, produced the best-selling volume *Brasil: Nunca Mais.*

Uruguay's situation had none of these facilitating characteristics. The military there had left power largely of its own volition, and certainly unbowed, while gross human-rights violations were occurring right up to the moment of its leave-taking—violations that affected a much wider proportion of the country's citizenry. The size of the country inevitably presented particular difficulties during the Uruguayan transition. Almost half of the population lived in the capital, and, even so, Montevideo was not a large city. When the exiled widow of the assassinated legislator Gutiérrez Ruiz reclaimed her family home following the return to democracy, it turned out that José Nino Gavazzo, allegedly one of the most notorious torturers, was living in a house just down the street; each morning, she faced the prospect of having to see him. Pérez Aguirre, for his part, had already twice encountered his torturer on the street. Such chance meetings were fairly common, and they happened even more often in the small towns of the interior.

It's not at all clear what, or whether, arrangements regarding all this were agreed upon during the negotiations at the Club Naval. For a while, Sanguinetti maintained in interviews that the subject hadn't even come up. At one point, he told William Montalbano, of the Los Angeles *Times,* "The question of amnesty for the military was not discussed in the negotiations, just as no one said that the jailed prisoners would be turned loose the day after an elected government took office. It was an intelligent omission. We were seeking ways to remove obstacles, not to create them. You can't make a peace treaty discussing the origins of the war."

Nevertheless, when that first amnesty was promulgated, within days of Sanguinetti's inauguration, violators of human rights were expressly excluded from its provisions. More recently, Sanguinetti's people have admitted that during the negotiations the future President assured General Medina that the executive branch would not itself launch any prosecutions of violators, though it would not stand in the way of private citizens' bringing claims through the normal judicial channels. Some observers feel that in fact there were also guarantees as to what would eventually be done about such judicial actions, but Sanguinetti emphatically denies this.

Very early in the new administration, Uruguayans began lodging complaints against specific individuals, alleging torture, kidnapping, disappearance, extortion, rape, murder, and other violations, and the judiciary undertook a deliberate and painstaking consideration of these claims. Presently, thirty-eight cases, involving almost 400 accusations against 180 officials (torturers, psychologists, doctors, supervising officers, and others), were wending their way through the courts. The military initially refused to allow any of its members to honor subpoenas to appear before civilian courts, on the ground that they could be tried only by juries of their peers—that is, before military courts. This issue sidetracked developments for almost a year while the question made its way up to the Supreme Court. The closer that court's decision loomed, however, and the clearer the indications that the court would decide in favor of civil jurisdiction, the more agitated the military became and the fiercer its demands for a speedy resolution of the entire situation.

In September, 1986, President Sanguinetti's Colorados proposed a blanket amnesty for the military. "Originally, I personally wanted some trials and a partial amnesty," he subsequently told Montalbano. "But once a general amnesty was declared for one side it became almost indispensable for the other." This sort of logic became the object of heated protest. For one thing, many victims of the worst repression had been ordinary citizens going about their ordinary lives; they had never belonged to any "side" of any putative "war." Furthermore, how could there be any basis for the claim of virtual equivalence between the situation of prisoners who had spent five or ten or more years undergoing continuous physical or psychological torments and the situation of those who had been administering the torments and had never suffered even the slightest inconvenience as a result? The Colorado Party's initiative was easily defeated by a coalition of Blanco and Frente legislators.

As the Supreme Court now began assigning civil jurisdiction in one case after another, nineteen retired Uruguayan generals issued a statement proclaiming the "irreversible solidarity" of the armed forces and declaring that no soldier would ever be required to honor the subpoena of a civilian court. "Armies cannot be tried after the fact for winning wars," the generals asserted, and then, in an eerie variation on the old Tupamaro slogan, "Either we are all responsible or no one is responsible."

In reply to this assertion, Pérez Aguirre declared that, on the contrary, not everyone in the military was guilty and that indeed it was only through the just application of the law that the innocence of the great majority of its members could be firmly established. But the Blancos, in particular, were growing increasingly nervous about the prospect of widespread and blatant military disobedience. Alberto Zumarán, a Blanco Party lieutenant, who had been Wilson Ferreira's stand-in during the 1984 Presidential election, warned, "The threat is not of a coup but of something worse: a sector of society that remains defiantly outside the law—a kind of permanent de facto coup." The Blancos proposed an amnesty of their own, covering everything but the most egregious cases. That, however, was too little for the Colorados, who were holding out for a blanket amnesty, and too much for the Frente, who were outraged because under this formula wholesale torture would not be considered an "egregious crime." On October 17, 1986, the Blancos' initiative, too, went down to defeat.

The military was growing more and more adamant in its refusal to allow itself to be judged in civilian courts, and at the same time the debate among civilians was intensifying. Sanguinetti asked rhetorically, "What is more just—to consolidate the peace of a country where human rights are guaranteed today or to seek retroactive justice that could compromise that peace?" It was becoming a question of how the future development of democracy could best be secured: by cautiously refraining from its full exercise at this delicate juncture or, rather, by boldly insisting upon it. "Democracy isn't just freedom of opinion, the right to hold elections, and so forth," one exasperated judge told me. "It's the rule of law. Without equal application of the law, democracy is dead. The government is acting like a husband whose wife is cheating on him. He knows it, everybody knows it, but he goes on insisting that everything is fine and praying every day that he isn't going to be forced to confront the truth, because then he'd have to do something about it." Eduardo Galeano offered a different analogy in an interview he gave *Report on the Americas,* the bimonthly magazine of the North American Congress on Latin America: "On the part of the government and some important sectors of the population, there is a belief that democracy is a fragile old lady in a wheelchair. If she moves too much she will collapse, and if you speak too loudly she will have a heart attack. So democracy is something that shouldn't be touched. These ideas are actually the enemies of democracy because true democracy must move forward, deepen, and develop."

Most Uruguayans had taken to lumping the various amnesty proposals under the term *impunidad*—"impunity." One Colorado Party leader told me that he didn't much like that term—that he'd rather characterize the process as "searching for peace." The search for peace, however, was hardly proving peaceful: debate was growing shriller. The Colorados were now tending to classify all the former prisoners as Tupamaros and to maintain that the opposition to the amnesty was principally a tiresome Tupamaro vendetta. Antonio Marchesano, Sanguinetti's Interior Minister, was even quoted at one point as justifying amnesty for rape, provided "it was intended to instill fear" in the prisoners.

Public opinion, however, seemed to be holding fast. Uruguayans were, if anything, more viscerally anti-militarist than ever. A major poll released in October showed 72 percent still in favor of punishing those convicted of human-rights violations (68 percent among the Colorado Party rank and file) and only 11 percent opposed.

As the first trial before which military officers were ordered to appear was fast approaching, leaders of the three parties convened for a live television debate on the night of December 3. The Colorado Party was represented by Interior Minister Marchesano, the Frente by General Seregni, and the Blancos by Wilson Ferreira. Marchesano and Seregni staked out predictable positions, but Wilson Ferreira adopted an increasingly abstruse stand and an increasingly tormented tone. (After all, as the military pressure grew it was the Blancos who were finding themselves the most under the gun.) He had hated the Club Naval negotiations all along, Wilson insisted; he had been in prison, and his party had had nothing at all to do with them, and rightly so, for secret deals had been struck and dark commitments made, and they were terrible and damnable and dastardly, but there they were, we were stuck with them. People watching the performance of this ordinarily smooth, assured politician couldn't get over the transformation: he was actually squirming.

The last evening of that first visit of mine to Montevideo, back in December 1986, I had one final conversation with Marcelo Vignar. We were ambling up and down the long narrow jetty that juts out into the water, protecting the enclosed harbor—walking out toward the setting sun and back toward town and then out again. The water was lapping gently among the broken stones. Lovers and children promenaded, everyone in shirtsleeves, savoring the wafting breeze of a rapidly approaching summer. "Back during the *dictadura,*" Vignar said at one point, as we were heading back landward, "you wouldn't have found a soul out here. Over there," he pointed toward a group of white stone buildings, blond in the evening light, "those Navy barracks were particularly favored by the torturers for some reason. On an evening like this, back in those days, anyone who happened to be out here would probably have heard horrible, horrible screams welling up from behind those grilled windows."

We turned around and headed out again. The warm breeze notwithstanding, Vignar was glum and subdued: the fix was pretty much in. It was becoming increasingly clear that before the end of the legislature's current session, Wilson Ferreira was going to swing the Blanco Party's congressional bloc behind some sweeping sort of amnesty. And this was indeed what then did happen just a few weeks thereafter. On December 22, the Colorados and most of the Blancos united to force through, well, not an amnesty exactly—nobody wanted to out and out admit to such a craven capitulation to the military's blackmail. Instead, they were calling it the *Ley de Caducidad de la Pretensión Punitiva del Estado,* the Law Declaring an Expiration of the State's Punitive Authority, as if that authority had just up and died by itself—but for all intents and purposes the results were going to be the same. Those saddened by Wilson Ferreira's *volte face* surmised that he was embarked on some elaborate courtship—hoping to assuage the military's anxieties regarding his personal reliability so that they, in turn, might finally countenance his victory in the next round of Presidential elections. What he actually said was, "The bottom line is we want to win the next election, and for that to happen, the elections have to take place." In any case, the whole project reeked of bad faith and a guilty conscience, and it was accomplished at the last possible moment. The next day, December 23, the first of the military subpoenas—one served on José Nino Gavazzo—was to have fallen due. Instead, that whole trial was now cancelled, all the trials were cancelled, there would be no further investigations, no truth-telling. The legislature debated into the wee hours of the morning before passing the bill—fistfights erupted in the chamber—and then adjourned for Christmas and the long summer vacation during which politics in Uruguay are always supposed to lapse into a sort of languid suspension. The law's promoters no doubt hoped that by March, when civil life resumed, popular rage would have subsided. Surely no one could have anticipated the truly astonishing turn that events would instead be taking.

But all of that still lay in the future that December evening as Vignar and I walked back out toward the setting sun. "This is such a sick little country," Vignar commented sadly. "All torn and twisted and broken, with so much of the brokeness concentrated around this notion of knowledge, of *knowing*: 'You can't possibly know what it was like.' 'We didn't know, we didn't realize.' The torturer's 'I know everything about you.' The victim's 'I don't even know what I said, what I did . . .' The torturer's 'Scream all you like, your resistance is completely futile, no one will ever know.' This point about no one's ever knowing was the very subject matter of the torturer's discourse, do you understand? That's what the torture was *all about.* That's why an amnesty will be so terrible, because it will perpetuate the torture itself."

By this time, we'd made it out to the very tip of the jetty. Everything ahead was orange sunglare playing on the water. Vignar sighed. "You know," he said, "everybody calls the water here *el mar,* the sea, but technically it's not sea, or not quite. It's not ocean and it's not gulf. On the map you'll see it's labelled Rio de la Plata, even though the river here is almost a hundred kilometers wide—way, way beyond the horizon over there you'd come to the Argentine shore. It's an estuary, I suppose—but a fairly unique one. Marine biologists come from all over the world to study its strange and curious life forms. Depending on the time of day, the season, the weather, the tides, it can be fresh water or salty. It's all confused, all murky." He paused, turning to head back in. "A bit, come to think of it, like our sorry Uruguay, the way the question is still hanging as to whether what we've achieved here is a renewed civil democracy or, rather, still, an only barely disguised military dictatorship."

2

Impunity

"Ignorance about those who have disappeared undermines the reality of the world." The Polish poet Zbigniew Herbert appears to have had the myriad European victims of the Second World War—or, perhaps, their survivors—foremost in his mind when he included that line in his poem "Mr. Cogito on the Need for Precision." But it was in Montevideo, Uruguay, just recently that the phrase kept returning to me.[25] Like the military dictators elsewhere in Latin America, the generals who dominated Uruguay for most of the past two decades were convinced, as a matter of doctrinal certainty, that theirs was but one battlefront in a Third World War that had already broken out—an absolute war, against Communism. Absolute wars leave absolute imperatives in their wake: Herbert's imperative of remembrance, but also, and sometimes in diametrical opposition, the imperative of renewal. These, at any rate, were the imperatives in contest during the past several years in Montevideo, and what was up for grabs, it often seemed, was precisely "the reality of the world."

Uruguayans are an intensely political people; they love sitting around their café tables, analyzing and disputing the intricate reconfigurations of power and strategy being played out in the public realm of their little city-state. At the time Wilson Ferreira made his celebrated about-face on the question of the amnesty, there was, as I mentioned earlier, a good deal of café-table speculation to the effect that he was trying to smooth things over with the military to clear the way for another Presidential bid in 1989. If so, Wilson Ferreira's strategy soon met with ironic truncation. Within weeks of the December vote, it was discovered that the legendary Blanco caudillo was suffering from terminal pancreatic cancer—and within a year he was dead. Montevidean café chatter occasionally drifts into a sort of magical thinking and once, on my next visit to the city, when I commented to some table partners on the tragic irony of Wilson Ferreira's death and how it had robbed him of the chance of ever reaping any benefits from his Faustian bargain, one fellow interrupted, "There was nothing ironic about it whatsoever. Wilson died *because* he made that vote—he couldn't live with himself thereafter." It's hard to know. Wilson Ferreira's defenders insist that Presidential ambition had nothing to do with his decision.

Juan Martín Posadas, a Blanco senator, who was the only legislator in Wilson Ferreira's faction of the party to vote against the *impunidad* law, subsequently told me how Ferreira had been tormented right up to the moment of the vote but had felt that his room for maneuver was shrinking precipitately. "Sanguinetti is a Florentine politician, and he played that gambit beautifully," Posadas explained. "The Club Naval pact was his masterpiece. Wilson Ferreira felt that he was facing a fait accompli—that to all intents and purposes the military had already been extended certain guarantees. And he believed that, in any case, if they continued to refuse to honor legitimate subpoenas the country would soon be facing the worst possible outcome—a sort of slow-motion de facto coup, in which one sector of society declared itself beyond the law. We had to redesign our strategy, he felt, for otherwise we would be relegated to a position outside reality. Reality had started down a road we didn't approve of and which we hadn't participated in choosing, but it was the road that had been chosen, and if we went off in a different direction we'd be reduced to a testimonial role. A political party is not a church, Wilson Ferreira would say—you have to be in a real situation. I myself disagreed with that analysis, but it was his analysis."

I asked if Wilson Ferreira continued to be troubled by his decision after the vote.

"In politics, you can't be Hamlet," Posadas said. "Once you make your decision, you go out and face the crowd."[26]

So there it was, a *punto final*—"period, full stop"—as everyone now took to saying, borrowing a phrase from the roiling debates in neighboring Argentina, where the Argentine military's officers were now demanding a swift end to all the human-rights investigations and trials. Their demands had teeth, too—the perpetual threat of a coup—and by late 1986 President Alfonsín himself was urging a *punto final* to those human-rights investigations. It was time to transcend the past and look to the future, Alfonsín argued. And an Argentine law was indeed passed, also in December of 1986, setting a sixty-day cap on the launching of any further prosecutions. Sanguinetti, for his part, now adopted an identical rhetoric: a year and a half of controversy was enough, it was time to move on, it was time for a *punto final.* "I don't have eyes in the back of my head," he declared. "I have eyes only for the future."

"But how can one even consider a *punto final?*" one of Sanguinetti's opponents had said to me at the time. "How can you have a period, end of paragraph, end of story, without any preceding paragraph, let alone any preceding story? Here in Uruguay, we've had no commission of inquiry, no officially sanctioned truthtelling. We've had no trials, no verdicts. All we have now is this period, hovering there in the middle of a blank page. It's unreal."

And, indeed, the period wasn't holding, it wasn't staying put. Late in February, 1987, a coalition of former torture victims, relatives of "disappeared" individuals, human-rights activists, anti-*impunidad* politicians, labor leaders, professionals, and other citizens inaugurated a campaign to overturn the *impunidad* law. As their vehicle, they would seek to use the referendum provision in Uruguay's constitution—something that had never before been done. "Our current constitution," Luis Pérez Aguirre, at SERPAJ, explained to me, "was based on the Swiss constitution, and we copied the referendum provision from the Swiss. However, our politicians endeavored to make the procedure much more arduous, by requiring the petition signatures of 25 percent of the total number of people who had voted in the immediately prior election. In Switzerland, for instance, with its population of over 6 million, you need only 50,000 signatures on a qualifying petition. Here, with less than half that population, we are required to get over ten times as many signatures—more than 555,000! That's roughly the same number of total signatures you'd need to collect to qualify a referendum in Italy, only there you'd be able to draw from a total population of 57 million people."

The remarkable 25 percent requirement may be unparalleled anywhere in the world. In California, for example, in order to qualify for a place on the ballot, a referendum campaign needs to secure the signatures of only 5 percent of those who voted in the previous gubernatorial election. Furthermore, in most places (as, again, in California) petition circulators need to secure only a registered voter's signature and voting address—a requirement that can be efficiently accomplished by, for example, moving down the lines outside popular movie houses. In Uruguay, however, a signer also has to provide his voter-registration number, a fairly arcane item; the form on which it's listed is likely to be kept in some drawer at home.

At first, many of the law's opponents were hesitant about embarking on this difficult course. The two principal party organizations would be throwing most of their weight against any attempt to revive the debate. All the television stations and most of the major radio stations and newspapers (many of them party-controlled) were on record as opposing such an attempt; it was doubtful whether the effort would receive much sympathetic coverage—or, for that matter, much coverage of any kind. One opponent, Sara Méndez, subsequently told me that at the time she herself had doubts about the referendum strategy. (The kidnapping of her nineteen-day-old son, in 1976, remains one of the most celebrated of the outstanding human-rights cases.) "The circumstances didn't exist yet for a fair debate on the issue," she recalled, "and I was afraid that the most likely outcome would be a *punto final* imposed by the people rather than the military." Eventually, however, she warmed to the campaign.

The coalition established itself under the name Comisión Nacional Pro-Referéndum and was co-chaired by María Gatti de Islas, the grandmother of a disappeared child, and Matilde de Gutiérrez Ruiz and Elisa de Michelini, the widows of the two revered politicians assassinated in exile in Buenos Aires in 1976. The Pro-Referendum Commission cast the widest possible net in terms of political allegiances: its membership included Frente Amplio types, dissident Blancos, and even some Colorados. The Tupamaros supported the referendum movement but did not play a major role. They remained a fairly marginal entity and were still resented by most Uruguayans. There were no Tupamaros on the Pro-Referendum Commission's steering committee.

During the first several weekends of the campaign, the commission was able to mobilize as many as 10,000 signature-gatherers and was averaging almost 10,000 new signatures a day. By March 16, they were already able to report 160,000 signatures, an astonishing number given the further obstacles they were suddenly encountering. The political establishment had initially reacted to the campaign with studied, almost imperious, silence (the establishment media was hardly reporting it at all), but the military were being decidedly less circumspect.

Without the generals ever actually saying so, the subtext of many of their well-publicized commentaries was "Fine, go ahead, sign the petition, that's the list we'll be using next time we come into power." The fact that they were registering any attitude, of course, went against the spirit of the new democratic order, in which they were supposed to remain absolutely subordinate to civilian control. Yet all they had to do was express misgivings about the course of the democracy and the unacceptable resurgence of "the treasonous left," and people felt a fresh waft of the terror that had so characterized the military's earlier tenure. People didn't need to be reminded about that system whereby the military had categorized almost everyone in the country as politically acceptable, suspect, or pariah. People knew that the archives upon which those categories were based were still being maintained. They knew that the fact of someone's signing a petition, say, against the United States invasion of the Dominican Republic in 1965, back in the days of the Great Democratic Exception, had come up ten years later, during the tortures and the summary trials, and that on the basis of little else such a person had received a prison sentence of five years, ten years, or more. And yet, knowing all this, they were signing. By May 26, 1987, the commission reported 438,000 signatures.

However, the tide now turned abruptly. In neighboring Argentina, during the Easter holiday a few weeks earlier, a small number of officers and soldiers had rebelled, under the leadership of a renegade colonel named Aldo Rico, and virtually none of the rest of the military seemed willing to move against them. Following the passage of Argentina's *punto final* law, in December, scores of prosecutions had been lodged at the last possible moment, and Colonel Rico wanted all of them quashed forthwith. Alfonsín called on the civilians, and hundreds of thousands of them rallied in defense of their reclaimed democracy. After a helicopter visit by Alfonsín to Rico's headquarters, the mutinous colonel and his men relented. There was a brief period of euphoria. Over in Uruguay, where signature-gathering had stalled, there was a sudden upsurge of activity.

But in the ensuing weeks it gradually became clear that democracy's victory in Argentina had been problematical at best. Alfonsín soon fired the chief of staff of the armed forces, whose ouster had been one of Rico's principal demands, and although Alfonsín continued to oppose a complete amnesty, which had been another of Rico's demands, he now moved quickly to propose a so-called due obedience law, which he managed to force through the Argentine Congress on June 5, 1987; this had the effect of voiding most of the remaining prosecutions of lower-ranking officers, who in many cases had been the actual torturers. In Uruguay, Sanguinetti used these developments to attack the petition campaign. Did Uruguayans really want to jeopardize the peace they had so precariously achieved? Was a Uruguayan Rico what they were asking for? New signatures became sparser and sparser. By October, the campaign had levelled out at 520,000 signatures.

Up to this point, the Pro-Referendum Commission had made a near-fetish of preserving the security of its completed petitions. People were being assured that their signatures would be kept secret, no one's business but that of the Electoral Court, which was charged with verifying the signatures and supervising any subsequent referendum (with the actual petitions presumably to be destroyed immediately thereafter).

But now a Colorado observer at the Electoral Court, a deputy named Rubén Díaz, proposed that once the petitions were turned over to the Court they should all be reviewed by the police, supposedly in order to weed out any known criminals or subversives. In reality, it was clear, the intent of his proposal was to intimidate would-be signers, and it seemed to be working. There was an immediate outcry from pro-referendum forces, and the proposal was temporarily shelved, but there was no guarantee of how the Electoral Court might eventually rule on it. Many of the activists on the commission began to abandon hope. Late in October, however, the commission launched a final offensive, mailing out 200,000 flyers. In response, it received enough signatures to go over the 555,701 goal, though it still continued to campaign, hoping to build up an adequate reserve. Finally, on the eve of Christmas, 1987, the Pro-Referendum Commission submitted petitions containing 634,702 signatures to the Electoral Court for verification.

In celebration, a group of activists went over to the front lawn of the notorious Gavazzo's house and began carolling. He came to the front door in a fury, armed with a loaded pistol, and fired several angry shots into the night air.

The government responded to the commission's exasperatingly productive campaign with the signature-verifying equivalent of a filibuster. Whereas the Electoral Court had at first predicted that it would require as little as four months to review the signatures, months stretched into whole seasons without any announcement. Every single signature had to be reviewed at least twice, and then finally against the original of the signer's registration papers—documents that in many cases were decades old and were lost in dusty filing cabinets buried deep in dusty warehouses.

Meanwhile, in January, 1988, over in Argentina, Colonel Rico launched a second mutiny. This one, too, failed—though again only barely—and it was followed by another tense, ambiguous period. Once again, Sanguinetti took to the Uruguayan airwaves, asking his fellow-citizens whether they were truly so mad as to desire such complications in their own placid country. Various generals, active and retired, expressed grave misgivings about the viability of democracy in Uruguay.

Far from reprimanding these soldiers for intervening in the country's political discourse, Sanguinetti appointed a retired general, Hugo Medina—the Army strongman with whom he had negotiated the Club Naval agreement, back in 1984—as the new Defense Minister in his civilian Cabinet. Sanguinetti's opponents were startled but couldn't help admiring the audacity of his gesture. "In what other country," I was later asked, "would a civilian President have the sheer imagination to appoint the head of the preceding junta as his new Defense Minister?"

Medina, for his part, began issuing pronouncements that some interpreted as threats. "The left is taking advantage of democracy," he said on television. "Rest assured that the armed forces are here to protect the country's sovereignty." He went on to point out that there had been only a few dozen disappearances in Uruguay. As everybody knew, there were many, many more in Argentina. In Uruguay, he said, "there were about five thousand political prisoners. There could have been four thousand disappeared." "And could yet be" was how most oppositionists understood the subtext of that particular observation. (Actually, the estimates on those incarcerated ranged considerably higher, but it's precisely one of the problems in Uruguay that there are no comprehensive official figures.) When asked point-blank if the military would obey the results of any eventual referendum, the most that Medina seemed willing to hazard was "Time will tell" or "We'll see" or "I don't know what would happen." When pressed by congressional committees for a clarification of such comments, he declined to oblige.

On July 18, a traditional holiday commemorating the signing of the country's first constitution, Sanguinetti granted his armed forces their first public parade in seven years. Two thousand soldiers, bristling with weaponry, marched briskly down the capital's main boulevard in an imposing show of force. At the end of the parade, Sanguinetti delivered to the assembled crowd, and to a nationwide television audience, a speech distinguished by its archly polemical tone. Alluding to recent events in Uruguayan history, the President declared, "I want 'the violent ones' "—presumably a veiled reference to the Tupamaros, upon whom he'd taken to blaming the whole petition campaign—"to know that the first shot will never come from these forces that are now parading, but that there will not be any hesitation in defending the constitution or guaranteeing peace against all threats." The military was apparently as heartened by the President's address as other sectors of the society were unnerved; which is to say that Sanguinetti probably succeeded in both of his intentions.

Meanwhile, in a particularly chilling development, early in August, Medina ordered that a Navy captain, Bernardo Gastón Silbermann, be relieved of his duties, arrested, and confined incommunicado for signing the referendum petition. Medina insisted that Article 77 of the Uruguayan constitution prohibited any political activity except voting by members of the military or the police. Such constitutional stickling on Medina's part seemed curious, since he hadn't shown himself to be particularly troubled by the far more inflammatory anti-referendum proclamations of various other serving officers. And, in any event, the constitution stipulated that a referendum could be signed by anyone with the right to vote. But constitutional analysis hardly seemed the main point in Silbermann's case (to anyone but Silbermann, that is). Rather, his arrest had clearly been designed to reveal that the Electoral Court was in fact no longer preserving the secrecy of the petition lists. That impression was heightened when, around the same time, a newspaper report quoted the Colorado deputy Rubén Díaz to the effect that the reason he had recently taken a trip to the town of Paysandú, on the Argentine border, was to deliver to the local Colorado Party boss a list of citizens in his area who had signed referendum petitions.

Soon thereafter, Pérez Aguirre at SERPAJ began receiving reports about citizens in the interior being visited by local precinct captains and quizzed on the subject ("There must be some mistake, old buddy. I'm hearing you signed that petition. I didn't realize you were a Communist"). Public employees were being made to fear for their jobs, retired senior citizens for their pensions.

As for the Electoral Court, it had announced that it would henceforth be accepting retractions of signatures from all those who might request to make them—an exceedingly peculiar undertaking, especially since the Court was no longer accepting additional signatures by any additional individuals who might make *that* request. Meanwhile, the Court was disqualifying whole batches of existing signatures. The grounds for disqualification often seemed capricious. For example, some names were disqualified because they were deemed, on their face, too silly. The required voter's-identification number—the *credencial cívica,* or CC—consisted of three letters followed by several numbers, but if a person put the initials "CC" (roughly the equivalent of "ID") in front of the three letters of his identification number, his signature was disqualified, because that made five letters where there were supposed to be only three. Signatures were disqualified in cases where the "V" in the letter sequence ("BVB," say) looked too much like a "U," or where the stem of a "B" was deemed too dark compared with the rest of the letter, or where the "B" could be mistaken for a "13," or where a single numeral was either darker or larger than the others, or where a pen ran out of ink and was replaced midway by another, or where a person who had moved and acquired a new CC listed both the old one and the new one, hence providing, say, six letters and ten numerals when there were supposed to be only three and five, or where a signer made a mistake and crossed it out and started over. Thousands of signatures were being disqualified in this manner. And all this was before the Court even started comparing the petition signatures with those on the original, often decades-old, registration sheets and disqualifying any with handwriting that had changed noticeably in the interim. The signatures of sixty veteran labor leaders were disqualified in this fashion.

The Electoral Court was supposed to behave in a nonpartisan manner, but in practice all its members were either Colorados or Blancos, and minority interests were represented only among the observers. Those minority observers, however, registered such vocal opposition to many of the proceedings that in March the Court began "suspending" signatures of certain sorts instead of disqualifying them outright—the idea being that the Court might go back and review them in some as yet unspecified manner.

But as the months progressed—June, July, August—the total number of acceptable signatures was steadily being whittled down, and it now began to look as though the total might soon fall below the necessary goal.

It was against this backdrop that I returned to Montevideo, in August of 1988. On my previous trip, I had spoken mainly with victims of the country's systematic human-rights violations. This time, I wanted to make a point of talking with some of the proponents of the amnesty law—particularly some of the leaders of the Colorado Party—because I sensed that they, too, had a case to make.

With Senator Manuel Flores Silva, for example. A handsome man in his late thirties, Flores Silva is a journalist and a professor, the scion of an important political dynasty, and the head of one of the more centrist factions of the Colorado Party. He had voted in favor of the amnesty—to the surprise of some, because during the transition of the early eighties he'd been a close collaborator of people like Pérez Aguirre, at SERPAJ, and a frequent, and very articulate, proponent of human rights.

"The problem of amnesty cannot be understood out of the context of the whole situation of our country," he said one afternoon when I visited him in his Senate offices. "Uruguay lived through a transition from authoritarian rule which was not at all typical. We didn't have the benefit of the classic situation in which the dictatorship suffers an external defeat, like Argentina in the Malvinas or the Greek generals in Cyprus, and therefore has to step down. We didn't have the other classic way out, either, in which the dictatorship loses as a result of an internal war, as happened in Nicaragua with the downfall of Somoza. Our way was to mobilize civil society and gradually encircle the regime until it accepted the transition. That was accomplished through a series of steps—the votes in 1980 and 1982 and 1984, for example—all of which were imperfect, which is to say they were not completely democratic. But each step made it possible to advance, and we achieved two things that no one else has achieved: democracy—which, for instance, Chile still hasn't—and a peaceful transition, without any deaths along the way.

"In all this the Club Naval pact was of key importance. It didn't speak explicitly, or even implicitly, about what would happen with regard to the past, but the military had a right to assume that a peaceful transition would entail a peaceful working out of the past. Now, if you were living in a dictatorship and I offered you elections in three months and democracy in six months, and you said you wouldn't accept such an arrangement until the dictators agreed in advance to go to prison, that would obviously be a wrong strategy. Naturally, two years later someone will say that this problem should have been included explicitly in the initial agreement—and this is understandable in theory. But we got rid of the dictatorship in reality.

"The trouble is that by mid-1986 we were falling back into the logic of extremes. Ironically, dictatorships freeze things, and, coming out of ours, we almost seemed to be back in 1972 and 1973—the same hatreds and polarizations all over again, leading toward an identical impasse and an identical probable outcome. We had to find a way out of that trap. It was very important, because it hasn't been shown anywhere that there is a law according to which dictatorships automatically fall. Sometimes they don't fall. For us to present an amnesty project, therefore, was not a matter of doing the necessary dirty work. It was a matter of making a moral decision to give priority to the possibility of a future of agreement over a past of division. We are consolidating democracy, which is the only guarantee of human rights."

I asked him what he could say to the victims of the abuses.

"We made a moral decision," he replied. "I didn't say it was an easy one. These abuses must never happen again. I can do nothing to change the fact that we lived under Fascism. What I can do is prevent it from happening again. Listen, as far as I'm concerned they should all have gone to prison. There should never have been any dictatorship, never any coup. I'm in favor of the Tupamaros' never having existed. But we did have Tupamaros, and war, and the logic of war, and Fascism—that's what happens in war, that's why you shouldn't start shooting in the first place—and my job is to give my son a country where we will again have civil government and democracy. That takes time, and peace."

Next I spoke with Vice President Enrique Tarigo, another hero of the transition, the lawyer who'd founded *Opinar* and then gone on to articulate, in a most courageous and convincing fashion, the "no" position during the 1980 televised debate regarding the military's proposed national-security constitution. Sanguinetti had subsequently chosen him as his running mate in part to capitalize on the honorable reputation he'd garnered on that occasion. In March 1985, Tarigo, like Flores Silva, had favored an amnesty that explicitly excluded the military from its provisions. But like Flores Silva, he too had changed his mind.

"In March, 1985, when we took over, we didn't think we should amnesty the military," Tarigo explained to me. Tarigo is a large, jowly man, reminiscent in his physical presence of the late Chicago Mayor Richard J. Daley. "We thought the justice system would be able to act independently and process the accused as individuals. But the system needs quiet as a context in which to work. You can't conceive of a judge having to rule on a case with the multitudes screaming at him. With the question of the military, the subject unfortunately became polarized. I think the leftists—the Communists and others—intentionally politicized it, publicizing photos, accusing individuals of crimes, spreading rumors with no evidence. The trials hadn't even begun and the military stood convicted. Now, there *were* crimes—you can't argue with that: twenty or thirty people were disappeared, and 'disappeared' is of course a euphemism. But the responsibility is difficult to establish, many were involved, it's all diffuse. And to have trials under those conditions would have involved the entire Army. A good part of the left was looking for exactly that, to put the entire Army on trial."

I pointed out that some of those I'd spoken with before, who'd opposed the amnesty, had insisted, on the contrary, that the entire Army was not to blame, only certain individuals, and that by isolating the guilty ones and removing them, the rest of the armed forces would be affirmed in their innocence. "But the thing is," Tarigo explained, "to secure convictions against, say, fifty military people, we would have had to have at least five hundred officers parading through the courts—as accused, as suspects, as accomplices, or, at any rate, as witnesses. It would have taken anywhere from four to eight years, because that's how long a penal process does take. If we had been able to plug all the information into a computer and get out all the verdicts on the same day—well, then maybe things could have been different. But, as it was, half the officers were going to be involved in one way or another. And I don't think any state can withstand having its armed forces destroyed in such a fashion."

I asked him what role he felt the armed forces should play in a small country like Uruguay. "We will have to deal with that. I believe the military should have less weight in the national budget. We have a military organized as if for the First World War, with a huge infantry, which makes no sense. But this is a subject which can be discussed only in tranquility."

I asked him whether he felt it would ever be possible to discuss such subjects when the current civilian government was still, in the opinion of many, under the military's domination. "I deny that we're living under the thumb of the military," Tarigo replied. "With the '86 law, we've given the military the tranquil knowledge that their past won't be revived, but the military in turn has assumed the responsibility of being subordinate. This is how we build democracy. As with all things in life, when a problem has been solved, it's better to let it be."

I quoted the Zbigniew Herbert line regarding the way "ignorance about those who have disappeared undermines the reality of the world." A democracy can have many components and attributes, I said, but didn't it at least have to be "real," in Herbert's sense? Could any democracy be built on a foundation of "undermined reality"?

"Of course it can," Tarigo countered vigorously. "We can do it perfectly well, as others have—Spain, for instance. When Franco died, a new page was turned, because everybody realized that to go back and review events of forty years earlier would be to provoke a whole new civil war. Life continues, life is made up of things that are not pretty, that are not the subject of a beautiful poem. And the function of a government is not to write poetry but to build a real future. In response to your poet, I would cite the political theorist Max Weber who distinguished between individual ethics and the ethics of those in positions of responsibility. I understand the point of view of the victim's family, but in the ethic of governance one has to weigh, for example, the question of justice for twenty or thirty individuals versus the possibility of losing democracy again in this country. This is what we had to do, and this is what we did."

Then I went to visit President Sanguinetti in his executive offices, which were in Libertad, the sleek, modern building that the military dictators had originally built for their Defense Ministry, and from which Sanguinetti had evicted them as one of his first Presidential acts. The building's interior, I found, was imposingly self-important—in fact, neo-Fascist —particularly the door at the end of a long hall which led to the

President's inner sanctum. Actually, the door *was* the end of the long hall: the entire wooden wall—floor to ceiling, side to side—pivoted portentously on a gleaming brass axis to admit visitors. But once I was inside the office and in the presence of Sanguinetti himself such observations tended to fade from consciousness, for the President was a genuinely commanding presence—tall, self-confident, firmly planted. Various observers of the Southern Cone (journalists, diplomats, academics) had told me that of the region's three civilian Presidents who had wrested power from their military counterparts within months of each other during the mid-eighties—José Sarney in Brazil, Alfonsín in Argentina, and Sanguinetti in Uruguay—Sanguinetti was far and away the most competent, the one with the greatest gift for politics and the finest feel for the job. Nothing in the hour I spent with him gave me reason to doubt that assessment.

At one point in our conversation, when I asked him to characterize the generals' dominion during their tenure, he replied, "They were omnipotent. They could do whatever they wanted. They overpowered everything else. We fought a lot against that dictatorship, a lot more than those speaking out now." He paused, and then added quietly, "But that's not important." That answer would no doubt have annoyed many of "those speaking out now," people who continued to criticize Sanguinetti for the way he sat out much of the dictatorship, declining to take a more active and public role in the opposition. But I'm sure he was being sincere: he is precisely the sort of person who would believe that only the crunch negotiation—*mano a mano,* leader squared off against leader, as he and General Medina were squared off during the secret talks at the Club Naval—could have had any serious relevance to the process that culminated in the military's withdrawal. All the acts of civil disobedience—the increasing grassroots activism, the hunger strikes, the women in their backyards at first furtively and then ever more boldly banging pots and pans in protest—had been simply so much background noise.

At any rate, I began by asking Sanguinetti why the military had been explicitly excluded from the March, 1985, amnesty, only to be granted what amounted to amnesty in the law of December, 1986. What had happened in between?

"The perspective changed," he said. "The reason that the amnesty for the terrorists and the political prisoners, as they're generically called, didn't include the military was that at the time it didn't seem that denunciation of their crimes would become so important. There might be a few accusations, but it wasn't going to be a big deal. Then things began to grow—accusations, confrontations, bigger confrontations."

Were the leaders unaware of the extent of the problem, I asked, or, rather, did they just think that there weren't going to be so many outright accusations?

"No. People pretty much knew what had happened. But such a generous amnesty in favor of the terrorists, it was thought, would serve to calm the society. Things looked different at the time from the way they look now."

So then what happened?

"Great numbers of accusations began rolling in, and we proposed an amnesty. Why? For many reasons. First, few of the accusations were going to lead anywhere—there wasn't enough evidence. It was going to disturb society, and there would simply be a lot of confrontation. Second, it was a question of moral equivalency: we felt that if we were going to have a settling of accounts for the left and the terrorists the military should be amnestied, too. A lot of those involved in violent left-wing groups had never been in jail at all. To begin the arithmetic of judging levels of responsibility, we would have been faced with complications of such magnitude that we thought it best to amnesty everybody—the left and the military. Third, it was necessary to have a climate of stability so as to consolidate democracy. Having lived through such turbulence for so many years, we felt we needed a more peaceful situation. If the country was going to insist on maintaining the old conflicts from before the coup, it was unlikely that we'd ever be able to consolidate democracy. And, finally, for historical reasons. Traditionally, after all great conflicts in a country the solution has been an amnesty for both sides."

Regarding this notion of moral equivalency, what percentage of those in prison was he classifying as terrorists? Weren't there many prisoners who were not even Tupamaros?

"Most were guerrillas—most of the long-term ones."

Wasn't that one of the outstanding questions? Shouldn't there have been at least a truth-telling phase, in which such facts could have been established, once and for all?

"We could have had a moral trial, an investigation followed by an amnesty. But that situation had all the problems and none of the advantages. To open that discussion would have been to preserve old wounds. One can always make mistakes, but, looking over the last four years, I'm convinced that I'm right. The experience of Argentina confirms it: the trials there were not permitted to continue—only the top generals were punished, and not those directly responsible for all the assassinations."

But in both Argentina and Brazil there have been truth-telling phases, either officially sanctioned or based on official documents. One knows how many prisoners were "terrorists" and how many were not. There has been nothing like that in Uruguay.

"That's why Uruguay is stable. The bottom line is that either we're going to look to the future or to the past."

Did he think it possible to have an honest disagreement on this subject—for example, that other people might feel that without attending to the past the future would be built on a faulty base?

"Obviously, on all these matters one can have other perspectives. But, while we were all responsible for what happened, those who carried out the violence on the right and the left were the most responsible. The majority of the country has rights, too, and the great majority don't want violence and do want their rights guaranteed, so they can exercise them today. And it's hard to have a balance when this sort of discussion is going on between minorities. However, more and more are coming to our view: the great majority want democracy and stability. The country still has to grow. During the last three years of the military government, Uruguay's GNP fell 17 percent; in our first three years, it rose 13 percent. Unemployment has gone from 15 percent to 8 percent. All of that is possible only because of political stability."

Was it really such a marginal minority who disagreed with his position? Close to 25 percent of the country's voting population had signed the petition.

"That's an argument in favor of my position. We've gone down a totally legal road. If there should ever be an actual vote, I'm convinced that it would come out seventy to thirty in favor of retaining the amnesty, and that would end the debate."

But if the referendum should be held and should pass—and, remember, this is an electorate that has surprised people before—what would happen?

"To begin with, you're talking science fiction. I have no doubt that the amnesty law would be upheld. But, if not, a period of very strong judicial and political conflict would begin. The country would suffer a lot. Most people understand this. That is why I'm so certain."

Before the December law was passed, soldiers had refused to answer subpoenas and attend trials. If in the wake of the referendum a new dispensation required that they do so, would they?

"I'm sure we'd have serious problems, and I don't want to make predictions. I think you should realize that the people in favor of the referendum are not people known for their defense of democracy. Prior to the coup, they were not defending democracy."

All 25 percent?

"No, no, no, but the Tupamaros, who are the ones in the vanguard. Some surely believe this is the better option, but the people who have all the money to buy up radio stations are Tupamaros." (Since June the Tupamaros had been leasing seventeen hours a day of airtime from an established radio station to present their own mix of news, interviews, and cultural programming; they were covering their expenses through the sale of advertising.)

What of the woman whose nineteen-day-old son was kidnapped? He was now twelve years old. For her, a legal process might reveal something and ease her future anguish. Weren't we talking here about the future and not the past? What could he say to *that* person, or to the widows of Deputy Héctor Gutiérrez Ruiz and Senator Zelmar Michelini?

"I have a great pain for them in my heart and understand their attitude. But what I'm really concerned about is its not happening again. That's why there can be two ways of thinking that are equally honest —their way, which is that the only means of overcoming the problem of the military is to have trials, and our way, which is that the only means is a pardon. The question is, Who can guarantee the future? I'm convinced that we will, this way, and they can't offer the same security."

Once again, I cited the Herbert poem, this time quoting a longer passage:

> *And yet in these matters*
> *accuracy is essential*
> *we must not be wrong*
> *even by a single one*
>
> *we are despite everything*
> *the guardians of our brothers*
>
> *ignorance about those who have disappeared*
> *undermines the reality of the world.*

I asked Sanguinetti whether he thought it possible to found a secure democracy on the basis of a sort of willed mass ignorance.

"That's not the basis of democracy," he replied. "The basis of democracy is the people's conviction that it's the best system and that everyone can expect to exercise his rights. The former terrorists now have their radios and newspapers, they shout insults at me at the top of their lungs. That's the basis of democracy—that everyone has a place under the sun. As for your poet—Ernest Renan, the great nineteenth-century French historian, who was very influential here in the Southern Cone, once said, '*Las naciones son plebiscitos todos los días. Y se hacen en base de grandes recuerdos y grandes olvidos*'—'Nations are a plebiscite every day, and they are constructed on the basis of great rememberings and great forgettings.' If the French were still thinking about the Night of St. Bartholomew, they'd be slaughtering each other to this day.

"This is a political, and not a moral, decision. It has to be resolved politically because it's a political conflict. Uruguay didn't fall apart by chance, and it's not going to be reconstructed by chance, either."

That evening, I visited the headquarters of the Pro-Referendum Commission, several sparse rooms in a second-floor walkup on a downtown side street. It was extraordinary to realize that such a vast signature-gathering operation had been marshalled from such modest quarters—and hard thereafter to take seriously the various aspersions regarding the supposed financial profligacy of the petition's organizers. Walls in the neighborhood, and for that matter throughout the city, were festooned with pro-referendum graffiti: *"Ni Olvido, ni Venganza, Justicia!"* ("Neither amnesia nor vengeance—justice!"); or simply, "Michelini!"; or simpler and more powerful yet, the repeated stencil image of an empty baby chair. There was virtually no anti-referendum graffiti anywhere, although it was explained to me that there didn't need to be: the referendum's opponents had free and daily access to the establishment papers, radio stations, and television, while for the pro-referendum forces, graffiti constituted a major portion of their publicity. Inside their offices, the peeling walls were covered with words and images—a grainy photograph of a group of pregnant women, lined up and stripped down to their underwear, their upraised palms splayed against a blank wall, a rifle butt protruding into the image from off-camera; a poster depicting a red rose with a single plucked petal, the rose itself bleeding; a poster declaring simply, "We have to have CONFIDENCE in Democracy"; a clipping with a 1982 quote from Sanguinetti himself, "A Referendum is so sacred that its results can never be questioned."

I was lucky to have chosen that particular evening, because it turned out to be the one set aside for the weekly meeting of the commission's steering committee, so a number of leaders and activists were gathering there. I struck up a conversation with a group of them and mentioned how their country's President had just told me that their whole campaign was principally a Tupamaro operation. "Well," said one, "that's an improvement: at least now he's recognizing our existence." Another one said, "Forget the Tupamaros, more people signed the petition than voted for Sanguinetti himself in the last election!" I also mentioned that in our conversation the President had characterized most of the worst victims of the military's repression as terrorists. "That's a huge lie, he's an incredible liar," an old man in a worn gray coat said, "and I want you to quote me on that." He gave his name, Enrique Rodríguez Larreta. "Although it's not *my* saying it that's important. It's that he *is* one."

Larreta pulled me aside and proceeded to tell me his story. Back in the sixties, he had been a journalist with *El País,* one of the country's leading establishment newspapers. In fact, his family had owned the paper. His uncle had once been Foreign Minister, and other relatives had been congressmen. He himself had resigned as a delegate to the Blanco Party's national committee in 1967, in protest against the lack of opportunity for young people in the country. His son became a student activist at the university, and was jailed and tortured for several months during 1972. After the 1973 coup, his son and his daughter-in-law fled to Buenos Aires, where the young man got a job as a reporter for a fairly conservative journal of economics.

Then on June 30, 1976, his son was kidnapped from out of his own apartment. Larreta rushed to Buenos Aires and, along with his daughter-in-law, began making urgent inquiries. He contacted the United Nations High Commissioner for Refugees and various ecclesiastical authorities; he presented a writ of habeas corpus at the Supreme Court, only to be told they'd already received six thousand such writs *that day*.

On the night of July 13, however, he and his daughter-in-law were themselves kidnapped, from the same apartment, and, hooded, were hauled off to one of Argentina's most notorious *chupaderos* (a slang term that literally means places that suck people up), in fact the same one where Sara Méndez was at the time being held, the torture center in the garage of Automotores Orletti. "Most of the kidnappers and all the guards there were Argentine," Larreta said, "but Uruguayan Army personnel participated directly in our apprehension, interrogation, and torture." As the weeks went by—and then through tenacious research in the years after his release—Larreta was able to identify a Montevideo police commander, Colonel Campos Hermeda (supposedly with the antidrug unit) and three army officers, affiliated with the Defense Intelligence Service, Jorge Silveira, Manuel Cordero, and the ubiquitous José Nino Gavazzo, as among the Uruguayan torturers.

At the time Larreta and his daughter-in-law were kidnapped, Orletti had sucked up more than sixty Uruguayan refugees, and that first night Larreta was hugely relieved to recognize his son among them ("partly through his cough, and partly because the sugar sack they were using to hood me was not tightly woven")—relieved but also greatly pained, because it was clear that the young man had been savagely beaten. "All night long, prisoners were being taken upstairs, one by one, for torture sessions," he said. "You'd hear them screaming and screaming, for hours, and eventually they'd be brought back down and flung on the cement floor and forbidden to drink any water, because, the guards said, they'd been through 'the machine.'

"The next night, my turn came," Larreta continued. His story seemed at once to bore and to compel him. "I was taken upstairs and stripped naked, except for my blindfold. My arms were pinioned behind my back, and I was strung up by my wrists from the ceiling, my feet dangling twenty centimeters or so from the floor. Then they strapped around my waist a sort of loincloth that contained a number of exposed electrodes. This was the apparatus they called 'the machine,' and they repeatedly connected it up throughout the interrogation, beating me all the while on my most sensitive parts. The cement floor was strewn with coarse salt crystals, in order to intensify the pain if you were somehow able to rest your bleeding feet on the ground. Night after night, they put us through this regimen. Once, because of the sweat streaking down my face, my blindfold loosened, and I caught sight of a large portrait of Hitler on the wall. The torturers frequently boasted of their admiration for the Nazis. All of us were asked if we were Jewish, and Jews got special attention.[27]

"OK, so this is one terrorist's story, what I'm telling you. One so-called Tupamaro—a father whose only crime was to be out looking for his kidnapped son. And I recognized many such 'terrorists' there: friends, and some of the most important labor leaders of Uruguay—León Duarte, Gerardo Gatti, Hugo Méndez—and several dozen others. Those three, in particular, never resurfaced. Most of the rest of us were luckier."

Larreta and his son and daughter-in-law were part of the group (which included Sara Méndez, minus her infant son) who were forcibly repatriated by military transport to Montevideo, where the younger members eventually formed the core cast for that black comedy in which the Uruguayan regime breathlessly announced the last-minute capture of a band of guerrillas who'd been attempting to infiltrate the country to carry out terrorist sabotage. "Come to think of it, maybe *that's* where Mr. Sanguinetti gets this idea about our having been terrorists," Larreta suggested sarcastically.

Most of the kids in the group, including Larreta's son and daughter-in-law, were tried and given prison sentences. Larreta himself was presently released; he fled Uruguay and settled in Sweden, where he lives to this day. (His son and daughter-in-law joined him there after they were released.) But he has been returning regularly to the Southern Cone, obsessively researching his case and those of the others, in the hope of achieving some measure of justice.

Recently, he told me, he had become part of a remarkable case in Buenos Aires, where a well-known human-rights lawyer named Jorge Baños had persuaded one judge, who could no longer rule on Argentine torturers, to agree to issue an extradition warrant for the four Uruguayan torturers Larreta had identified as operating in Buenos Aires. The amnesty protecting them in Uruguay did not affect their status within this judge's jurisdiction, nor did the one protecting Argentines. The extradition warrant was currently bottled up in the Uruguayan Foreign Ministry, under extended study, but Larreta was back in town doing his best to move matters along.

Another activist I met that evening, a short, exuberant matron whom everybody fondly referred to as Tota (I asked her what her actual name was, and she replied, "You know what, I've forgotten!"), related another story with international ramifications. On June 24, 1976, her daughter, Elena Quinteros Almeida, then a thirty-year-old teacher and a leader of the teachers' union, was arrested in Montevideo. On June 28, she escaped her captors and ran into the grounds of the Venezuelan Embassy, with two soldiers in pursuit. Disregarding the Embassy's status as a sanctuary, the soldiers beat her and also several Embassy personnel who came to her assistance. She was eventually dragged away, and was never seen or heard of again.

Venezuela broke off diplomatic relations with Uruguay over the incident, and resumed them only in 1985, when the new civilian government promised to reopen the case and track down those responsible for her disappearance. To all intents and purposes, the *impunidad* law had voided that promise. Tota told me this story sombrely, but what she really wanted to talk to me about was what it had been like, during the past eighteen months, collecting signatures in the shantytowns ("People came pouring out of their shacks, waving their national documents in their hands"), and receiving them here at the headquarters when she was on desk duty ("Two blind men came up and could only offer their fingerprints but did so with enormous conviction"). Relating these stories, she seemed almost transported. "And no wonder," one of her colleagues remarked later. "For over a decade out there, looking for her daughter, she was alone in the wilderness, and now she suddenly knows she has 634,000 allies."

Others also spoke of the international aspects of the *impunidad* law. "Some laws can be valid domestically and yet invalid with respect to international law," one lawyer commented. He cited several UN and OAS conventions, to which Uruguay was a proud signatory, and which the *impunidad* law flagrantly violated.[28] Another person recalled how one of the new civilian regime's first acts, back in April 1985, had been to send the Blanco leader Alberto Zumarán, the man who'd served as the banned Wilson Ferreira's stand-in in the 1984 Presidential elections, to the UN Human Rights Commission in Geneva to deliver personally the new Uruguayan government's assurance that all human-rights violations would be documented and their perpetrators prosecuted. Now, of course, Zumarán, who'd become the top Blanco leader in the wake of Wilson Ferreira's death, was one of the *impunidad*'s most outspoken advocates.

"But the violation of international standards isn't the main issue," a psychologist put in. "It's the violation of our *own* standards, the violation of our hope for the future of democracy here in Uruguay." Unwittingly reversing a point made by Senator Flores Silva, he went on, "There's no historical law according to which Uruguay or Chile is inevitably destined to return to permanent democracy. Sanguinetti in effect says he wants to consolidate 51 percent of democracy today and maybe go on to 53 percent next year and 58 percent the year after that. But it's just as likely that we could go the route of Bolivia or Brazil, with endlessly recurring cycles of misery and Fascism, especially if we evade our own history. It's Oedipus, it's Hamlet: the curse of the unpunished crime. When murder is not atoned for in some way, it will out in other ways, and here you see how it's already warping us: basically decent people—Sanguinetti, Wilson Ferreira, Zumarán—have been acting completely crazy."

"Oh, I don't know that Sanguinetti is being so crazy," another observer said. "He *needs* the military, and he needs a strong military—it's a charade that he's only just barely able to keep them in check—to be able to force through his economic program. He's intent on paying off our incredible foreign debt—amnesty for the torturers, yes, but no amnesty for their debt. And why? Because the debt is history, and we have to honor our historical obligations. Justice, of course, isn't a historical obligation. Well, if he's going to pay off that debt as dutifully as he seems to want to, he has to impose a stiff austerity program, and to do that he'll have to discipline the unions. Did you hear him in that speech the other day? 'The country has to be protected from them'—only the 'them' we had to be protected from wasn't the military, it was the unions."

"Yeah," said someone else, "and then in that other speech: 'They've suffered so much over the past year'—and the 'they' in question turns out not to be the victims of the abuses—no, it's the military."

They all laughed. "You know all that business about the equivalency they're always claiming," another lawyer broke in, "about how they amnestied one side so that now in fairness they should amnesty the other as well. That, too, is so much nonsense. Leaving aside the huge imbalance in the suffering exacted before the amnesty, the fact is they didn't actually 'amnesty' the prisoners back in March, 1985, when they let them go. What happened was that they reviewed the trials that had resulted in those long prison sentences and they found them so utterly lacking in even the barest semblance of due process—they were all just a bunch of kangaroo courts, drawing on confessions elicited during torture, every one of them—and the sentences imposed were so utterly arbitrary and out of proportion to the alleged offense, and the conditions of imprisonment were so appalling, that they simply legislatively decreed that henceforth one day of actual time served would be considered the equal of three days of the original sentence. And that had the effect of freeing everybody. We're not asking that due process be suspended in the cases of these human-rights violators; in fact, we're insisting that it be observed."

But what of the danger to democracy in forcing the issue, I asked. How did they answer those who feared that a positive vote on any eventual referendum might provoke a coup or that the military would still refuse to obey subpoenas? Zumarán, for instance, had recently said that the referendum might be just, but that the civil forces simply didn't have the strength to enforce it at this time. What was their answer?

"That's one of the forms the campaign of fear is taking," a young activist named Milton Romani acknowledged. "I think first of all we have to see it as a tactic, as a means of disheartening us. But, in fairness, it's a subject we haven't had a coherent position on—what will happen if the law passes. The referendum won't be any sort of magic wand—it will be only a beginning. But it will clarify things. And, anyway, impunity is a political problem, but it's also an ethical one, and those have different ground rules—absolute ground rules. There's a profound sentiment in this country—and it hasn't been expunged—that if you commit a crime you should be held accountable. The Colorados are just as convinced of that as I am. That's why they're so scared of this referendum—why they're so eager to prevent it or at least postpone it."

One striking aspect of the conversations I had with these activists and with most of the supporters of the referendum was the apparent absence of any spirit of rancor or vengeance—the anti-referendum propaganda notwithstanding. (Ironically, the referendum's supporters seemed far angrier at Sanguinetti and Tarigo and Wilson Ferreira and Zumarán than at the torturers or the generals—and that's no doubt precisely the way the military wanted things.) Over and over, I heard it said that, once there was a true accounting, nobody had any interest in anyone else's going to jail.

"Only God can pardon, but even with Him only after confession," Larreta said. "You can't pardon someone who's convinced he has behaved well. Someone asks for a pardon, having repented. I don't care whether anyone is incarcerated, as long as he confesses, repents, and *then* is pardoned."

That morning, I had talked with Pérez Aguirre and asked him if he could imagine ever pardoning his own torturer. "I already have," he replied. It turned out that twice on his daily rounds he'd encountered his torturer on the street. "He tried to avoid my gaze," Pérez Aguirre recounted. "But I took the initiative. I called him over. I said hello, how was he. You see, I wasn't acting the way he expected. He told me he was very depressed. He is one of the foremost accused. He said that he felt his life had become terribly complicated, that it was not good for him or anyone to live in this state of ambiguity. I showed him in a practical way that I was not angry. I told him if he needed anything to come to me. And I told him I forgave him. It's a personal, internal process that I went through, from profound Christian conviction. It's not a very simple process. It takes a lot of internal effort. You need a strong conviction of the power of pardoning—the power of love and reconciliation—and how it affects the other person. But it has to be true reconciliation. And it's something I have to do—the state can't claim to do it for me. If there should be a truth-telling, I'm sure people would find ways of pardoning most of the torturers. We have a tradition of mercy."

Similarly, that evening, Rafael Michelini, the twenty-eight-year-old son of the murdered senator, expressed remarkably little bitterness. Michelini was currently a Frente representative on the Montevideo city council and was also active in the pro-referendum movement, while his mother was one of the commission's co-chairs. Inviting me to a café, he mentioned that he was just back from the United States where he'd been the personal guest of Senator Edward Kennedy at the Democratic Party convention in Atlanta. That fit. *Kennedyesque* was exactly the adjective that came to mind. His was the perfect young politician's face: every feature an icon of destiny—piercing blue-green eyes, "tokens of lucidity"; a straight nose, "heading straight toward its goal"; full black hair, parted down the middle, "the wave of the future."

I told him of the way Sanguinetti had cast the referendum movement as principally a Tupamaro campaign.

"That's a lie," he said softly, almost sadly. "My mother is no Tupamaro; Mrs. Gutiérrez Ruiz is no Tupamaro. How can he take a movement that got almost 30 percent of the electorate to sign a petition—the equivalent of 50 million people in the United States—and dismiss it as the work of Tupamaros? No," he continued, "we're a movement of reconciliation, of peace by constitutional means. Basically, we have three goals. First of all, once the law is annulled, to show the military clearly that it must obey the civil government. Till that is understood, there's *no* future, especially since the law was passed under pressure. Second, to separate from the military those officers who wrote the darkest pages in our history—to stop their being promoted or having others pay homage to them. And, third, to know the truth, to have a serious investigation to find out what happened to the disappeared, so that families may at last be permitted to mourn their dead; so that grandparents can find out what has become of their still living grandchildren; so that we can be at peace."

Did he have any idea who had been responsible for his father's murder?

"We think we know, but I want to be prudent. We're not judges. And, anyway, the problem isn't getting them into jail—it's getting them out of the armed forces. We have to look toward the future, not the past."

I asked him about the danger of a coup or of the military's refusal to honor any eventual subpoenas.

"Blackmail is an important part of politics, and the referendum will be presented as a choice between tranquility and chaos. I don't know the conscience of every Uruguayan, but I'm positive that if the referendum passes and the law is annulled, the military would testify. Not everyone thinks this, but I'm positive. To do otherwise would be to destroy the country simply for the sake of saving thirty or forty officers from testifying. To refuse to recognize the power of the majority would be to put a time bomb at the heart of our democracy. Faced with a historic decision between democracy and the military, I'm convinced Sanguinetti would choose democracy. As for the military, in 1980 they respected the results, why wouldn't they do so now? There's a great sense of honor in the Uruguayan military. They're Uruguayans. And it's not at all clear that the entire armed forces would be willing to sully their image to save forty or fifty scoundrels. The expression of the popular will would have such impact that Sanguinetti would order Medina to make them obey, and Medina would do so, personally jailing anybody who defied him."

And what about you, I asked. What if they finally held the referendum and it lost? Where would that put you with respect to your father? Where would it put the movement?

"There must be total respect for the outcome of the vote," Michelini replied earnestly. "We'll play that absolutely clean. If anyone breaks off and goes beyond the law, we will be the first to condemn him. There's no future for Uruguay if the will of the majority is not respected."

He paused, then added, "Listen. If you ever get a chance to interview Medina, tell him I said so—tell him Rafael Michelini says he would obey. I'd love to hear his reaction."

I did get a chance to interview General Medina. Arriving for my appointment at the compact, elegant onetime hotel that had been recast as the new Defense Ministry following the return of civilian rule, I experienced a momentary shudder. As the soldiers stepped up smartly, reviewed my papers, and waved my taxi in, I realized that this felt exactly like something . . . this sensation of leaving the realm of superfluous epiphenomena and entering the zone of true power. It felt—*that* was it—exactly like entering the Soviet Embassy compound in Warsaw, back in 1980: sure, everything on the outside was real and authentic in its way, but it was obviously here, inside, that the parameters of the allowable were being set.

I had spoken with various people in town about Medina, who was the subject of a good deal of intense speculation. Some spoke of the crisis he'd faced back in April, 1984, when, just as he was about to become Army commander-in-chief, a doctor named Vladimir Roslik in the interior region he was at the time heading turned up dead, supposedly of a heart attack but with clear evidence of having been tortured. Many people hypothesized that the incident had comprised an elaborate provocation, designed to derail Medina's impending promotion, but if so it backfired, as the general made personal assurances that the officers involved would be courtmartialled, and in his subsequent inaugural speech, he recommitted the Army to an honorable exit. One sociologist suggested to me, however, that despite such behavior, Medina was in fact a *duro*—a hard-liner—and that he'd begun favoring a return to civilian governance back in the late seventies and early eighties, not so much out of some suddenly nascent concern over human rights, as out of his ongoing, and increasingly urgent, concern for the institutional integrity of the military itself. He had become troubled by growing corruption inside the armed forces and by a breakdown of internal discipline, which, as in the Brazilian case, seemed unavoidable by-products of totalitarian military rule. Medina's only purpose in life, an opposition senator said, was to protect and preserve the institution of the military. (Medina came from a military family.) "Most of the other generals are gorillas," the senator continued. "They have no feeling for nuance. He does. And also in his favor is the fact that he's one of the few who didn't profit personally from the years of the dictatorship. I respect him. I respect him as an enemy." Everyone agreed that, along with Sanguinetti, Medina had been the principal architect of the Club Naval agreement and had been the person who managed to sell it to his often reluctant colleagues in the military.

A military officer ushered me into the building's central lobby—inlaid mosaic floors, murals of pastoral scenes, stained-glass windows, a dark wood balustrade girdling the mezzanine, a curious fresco of a half-naked Venus carrying a club—and I noticed that virtually every man moving about this ministry of a civilian government was in uniform. (There were no women to be seen.) Presently, Medina emerged from his office and beckoned me in. *He* had shed the uniform (he retired as general before assuming the post of Defense Minister) and was dressed in a modest gray suit. He was mustachioed, with graying hair and washed-out blue eyes. During the interview, there were moments when he seemed grandfatherly, moments when he looked a bit like Chile's Augusto Pinochet, and other moments when he looked like the banker on the old "Lucy" show. But throughout he radiated confidence and self-assurance.

We began our conversation with a historical review of the events that had led to the 1973 coup. "The panorama before the military coup was increasingly critical, owing to a lack of responsibility on the part of Congress and some agencies, and labor instability. All this made the country increasingly difficult to govern," Medina said. "This ingovernability was exacerbated by the actions of a seditious group called the Tupamaros, who acted—and let's make this clear—against the constitutionally elected authorities." His account was considerably fairer and more measured than the one I was being offered by many of the current civilian authorities, who seemed willing to place the blame for almost everything exclusively on the Tupamaros.

I mentioned that the military had resolved the problem of the Tupamaros months before the coup in 1973.

"That was true in the case of the armed apparatus," Medina agreed, "and when one speaks of the Tupamaros' defeat one speaks of their military defeat. But in neither the political nor the ideological sense were they defeated—witness the fact that they continue to exist to this day." He went on to give a reasonably balanced evaluation of the accomplishments of military rule ("We put the country back in order") and of its shortcomings (the economic debacle of the early eighties).

I asked at what point the decision was made to begin returning governance to the civilians, and he said, "The decision to return to democracy always existed in the armed forces, from the beginning."

I asked him if he felt that the armed forces were insufficiently appreciated.

"Well, I would have to say perhaps yes—that there has not been a recognition of the real labor performed by the armed forces. There are things that prevent things from being seen as they are. I can say in all sincerity that at every moment the objective of the armed forces was the well-being of the public. There may have been some mistakes, some errors, along the way, but we always felt that the country, its interests, and its inhabitants came first, before any personal gain. The armed forces always acted as an institution: we never permitted the appearance of a messianic leader, a single man who would take over the process. And when, after 1980, we committed ourselves to the timetable of transition, it was a commitment of honor, and was maintained against all opinions favoring our continuing in power."

I asked if he was proud of the Uruguayan tradition of democracy.

"In the first place, it is, as you say, a tradition—a long history of democratic life. Secondly, I am proud of this, yes. The armed forces understood that while individual men could be questioned, the system should not be—not the parties or the democratic system, which are almost as old as the country itself." He paused. "Actually, many people in this country are not as democratic as one is led to believe. The democratic fervor is not as great as they try to make it appear now. When the moment comes to defend democracy, there are not many people who defend it. At least, that has been the history."

We went on to discuss the Club Naval agreement, and, like President Sanguinetti, Medina declared that the issue of the military's eventual liability for human-rights violations never arose: "It was purposely not considered: touching on this subject would have made it very possible that no agreement could have been reached."

I asked whether he, like President Sanguinetti, had been surprised at the intensity of feeling about the subject after the transition.

"You are putting me in a difficult position, because I must say that on this point I do not agree with the President. Having observed the behavior of people carrying on this campaign to disgrace the armed forces, and knowing the kind of people involved, having had direct contact with them in the battle and in prison, made it easy to predict. Maybe not the degree of intensity—but there was obviously going to be trouble."

Many of the prisoners had not been part of any armed apparatus—students, labor leaders, and so forth. How would he characterize those people?

"During the struggle against subversion, elements were captured from all the sectors—the Tupamaros, the Communist Party, for the Communist Party had been declared illegal by that time. People were captured as a result of being denounced, as a result of the detention or the testimony of other jailed Tupamaros or Communists." A strange smile began to spread over his face. "A man after being arrested was interrogated, according to his characteristics, energetically or mildly . . ."

Energetically?

"Energetically in the case of a man who refused to speak."

Energetically meaning what?

He was silent for a moment, his smile steady. For him, this was clearly a game of cat and mouse. His smile horrified me, but presently I realized that I'd begun smiling back. (It seemed clear that the interview had reached a crisis; either I was going to smile back, showing that I was the sort of man who understood these things, or the interview was going to be abruptly over.) So I smiled, and now I was doubly horrified by the very fact that I was smiling. I'm sure he realized this, because he now smiled all the more, precisely at the way he'd gotten me to smile and how obviously horrified I was to be doing so. He swallowed me whole.

"Listen," he said at length, turning suddenly serious. "In many instances, the life of one of our comrades was in danger, and it was necessary to get information quickly. That is what made it necessary to compel them.[29] But after that was done the subject would just become one more prisoner. That was the focus of our struggle. We do not reject the accusation of *apremios*"—instances of compulsion—"in dealing with the prisoners. Because there were *apremios.* But if we had done what they did in other countries—this is my own reflection—if we had given way to other kinds of repression, then, of the five thousand or so prisoners that there were in this country, four thousand or so might have been killed."

He had said something similar on television the other day, I pointed out, and some people interpreted it as a threat. Had he meant it that way?

"No, I don't mean to threaten. It's simply a reflection—something I truly believe could have happened here. And that it didn't happen here was because of the humanitarian spirit of the armed forces."

I asked if their allies in Argentina, for example, had urged them to act more along Argentine lines and they'd chosen not to.

"Your question is based on a faulty premise. You spoke of allies. We didn't have allies. We were fighting against people in our country; they were fighting against insurgents in their country. There was an interchange of information, logically. . . ."

Was there ever a situation where an Argentine or Chilean President or leader said to him or his colleagues, "I don't understand why you don't do what we do"?

"No, no. There were interchanges of opinion, people who had connections from before the war, people for instance who'd become acquainted while serving guard duty on opposite sides of the border. But they never—nor would we have permitted it—received suggestions or orders."

Were there people here who favored a more Argentine-style approach and were overruled?

"There were lots of opinions. What is important is what was done."

Before the final amnesty debate in Congress, in December, 1986, a group of retired generals, in a kind of palliative gesture, had submitted a statement in which they conceded that there had been some transgressions, though they insisted that the investigations should now cease. He himself, earlier in our interview, had mentioned mistakes and errors. What sorts of mistakes, errors, transgressions did he have in mind?

"Yes, the commanders-in-chief submitted a letter in which we recognized errors and pointed out how, in a situation like that, one loses one's point of reference. But we noted that the errors were committed by men acting as part of a hierarchy, and that to permit those men to be punished would be to risk the loss of authority of the leaders in whom these people had trusted when they were carrying out their orders, so that the leadership would thereafter assume full responsibility. The letter was published, and understood, and the law followed, on December 22."

What sort of errors did he have in mind? People killed? People imprisoned who perhaps shouldn't have been?

"In talking about errors, one talks about all of them, from the smallest to the largest—one doesn't discriminate. All the errors that you can imagine might have occurred. But I very clearly informed all the Army units that there would be complete protection for those who were carrying out orders in the line of duty."

I pointed out that approximately a quarter of the voting population of Uruguay had signed the petition calling for an annulment of the amnesty—a significant proportion in any democracy. Many of the signers whom I'd spoken with, I told Medina, didn't seem to have a particular interest in having anyone else go to jail. What they wanted was a truth-telling. Was there any way the military would be willing to accept some official historical investigation, which could evaluate the role of the Tupamaros, the politicians, and so forth, and, within that context, the behavior of the military?

"I would ask you who would be benefitted by such a study," Medina replied. "What reasons do those who are searching simply out of curiosity have—and here I'm not talking about you, about the sort of thing you're doing—to return to the past, and make the country lose time and money? I think that doing so simply to satisfy a curiosity, which I think is close to morbid, would have no positive results. Positive results are achieved by work, dedication, and, as the President says, looking toward the future." He went on to say that though the referendum movement was employing a legitimate means, there were countless irregularities in the signatures on the petitions. "I think and hope there will not be enough signatures—not because it would be better for the armed forces but because it would be better for the country," he said. "The positive aspect of an election would be that the healthy sector of the country, I'm sure, would win, and by a landslide, so that the subject wouldn't have to be discussed any longer—it would be over forever. But at what cost? Just the fact of the campaign, with all the propaganda before the vote, with emotions heating up, with all the confrontations and unfortunate incidents that would no doubt occur—that's what I'd want to avoid."

A completely hypothetical question: If there should be a vote and if the law were overturned, if soldiers should be subpoenaed, would he, as the Defense Minister of a constitutional government, order them to obey the summonses?

"They are not going to win. I consider it fruitless to speculate on events that are not going to occur. I am not going to talk about it."

I mentioned that I had been interviewing Rafael Michelini and that he had said two things that might interest him: first, that if the referendum lost the activists would have to obey the will of the majority; and, second, that if it won he, Michelini, was convinced that the President would follow the will of the people and so, specifically, would General Medina.

Medina smiled significantly. "That," he said, "is Rafael Michelini's opinion."

He laughed, I laughed, and I decided to change the subject.

I mentioned the woman I had interviewed whose nineteen-day-old son had disappeared twelve years ago. She couldn't sleep at night, wondering where the boy was. Could he empathize with that? What should she do?

"Well, sympathy? No. I feel the natural pity for her that anyone might feel when faced with the misfortune of another. That is something that did not occur in this country, and I have no suggestions."

We're not talking about punishing anyone—simply finding the child.

"These cases have been investigated by military justice, and the families of the disappeared have refused to testify in military courts, so it's very difficult. In addition to being difficult, it's not in my mandate." (It is a fact that some of the disappearance cases were specifically excluded from the 1986 law. Congress empowered the President to pursue them as he saw fit. To the outrage of the families and many congressmen, even of many supporters of the bill, Sanguinetti chose to assign the cases to a military prosecutor. The families did refuse to collaborate in what they saw as a whitewash; the prosecutor, for his part, quickly dismissed the cases. Amnesty International recently criticized the military prosecutor's handling of these matters.)

Couldn't he at least make personal inquiries?

"When the way of obtaining such collaboration is a public scandal, and there is all this shouting, it's very hard to get the cooperation of the authorities."

Did he mean that if the shouting stopped, it would be easier?

"The scandalous shouting has already occurred. You can be sure that if I, as a human being, were to encounter the child and could return it to its mother, I would do so. But in the context of my function in government I don't see any reason for me to intervene."

Uruguay, I pointed out, had a military budget proportional, in terms of the national budget, to the military budgets of countries like Israel and Nicaragua and Cuba and Iran—countries that consider themselves at war, to varying degrees. What did he see as the long-term role and budgetary requirements of the Uruguayan military?

Medina began his answer by disputing my premise, pointing out that all kinds of civil functions were undertaken by the military in Uruguay (the weather service, Antarctic research, customs monitoring, and the like), so the actual military proportion was much smaller. Furthermore, 70 percent of the defense budget went for salaries. "If the budget were reduced, obligatory military service would have to be imposed—an option that has traditionally been rejected by public opinion."

But the military today was much larger than it had been in the sixties. How big did it have to be?

"Since March of 1985, we have reduced the armed forces by 5,000 positions"—from 31,000 to 26,000 compared with about 15,000 in 1968. "The other day, I said that if we continued to reduce the size of the military I myself would end up having to work as a guard."

What did he see as the role of the armed forces in Uruguay? Neither Brazil nor Argentina was likely to invade. This was a country at peace.

Suddenly, Medina, who had stayed completely unflustered through all the difficult terrain we'd covered up to this point, almost began to shake. "Will you give me a guarantee that they will not invade?" He raised his voice. "We have the mission to defend the sovereignty, the borders, and to maintain order within the country when we are required. We may be a small country, but we have dignity. And if we were a country without an army we would be very close to being a country without dignity."

He was speaking with desperate intensity. And, indeed, I felt that we had come to the very nub of the matter. It had something to do with this matter of the wandering "we" in his answer: the "we, Uruguay" shimmering, vibrating, blurring into and out of "we, the armed forces"—the dignity of the country being wrapped up in the dignity of its armed forces, whose raison d'être seemed to be their own dignity.[30]

Pushing things a little further, I pointed out that throughout the world today Communism seemed to be much less of a threat than it must have seemed a decade ago. Gorbachev seemed almost to be dismantling Communism in the Soviet Union itself. Did he, Medina, still perceive Communism as a threat to Uruguay's internal order?

"From what I have been able to see, there has been no substantial change in the foreign policy of the Soviet Union. And our Communist Party has its guidelines set in Moscow. I haven't seen the Berlin Wall being dismantled. I haven't seen the Jewish people permitted to emigrate." (This was rich!—a Southern Cone general expressing concern over the fate of Jews in the world!) "I haven't seen an amelioration in the subversive tendencies of some of the Soviet satellites. Therefore, I would prefer to wait to give a final opinion."

Did he think that subversion in Uruguay was directed from the Soviet Union?

"I have no material proof. But I have my suspicions, yes."

One last set of questions. Back in the middle of the interview, he had indicated that the leaders of the military took responsibility for all that was done under their command. Could that lead to a situation down the line where if there were going to be any trials he would insist that it be the leaders who were tried?

"When the leaders assumed that responsibility, it was with all its consequences."

I now broached the case in which the Argentine judge was requesting the extradition of the four Uruguayan officers.

Medina interrupted me angrily. "That case was just pulled out of a hat," he said. "Here there's an amnesty, there there's an amnesty. Personally, I think the action of that judge leaves a lot to be desired. Because he can't judge the officers in his own country, now he's looking for officers in other countries."

But, over and above the quality of the judge, here we were dealing with extradition laws. Faced with a situation like that, would he assume the legal responsibility for those individuals?

"Look," Medina said sternly. "I won't enter into that kind of speculation. I am not going to tell you whether officers will be turned in or not. What I'm saying is that it's not rational, it's not logical, *it's not just.* When, or if, I see the extradition papers, then we'll see."

He paused. "We're not responsible for the kidnappings and the killings—those crimes were amnestied." Again, the complicitous smile. "But I am the one responsible for those officials in Argentina. Obviously, those people didn't just show up in Argentina. They were there carrying out orders—not the Michelini case, that was not our case, we don't know who did it. They were there carrying out somebody's orders, and they were *our* orders."

And with that our conversation came to an emphatic close. As he was escorting me to the door, he laughed self-depreciatingly and said, "When this appears, they're going to hang me." He nodded in the direction of the officers milling around in the lobby. But he didn't seem too worried.

Luis González, the premier political pollster in Uruguay, is stone deaf. It's curious that this master of the art of political soundings (the French word for polls is actually *sondages*), this man with his ear to the ground of his country, cannot actually hear a thing. But he can lipread marvelously, fluently, in both Spanish and English (he was trained at Yale), and though his speech is vaguely slurred, it's hearty, expansive, and eminently understandable. The only scary part is when he insists on conversing while driving. To keep up your own end of such conversations is simply to risk death. It was, at any rate, on one such drive that Luis González laid out for me the results of the latest polling that his organization, Equipos, had done on the question of any eventual referendum vote. "When you study the data, three main points emerge," González said. "Everybody knows that there were huge violations of human rights. Most people think that the military men responsible for those violations should be held accountable in some manner. Yet most people have the idea that it won't be easy, or even possible, to hold them to account. People are generally not as worried about any imminent coup as they were in the early days of the transition—except when you bring up this question of the referendum. Then the anxiety level rises sharply. The figures are very clear and remarkably steady. Early in 1987, we predicted the number of people who would be willing to sign the petition, and we got the numbers almost exactly right. Now we're predicting that if there is ever an election, at most 40 percent and probably a bit less (right now, it's about 35 percent), will vote to overturn the *impunidad* statute. It's not that people approve of *impunidad*—they emphatically don't—but that they just don't see any alternative."

Waiting till we'd come to a red light, I asked González if he himself felt that it would be healthy for the country, in the long run, to ignore its history.

"That's not the right question," he replied. "It assumes that you have a single wrong actor, and that this devil is the military. But that isn't fair. We know that it was guilty of terrible violations, but why restrict the blame for those to the military? From 1971 on, certainly, the military had a clear mandate from the politicians—it had been ordered to impose order on the country, and nobody was bothering to tell it how. The politicians brought the military in. But if we acknowledge *that* huge problem, where does that put us? Perhaps it's better just to start again from scratch." He paused. "You know," he said, sighing, "what was instrumental in the earliest building of democracy in Uruguay—when the country was emerging from that series of fratricidal wars between bands of Colorados and Blancos at the turn of the century—was that there would be, as people said, 'no winners and no losers.' Perhaps such an approach can be instrumental again in the current reconsolidation of democracy. I don't know."

I met a lot of people in Uruguay who had not signed the petition—often, especially in the case of public employees, out of fear for their jobs or their pension—but who said that in the event of a referendum they would vote to overthrow the *impunidad* law. I also met several who said that though they had signed the petition, they intended to vote against the referendum. "From an ethical point of view, it was important to sign," one woman explained to me, "but politically it's not the right time."

When, I asked her, would it be the right time?

"There will never be a right time," she replied sadly. "It's all just too risky."

Over and over during my stay in Montevideo, I encountered this distinction between the ethical and the political. With that young woman, the two were held in a kind of self-consciously dynamic equilibrium. But more often one side predominated, almost to the exclusion of the other. People who saw the issue as essentially a political one—that is, susceptible to negotiation, concession, compromise, the interplay of power centers on the field—considered discussion of its ethical component a frivolous self-indulgence. Conversely, those who saw the issue as an ethical one—a matter of absolute principle, by definition nonnegotiable—were appalled by what they considered the spineless opportunism of the so-called pragmatists.

Carina Perelli, one of the finest of the new generation of Uruguayan sociologists, has argued that the rise in ethicist thinking is in an ironic sense an outgrowth of the dictatorial period itself. In a fascinating essay, "The Legacies of the Processes of Transition to Democracy in Argentina and Uruguay," she recalls what it was like for average people (like herself—she was a teenager at the time) to go about their daily lives under conditions of such total repression: how people had to "split themselves into person and persona, playing the role of 'the good citizen,' making sure that the length of their hair, the look of their clothes, the expression on their faces, the tone of their voice, were in line with the parameters of the mask they ought to show in the world. . . . Surviving implied being capable of blending in, maintaining anonymity, of not standing out. This in turn implied a rigorous self-control of the personal: a self-assault, in order not to be assaulted. . . . The first inxile is then the one that takes place in the individual's own body. Thus the body becomes political to the extent that it becomes a sphere in which struggles for power take place."

Perelli outlines the legacies of "this invasion of the public into the most recondite parts of the private": "When the personal is political, then the political ceases to be analyzed in the light of cold reason, of realistic calculation, of party traditions. The political comes to be lived as personal and to be ruled by the norms that govern, in essence, private life, which is to say, *ethical principles.*" Thus, according to Perelli, the military, through its style of repression, unintentionally spawned a new sort of citizen—one who would be singularly uninterested in any sort of pragmatic accommodation.

Perelli herself, I found, did not celebrate this condition, and, indeed, had little patience with the referendum movement. "It's a return to the Uruguay of the past," she said one day when we had lunch together. "A return to the days when you could do whatever you wanted, regardless of the consequences. And I also disapprove of its black-and-white schema—how it makes the Army the scapegoat for everything. I would vote for a referendum that would judge the whole of Uruguayan society, because everybody, even in my generation, was guilty. We accepted the Tupamaros, we smirked at their antics, we accepted the descent into violence. We were like the French during the Occupation, sitting on the sidelines and waiting to share in the spoils with the winners. Everybody played a disloyal game at the time. It's not a black-and-white issue, and in transforming it into black-and-white you lose the shades of gray, which, as you know, my friend, is the color of intelligence."

Carina Perelli pointed out that the same tension between pragmatic and ethical modes of being also existed inside the military, only in the military the ethic involved such notions as unity, mission, honor, doctrinal purity, obedience, and subordination, and its champions refused to even entertain the notion of the military as an institution subject to any sort of civilian oversight. Ironically, Perelli pointed out, the more the civilian ethicists pushed, the more the military ethicists rose up in response. I subsequently heard a story about how, in mid-1985, Medina had secretly suggested to Wilson Ferreira that the military might be willing to give up certain officers for trial—for example, Gavazzo, who had been implicated in significant freelance corruption alongside his more professional activities as a kidnapper and torturer. Gavazzo reportedly got wind of these tentative talks and let it be known that if he were ever tried, he'd spill the beans on at least three hundred other similarly compromised officers. After that, he wrapped himself in the mantle of the pure military ethicist—an absolute champion of the institution itself—and as such he has since become the idol of many of the younger officers.

"When the dictatorship was ending," Perelli added, "everybody assumed that following a talking-out period, a catharsis of some sort would take place. But it didn't. The politicians blew it. The terrible thing is that we've arrived at a situation where in order to deal with the past at all, a referendum has become necessary. That's the politician's fault."

Juan Martín Posadas, the only senator in Wilson Ferreira's faction of the Blanco Party to have voted against the *impunidad* legislation, was similarly bleak. "During the first six months," he suggested, "a resolution of the situation would have been possible. Civil society was strong and the military uncertain, and we could have pressed the issue. I still don't know why we didn't. Maybe this delay was built into the Club Naval agreements. Time passed, that whole year-and-a-half while the question of civil versus military jurisdiction wended its way up to the Supreme Court, and by the time the Court ruled in favor of civil jurisdiction, it was too late. When you ask Medina today about the continuing applicability of the understanding he achieved with Wilson Ferreira back in '85 regarding the prosecution of particuarly corrupt individuals, he says a lot has happened since then and now everybody will be protected." Posadas sighed. "The future of democracy would have been different if we had been able to resolve this transition with a minimum sense of justice. It's really tragic. We had a chance, and the opportunities are so rare."

I asked him how he was going to vote if there ever was a referendum.

"I favor the referendum," he said, tiredly.

Didn't he think the referendum might provide a vehicle for rectifying the situation?

"I don't know where the enforcement process would break, at the level of Sanguinetti or at the level of Medina. But the hypothesis that the military today would under any circumstances allow itself to be brought to trial escapes the bounds of this reality. I can't even entertain that hypothesis, because it's not going to happen."

Even following a majority vote overthrowing the amnesty?

"People's Power is not a fantasy, it's a fact. But it has the limits of a fact. In 1985 this fact would have weighed ninety tons. Today it weighs five tons. It's not going to happen."

Around the time I visited Uruguay, Jorge Baños, the Argentine human-rights lawyer, somehow obtained secret papers (which he subsequently disseminated) from the Seventeenth Conference of American Armies, a convocation of high-ranking officers from fifteen countries, including the United States, which had been held in November, 1987, in Mar del Plata, Argentina. (Baños clearly had some impressive sources inside the military: these were highly revealing documents.) They proved that Latin American military men were by and large as committed as ever to the doctrine of national security.

Indeed, the doctrine had received some subtle elaborations at Mar del Plata, in the light of recent developments. A frequently recurring theme in the papers was the ongoing resort of the International Communist Movement (MCI, by its Spanish initials) to "terrorism" (overt violence) and "subversion" (more insidious, often cultural, stratagems)—the two were considered equally treacherous. There were particularly caustic references to liberation theology ("that subtle and substantive means for the MCI to penetrate society"), human-rights initiatives (effective in "limiting the freedom of countersubversive action"), and even parliamentary democracy (which was now being used by the MCI as a "substitute" for the more traditional "dictatorship of the proletariat" as a way station on the road to victory).

When Medina was subsequently called before the Uruguayan Congress to discuss the participation and attitude of Uruguayan military officers at the conference, he declined to answer questions on such matters in anything beyond the sketchiest details. But the tenor of much Uruguayan military thinking in the wake of Mar del Plata was soon conveyed in a widely publicized statement included in an intraservice newsletter: "Uruguay is infested with the guerrillas who at a certain moment were brilliantly crushed but today are back among us. Uruguay is one of the battlegrounds of the cold war waged by Communism with its intent to dominate the world."

According to Juan Rial, one of Uruguay's leading political scientists, the whole question of *impunidad* was part of a much broader horizon of issues regarding civil-military relations, and it would take years and years before any semblance of normalcy returned to those relations, if ever. (Rial was Carina Perelli's husband. Three-quarters of a generation older than his wife—which is to say, a university student during the tumultuous late sixties—he'd been part of that sector of Uruguayan society that had borne the greatest brunt of the military's repression. He himself had been blacklisted out of a succession of jobs and had come away from the experience with a healthy, almost consuming sense of the military's potential ferocity, and a decided reluctance ever to test it again. He was like a mouse authority on the claws of cats—the military had become the principal focus of his studies.) "In Congress," Rial elaborated for me, "there are two committees that currently oversee the defense establishment, one on the budget and the other on the promotion of personnel. But in both cases, up to this point anyway, they just watch, they don't control. This year, the military academy was closed for the first time to first-year students while they reformed doctrinal training—but it's the military that's doing the reforming, not the civilians."

And indeed, for all the protestations to the contrary on both sides, any eventual referendum would obviously be about much more than the fate of several dozen, or even several hundred, violators of human rights, or even the attaining of a modicum of justice for several thousands of their victims. The reason the military was so hesitant to countenance the open public airing of these countless instances of depravity —and conversely, the reason others were so insistent that such an open public airing take place—was that the depravities went to the very core of the military's wider concern, which was its fundamental legitimacy: its right, in effect, to strut, and the future of that strut. A military which could be shown—not just known, but *shown*—to have indulged in such systematically dishonorable, disfiguringly dishonorable activities might begin to lose its honor. Or not so much its honor, which had always been a sort of fiction, but the populace's suspended disbelief in that fiction. These were potentially *magic* truths which were being bandied about: it wasn't just a question of saying them, but saying them aloud in a particular venue. Were such a particularized saying to take place, there might eventually be real-world consequences for the military, in terms of such things as budget, assigned mission, continued control over its own indoctrination and promotion practices, its tutelary power over the wider populace, and so forth. *Who finally knew how far the military would go to prevent such things from being said in such a context?* That was the scary part, the reason why so many Uruguayans were saying that were things to come to a vote, they'd probably end up opposing the referendum.

When I went to visit Senator Carlos Julia Pereyra, the leader of the one Blanco faction that had voted en masse against the *impunidad* statute, he started out by voicing exasperations similar to Juan Rial's. "Ten days ago," he told me, "General de Nava, the commander of the Third Army Corps, in the North, gave a highly publicized speech in which he proclaimed that the armed forces were preparing to defend the country from the advances of leftist elements. This provoked a considerable reaction. Medina tried to smooth the situation over by saying that de Nava's speech had been directed not at public opinion but, rather, at the soldiers. If you ask me, that's far worse. And it's got to be made to stop. We have to stand up to the military."

He turned to the subject of the *impunidad* law. "Any form of amnesty invites a repetition of human-rights abuses. Someone who has done such things and is not punished is inclined to do them again." (Sometime later, General Alfonso Féola seemed to confirm Pereyra's point, though from the other side of the argument. "Who in the future will fight against subversion," he asked, "if he knows that at any moment he could be tried?") "If you ask me," Pereyra continued, "it's relatively simple: to show signs of weakness or fear in the face of challenges to these basic principles would be the greatest single stimulant to the reappearance of dictatorship."

But what if the election took place and the law passed and then it was disobeyed, I asked Pereyra. Then where would they be?

"I think that if we get to that moment, that will be the moment of truth, the hour in which Uruguay will decide whether it is living in a democracy or whether what we've been living the last four years is a farce. We'd have to run through the usual constitutional remedies—hearings, inquiries, up through impeachment, if necessary—and if they all came to nothing it would be time to go home. There would be no point in our going on occupying these congressional seats. As a citizen and a politician, I prefer to know the truth, even if it means we have to begin all over again."

As I was packing my bags in preparation for my return to New York, I decided to phone Jacobo Timmerman, the Argentine journalist and former torture victim. I was curious about his view of the ongoing drama in a neighboring country, and then somewhat surprised at how torn he was. "One wants to do the ethical thing," he said. "But what does one mean by ethics—short-term (ethical in terms of the next year, say) or long-term (ethical in terms of fifty years from now)? Fifty years from now, the particular fate of individual victims or perpetrators won't matter. Whether there's still a democracy is what will matter. I mean, I'm not coldhearted, I'm not made of stone, I'd really like to see justice done. But I don't know."

He paused. "It reminds me of something the Israeli novelist Amos Elon once told me, how once when he was studying with Gershom Scholem, the great professor of Kabbalistic studies at Hebrew University, he went up to him after class and said, 'Before I thought I understood, but now I'm getting confused.' 'Ah,' Scholem told him, 'that means you're beginning to understand.' "

During the ensuing weeks (in the meantime I had returned to New York), the Electoral Court continued steadily about its work. In October, it issued a new round of signature disqualifications, which included the signature of Senator Pereyra. (His was one of eight thousand signatures eliminated, subsequent studies revealed, owing to simple transcribing errors on the part of Court employees.) The Uruguayan author Eduardo Galeano, writing in the independent leftist weekly *Brecha,* recorded another instance, the disqualification of the signature of a janitor who worked at the Court itself:

> He was right there . . . at the moment of the verification of his signature.
>
> "Mariño," said the official. "Did you sign?"
>
> "Yes," answered Mariño.
>
> "The signatures do not coincide," said the official.
>
> "But it's my signature," said Mariño.
>
> "I am very sorry," said the official, "but they do not coincide."
>
> In vain, Mariño insisted, crying, "But I am me!" And the official gave him a look as if to say, "You thought you were so clever, young man, but you haven't fooled us."

The signatures of one-time illiterates, who had had to register with their thumbprints years earlier and had subsequently learned to write, were automatically disqualified. For that matter, the thumbprint signatures of all the remaining illiterates were set aside, on the suspicion that —who knew?—they might have attempted to forge their thumbs.

Perhaps the last straw was the disqualification of the signature of General Líber Seregni, the leader of the Frente Amplio and one of the referendum's most outspoken supporters, because, it was explained, the "S" in his current signature did not coincide with the "S" in his signature forty years ago, when he first signed the voting register. At that point, the Pro-Referendum Commission denounced the entire process as a charade and withdrew its observers from the Electoral Court. The matter was brought before Congress, but, following a passionate debate, which lasted an entire day and until five o'clock the next morning, Congress voted, along exactly the same lines as it had voted in passing the *impunidad* law, to uphold the probity of the Electoral Court's procedures. The military, for good measure, summarily fired two civilian employees of a military hospital (employees of fourteen and eighteen years' standing) for signing the petition, and intimated the impending dismissal of thirty more on the same grounds.

Late in 1988, Americas Watch, the New York-based human-rights monitoring organization, sent Robert K. Goldman, a professor at the American University Law School, in Washington, D.C., and a veteran observer of the Uruguayan scene, to Montevideo to head a team assessing the situation. They spent a week interviewing the principals but were denied access to Sanguinetti, Medina, and most other high government officials. On the last day of their stay, Goldman held a news conference at which he declared that Americas Watch was viewing ongoing developments with serious misgivings. A few days later, back in New York, I had a chance to speak with him.

In an exquisite turn of legalese, Goldman noted his concern over the Court's "ambulatory criteria with respect to eligibility for signing," and he gave a number of examples. But, he said, the thing he and his team had found most troubling was the attitude of the distinguished Colorado Party veteran Renan Rodríguez, an old man who, in his last appointment, was heading the Electoral Court. "We met with him, and he seemed tired and frail and clearly under crushing pressure," Goldman recounted. "His wife died earlier this year. He seemed authentically 'mortified,' as he put it, by all the criticism the Electoral Court was receiving. But when we asked him specific questions about procedures he kept avoiding answers, and finally he just blew up. He became extremely agitated, and ended by insisting that all the people who had signed the petitions were little more than Tupamaro sympathizers. Now, it's one thing for the Colorados to take that line rhetorically, but this was the head of a court that was supposed to be maintaining a position of punctilious neutrality. It was really shocking. And it was sad, too, because Rodríguez seemed a fundamentally decent and honest man; he had just reached his limit. It's terrible what they're doing to him."

I said that this seemed to be a frequent pattern in transitional democratic regimes still dogged by their military predecessors. In Guatemala in 1987, for example, the new civilian President, Vinicio Cerezo, created the post of human-rights ombudsman with great fanfare and then filled it with a distinguished political veteran who was so old and rickety that he was literally unable to hold the pages of his acceptance speech the day he delivered it to Congress. Thereafter, he was shunted aside to a villa on the edge of town, miles from any bus line and hence virtually inaccessible to any of the poor peasants who might have been expected to form his principal clientele; he wasn't even heard from for over a year, at which point he roused himself, for the first and only time, in order to protest an increase in the electricity rates.

"Yes," Goldman agreed. "But it's also important to say that Uruguay isn't Guatemala. The Tupamaros *have* been released, the political prisons *have* been shut down, fired workers *have* been rehired. There has been a genuine attempt to compensate some of the victims. This is not merely a 'technical democracy,' like El Salvador, where sham elections and institutions barely disguise the true nature of military rule. The Uruguayan elections *were* legitimate. The Uruguayans *are* trying to carve out an authentic space for civilian life. That's what makes these irregularities all the more troubling—Sanguinetti's assignment of the disappearance cases to a military prosecutor, for example, and this signature-verification process, in which it's as if a signer were assumed to have been acting fraudulently unless it's proved otherwise. I'm afraid they're really blowing it."

On November 28, 1988, almost a full year after the submission of the referendum petition, the Electoral Court announced its final tally. With 555,701 signatures necessary in order to trigger an election, even the Court had to admit that 532,718 signatures were indisputably valid. That left a shortfall of 22,983 signatures. However, according to the Court, 36,861 signatures were "in suspension"—that is, not totally disqualified. And this was what the Court was going to do: it was going to publish those names (an immediate uproar arose from all those who were still insisting on the confidentiality of the petition rosters), and, less than three weeks hence, on the weekend of December 17 and 18, it was going to open up a hundred offices around the country. If 22,983 out of those 36,861 people showed up that weekend (and the following day—Monday, the nineteenth—when a smaller number of offices would be open, to handle cases of individuals who had moved away from their original precincts) and confirmed that they had indeed signed the petition, then there would be a referendum. Otherwise not.

It was not lost on anyone that the weekend of December 17 would fall just after the traditional start of summer vacation (a week before Christmas), and, therefore, a sizable percentage of individuals might already be gone. The Court, for its part, would make no effort to contact the people in question, beyond publishing the list in the *Diario Oficial,* an ordinarily obscure government publication with a circulation of only 8,000. Back in New York, Goldman pointed out the perversity of the process: people were being asked to confirm that they had indeed signed, though it would have been much simpler to publish a list and ask any persons who had not actually signed to come forward.

In Montevideo, meanwhile, the military stepped up its fear campaign once again. Medina declared that anyone who had signed the petition was "mentally ill," and Sanguinetti, for his part, denounced the Pro-Referendum Commission for persisting in its "campaign of hate." There was no question that for someone specifically listed by name to come forward and confirm his signature was going to require even more courage than the initial (ostensibly confidential) act of signing.

On November 29, the steering committee of the Pro-Referendum Commission met for several hours, debating the wisdom of even attempting to jump through this latest, most arbitrary, and undoubtedly most formidable hoop. Some members, like Pérez Aguirre, considered the prospect for success on such short notice to be dismal at best, and the prospect of even trying almost beneath their dignity. (One person pointed out that the Court, which had given itself almost a year, was now going to give them less than three weeks.) They advocated shifting the struggle to some different form and venue (street demonstrations, civil disobedience, electoral politics, international courts). But other members insisted on going ahead with the challenge, and they eventually won the debate by the slightest of margins.

Just a few days later, on Friday, December 2, the Argentine military attaché in Panama, Colonel Muhammad Ali Seineldín, secretly returned to Argentina, took command of an infantry school, and launched a third attempted coup, reportedly demanding, to begin with, the freeing of imprisoned officers, the suspension of any outstanding human-rights trials, the sacking of the new chief of staff, and a big pay increase for the military. It quickly became apparent that the last stop on his secret way back to Argentina had been in Uruguay.[31] These developments, of course, could not have come at a worse moment for the Pro-Referendum Commission. Seineldín's attempt narrowly failed, like the others before it, with the same ambiguous denouement. (The new chief of staff did announce his resignation, the soldiers did get a pay increase.) Once again, Sanguinetti was able to point to these developments with alarm.

In the midst of all this, Uruguayan government lawyers began floating the notion that even if there ever were enough signatures to force an election, and even if the referendum passed, its effect would be moot, since on grounds of double jeopardy, it would be impossible for anyone to rescind an amnesty once it had been granted. Pro-Referendum Commission lawyers pointed out that, technically speaking, no grant of amnesty had ever been made: on December 22, 1986, the government merely declared, as the law's title explicitly stated, the expiration of its own punitive authority. The government hadn't vested any rights in the defendants in the various human-rights cases; it had simply decided, unilaterally, not to go ahead with their trials. That was the decision the law was seeking to overturn, and that decision was eminently revocable. A senator from the majority (pro-*impunidad*) wing of the Blanco Party named Gonzalo Aguirre now submitted a bill declaring that were an *impunidad* referendum ever to succeed, its effect would be to derogate rather than to annul the law, which was to say that its effect could only be prospective rather than retrospective. Aside from the fact that that's not what the petition had said—and the petition's wording was what everybody was going to be voting on—people had a hard time figuring out what could possibly be meant by the *prospective* implications of the repeal of a law whose only subject had been the dismissal of *past* charges. Even the *impunidad* law's supporters couldn't quite get their heads around that riddle, and Gonzalo Aguirre's bill languished. If all this sounded confusing, that was, of course, the idea: it was intended to confuse, and to confound, and to dishearten, and to get fewer people to show up on December 17 and 18.

The next three weeks saw frantic organizing by the Pro-Referendum

Commission. Now that the list had been published, and the military had it anyway, it became imperative that the list receive the widest possible dissemination, so that those involved would at least know that they were on it. The government promised to post the complete list in public buildings (post offices, pension bureaus, and so forth) all around the country, but it never did so. The two main dailies, the Colorado-controlled *El Día* and the Blanco-controlled *El País,* declined to print the list and, for that matter, downplayed the whole story, as did all the television stations (the government station refused even to run the pro-referendum campaign's paid commercials). Only two of nearly forty radio stations agreed to cooperate with the Pro-Referendum Commission in any way: CX30, the station of Germán Araujo, a former anti-*impunidad* legislator who had been expelled from the Senate following brawls that erupted inside the chamber in the early hours of December 22, 1986; and CX44, the station run by the Tupamaros (the establishment's contention that the Tupamaros were playing a central role in the whole campaign had thus become self-fulfilling).

The Pro-Referendum Commission opened seven impromptu offices, with hundreds of volunteers manning phone banks to try to get the word out, though they soon realized that over 40 percent of the people they were attempting to reach didn't have phones. People with similar names were called, leads developed, cars and bicycles dispatched to far-flung neighborhoods. The two radio stations punctuated their programming with urgent queries: "We are looking for a Juan Pérez Martínez; it appears he used to work at the ANCAP filling station in Pocitos; anyone with information as to his whereabouts should call . . ." Outdoor tables sprang up all around town, manned by grandmothers and students and others who urged all passersby to examine increasingly tattered copies of the master list to see if their names appeared, or the names of people they knew. The organizers began to arrange transportation for every single listed person they had been able to locate. People started leaving on their vacations. The clock was winding down.

From the reports I was getting back in New York, Montevideo must have presented an eerie aspect that weekend of December 17 and 18. (I'd taken to calling every few hours.) A tremendous amount of almost frenzied energy was being focussed upon a minuscule proportion of the population. Everybody in town was aware of the concentrated activity, and most people (both for and against) were deeply concerned about the outcome. Yet the campaign was still being virtually ignored by the major media.[32]

Cars in Montevideo were racing about town, picking up homebound signers and ferrying them to the Court's various outposts. (The Court had fifty such outposts set up in Montevideo, with another fifty scattered around the rest of the country.) The two pro-referendum radio stations were on the air around the clock, announcing the latest updates on the confirmation totals, and inquiring after missing individuals: "Does anyone know the whereabouts of María Flora Sánchez?" "We've just received word that Carlos Julio Paz is out fishing in the middle of Lake Castillos—can somebody get a boat and bring him back in so he can confirm his signature?" At each of the Court's outposts around the country, three Court representatives reviewed all confirmations. In addition, there was a Colorado Party observer, who often objected, for example, about the discrepancies between a fifty-year-old signer and his I.D. photo, taken when he was eighteen. A pro-referendum observer was there as well, conveying the latest totals back to headquarters every half hour or so. It was thus possible for the two radio stations to be running up-to-the-minute totals all the way through the weekend. (Araujo himself stayed on the air for fifty hours straight.)

In order to succeed, the pro-referendum organizers were going to need to get 64 percent of the 36,834 suspendees to step forward and confirm their signatures. By the end of Saturday, about 36 percent had done so—significantly fewer than the organizers had hoped for—and by Sunday night they were still 1,467 confirmations short of the 22,983 required. On Monday, far fewer Court offices were going to be open for business (in fact, only three in the whole country, one near the Argentine border at Fray Bentos, another in the interior, and the last at the Court's headquarters in Montevideo), and they would be accepting confirmations only from individuals who had moved out of their original precincts. Furthermore, with the onset of the summer vacation, they would be keeping holiday hours and closing at 2 P.M. Even some of the strategy's most enthusiastic proponents were turning pessimistic.

Things weren't helped any when, early Monday morning, the country awoke to a spectacular electrical storm that lasted well through the first several hours of the process, snarling traffic throughout the region. The Pro-Referendum Commission's lawyers appealed to the Electoral Court to extend office hours on account of the storm, but the Court turned down the request, by a vote of six to three. The two radio stations crackled with desperate exhortations. Seven buses loaded with Uruguayan signers temporarily residing in Buenos Aires had set out early in the morning, headed for the border town of Fray Bentos. Now came word, over the radio, that the ubiquitous Colorado deputy Rubén Díaz was at the border, trying to deny the buses entry into the country, or at least to delay their entry past 2 P.M. He had no grounds for doing so (critics pointed out that Rubén Díaz had never displayed such zealous concern over the sanctity of the country's borders back in the days when Argentine torturers were being given free passage in and out—nor, for that matter, just a few weeks ago, when the Argentine mutineer Seineldín was permitted to slip into and out of Uruguay on his way down from Panama), but he in fact did succeed in holding back two of the buses, with over eighty-five signers.

Late in the morning, with numbers still lagging, a spirit of exhausted desolation began to pervade the Pro-Referendum Commission's headquarters. The final morning edition of the Colorado daily *El Día* had suddenly taken note of developments with its banner headline "LOOKS BAD FOR REFERENDUM." At noon, however, came word from Canelones province, just to the north of Montevideo, reporting five hundred fresh confirmations. Spirits buoyed: it was going to be a real race after all. And, indeed, Eduardo Galeano subsequently described for me how "at one-fifty-nine, the streets leading up to the Electoral Court's headquarters in Montevideo were lined with referendum supporters, urging on the last of the stragglers, who came running up, waving their identification documents in their hands, the crowds cheering wildly, exactly like at the Olympics." All over the country, people waiting outside the Court offices now jammed themselves through the doors as they were being closed—"We were here! It's not our problem if you're being so slow. You have to count us!"

From the reports I was getting, the whole country now seemed to fall momentarily silent, awaiting the results. Patricia Pittman, an American journalist and human-rights monitor based in Buenos Aires, who had been sent by Americas Watch to observe the weekend's developments, later recalled for me what happened. "The outcome wasn't really clear till 2 P.M. on the dot," she said. "I was sitting in a café, and suddenly cars started honking all around, everyone was throwing papers into the air and banging pots, throngs of people took over the Avenida 18 de Julio, celebrating." The first announcement from the Pro-Referendum Commission, instantly conveyed over the two radio stations, listed a final total of 23,003 confirmations—a figure that was subsequently increased to 23,166, a decidedly more comfortable wafer-thin margin. A woman I reached at the Pro-Referendum Commission's headquarters described to me how, earlier in the day, Tota Quinteros (the mother of the young woman who'd been dragged out of the Venezuelan Embassy in 1976) had begun suffering from a heart fibrillation. Paramedics had been called to take her to the hospital, but she'd refused to leave. She spent the rest of the day on a makeshift cot in a corner. Just after two in the afternoon, however, as everyone started celebrating, she insisted on getting up, pushing away those trying to restrain her. "Let me go!" she was shouting. "Let me go! If you don't let me dance, I'm going to have a heart attack!"

"This incredible grin seemed to come over everyone's face," Pittman, for her part, reported. "It was very Uruguayan—this low-key but incredibly wide grin. Shy, almost embarrassed. 'Congratulations,' people were saying to each other. 'Congratulations to *you.*' 'No, congratulations to *you.*' There was this grassroots sense in which every single person counted—and, in fact, every single person *did* count. And there wasn't any showboating, various factions claiming all the credit, the way there would have been in Argentina. In Buenos Aires, you'd have had the different contending factions parading under their separate banners, jostling with each other as each of the various supposedly united leaders tried to hog the show, glaring angrily at the other. But that wasn't the way it was here."

As Pittman was saying this, I recalled the explanation Galeano had offered when I asked him why, since he is half Uruguayan and half Argentine, he had chosen to make Uruguay his home: "For one thing,

I like smaller towns, so I prefer Montevideo to Buenos Aires. But mainly it's that I like to be able to know that if I'm ever going to be shot the bullet that kills me will have been fired by an enemy, and not by some alleged friend. In Argentina, I could never be sure of that."

Uruguay's main labor confederation now declared a spontaneous celebratory strike, and everybody took the rest of the afternoon off. An ashen-faced Sanguinetti was portrayed on the news huddling with Zumarán, the Blanco leader, discussing the day's "notorious" developments. Amid all the celebrating, there remained a wisp of anxiety: the Electoral Court still hadn't made the results official. But a few days later the Court finally did so, and a few days after that Congress scheduled a referendum for Sunday, April 16, 1989.

Soon after the pro-referendum movement's December victory, *Búsqueda,* the most respected establishment journal in the country (a sort of Montevideo version of the *Wall Street Journal*) tried to reassure its readers with the headline "IF THERE ARE NO UNFORESEEN CHANGES IN PUBLIC OPINION, THE AMNESTY LAW WILL NOT BE OVERTURNED." The figures underlying that assertion, however, which were drawn from the most recent Equipos poll of Montevideo voters, showed that while only 39 percent were saying they'd vote to overturn the amnesty, still fewer (only 30 percent) were saying they'd vote to sustain it, with 31 percent still undecided—this after two years of incessant government and establishment-media attacks on the referendum project.

In the meantime, General Medina went on television to warn of the danger if the process should "run out of control." More forebodingly, General Washington Varela, the director of the Military College for Advanced Studies, warned, "There won't be any progress, peace, or reconciliation if, in a spirit of vengeance or frivolity, we put blame for all errors on only one side and refuse to admit our own errors." (This was a novel use of "we.") Just to be certain that there would be no misunderstanding his flight of rhetoric, Varela continued, "We won't be taken by surprise by those who encourage violence and oppose reconciliation. If need be, we will close ranks to block their path."

A few weeks later, on January 23, 1989, in Argentina, an astonishing, confusing, and deeply troubling event took place—one with enormous ramifications for Uruguay. A band of about fifty heavily armed men and women, some of them outfitted in camouflage fatigues, took over the Army barracks at La Tablada, just outside Buenos Aires. At first, everyone assumed this was just another—a fourth—attempt at a right-wing military coup. But the insurgents turned out to be members of an extreme left-wing fringe group. Holed up in La Tablada, with several dozen young recruits as hostages, the guerrillas were calling "the people" into the streets. The people, however, stood by aghast, as the armed forces responded by training tanks and heavy artillery on the surrounded barracks; a thirty-hour bloodbath ensued, which was broadcast live over Argentine television. (This time, the Army betrayed none of the squeamish hesitancy it had on the three earlier occasions—it didn't even pause to attempt negotiations.) When the battle was over, there were thirty-nine corpses (twenty-eight guerrillas, eleven security personnel), some seventy injured, and eighteen guerrillas taken prisoner. Most astounding of all, one of the corpses turned out to be that of Jorge Baños, the human-rights lawyer.

The Argentine right had a field day—the incident seemed perfectly designed to confirm every one of its stereotypes about the left, and in particular its standard claim that human-rights activists were all Communist insurgents in disguise.

There were several curious aspects to the drama, however. Early in the siege, a representative of the insurgents indicated in a phone interview with a radio station that they'd taken over the barracks in order to break up a meeting they'd been told was taking place there between followers of Rico and Seineldín, who were said to be plotting yet another coup attempt. No such meeting was in fact taking place in the barracks, and some people have since speculated that Baños in particular was set up: whoever had leaked to him the Mar del Plata documents had done so in order to gain his trust, so that he'd believe any subsequent leaks. Furthermore, one of the principal leaders of the insurgency, a notorious guerrilla veteran named Enrique Gorriarán Merlo (he'd been second-in-command of the bloodiest of the Argentine guerrilla organizations during the "dirty war"), was not apprehended. Nor was this the first time he'd emerged, unscathed and uncaptured, from an incident of this sort. Those who'd taken to assuming he was an Army plant or agent—or, at any rate, someone so crazed that the Army had no interest in apprehending him, since he could be counted on to play into its hands in precisely this manner—saw no reason to change their opinion.

Argentine politics lurched suddenly and dramatically to the right. Although the prisoners were turned over to civilian courts—to that extent, Alfonsín's struggle to sustain constitutional governance had held—most politicians moved noticeably closer to the military. A few days later, at a military rally to celebrate the fifteenth anniversary of Operación Independencia, a key offensive during the "dirty war," the new armed forces chief of staff declared, "We must prepare ourselves to fight against subversion, armed and unarmed," and Alfonsín, in the audience, was shown on TV to be applauding the speech. He soon created a National Security Council to confront the allegedly resurgent terrorist threat. Headed by a retired admiral, the council included a seat for the military's intelligence services, in express contravention of a 1988 law that had prohibited the armed forces from domestic intelligence-gathering.[33]

For Uruguay, of course, this was precisely the sort of thing that Sanguinetti had been warning about all along, and the referendum's opponents didn't hesitate to reiterate the point. The Tupamaros, for their part—to the intense consternation of everyone else in the pro-referendum movement—refused, at least at first, to condemn the actions of the La Tablada insurgents. "They were *compañeros,*" the Tupas declared. "They paid with their lives—that is sufficient. They deserve respect." Four weeks after the La Tablada incident, the Uruguayan military staged an unprecedented and highly publicized war-game exercise, simulating the retaking of a hijacked battalion headquarters. Afterward, Medina sought to reassure a jittery public—"At the moment, anyway, and at least until after the referendum, we don't have any problem with subversives"—but his words only added to the jitters. According to Luis González, at Equipos, support for the referendum had apparently peaked: his February figures showed virtually no change; none of the undecided were coming over to the pro-referendum column, which was stuck at 39 percent.

Just to be on the safe side, as the referendum vote approached, its congressional opponents undertook one last gambit to undercut its chances. They passed a version of Blanco Senator Gonzalo Aguirre's bill providing that, even if the referendum were approved, individual judges would be empowered to declare its effects exclusively prospective rather than retrospective—a legislative twist designed not just to confuse matters before the vote, but to confound them, if necessary, thereafter, insuring another several years of judicial deadlock.

By March, even though the Pro-Referendum Commission had embarked on a campaign to have volunteers visit the home of every single voter in the country, the referendum's prospects could hardly be described as sanguine.

"Even if we don't win on April 16, it's going to be all right," Galeano told me over the phone a few weeks before the election. "This is already a tremendously important achievement. It's the first time in history that a people has risen up like this, peacefully, against such odds, with all the wind against us, and in such numbers. No one else has ever succeeded in chasing an *impunidad* law this far. Of course, we hope we'll be able to chase ours still farther, but this is already quite something. We're still the Great Exception. And I wouldn't count us out. The odds seem insurmountable. But in Uruguay, already several times in the past decade, stranger things have happened."

During its last few weeks, the campaign leading up to the election recapitulated all the major themes of the preceding years' debates. To simplify matters, it was decided that the ballot for the eventual plebiscite would be color-coded: those desiring to overturn the amnesty would be invited to put a green ballot in their secret envelope, while those desiring to reaffirm the law would insert a yellow ballot. The yellow (or "gold," as its proponents preferred to characterize it) side continued to enjoy the fervent endorsement of the major media and most of the leaders of the two principal parties. Its backers argued that only through a yellow vote could the continuity of a democratic future be assured. By contrast, were green to win, as President Sanguinetti said, "I can't promise anything; it would be like entering a blind alley." In the days just before the election, General Medina simply warned,

"The pacification, the future's calm, and the army's dignity will be at stake on April 16"—whereupon he made a great show of going off into the interior to consult with some of the prior regime's retired generals. One of those generals, addressing a military rally in Montevideo on the eve of the election, baldly asserted that the Uruguayan military would never tolerate being insulted or being separated from power.

The green side's supporters, for their part, urged voters not to succumb to this fear campaign; once again they tried to argue that the only true guarantee of democracy's future would be a sense of justice regarding the past. However, they continued to have problems getting this message across. The Pro-Referendum Commission, for example, bought time on all three television stations for the Friday before the vote. The ad, which they delivered for broadcast that morning, was a simple one: Sara Méndez recounting the story of her nineteen-day-old son's kidnapping and explaining how only through a repeal of the *impunidad* statute could she ever stand a chance of seeing him again. None of the television stations would air the commercial. When lawyers for the Pro-Referendum Commission demanded an explanation, they were told that the decision to ban the ad had been made "at the highest possible level."

Meanwhile, President Sanguinetti's Education and Culture Minister, a woman named Adela Reta, went on television to insist that no children had ever been disappeared in Uruguay. The Argentine grandmother of a child who had in fact been disappeared in Uruguay happened to be in town for the elections, and when she objected vehemently, Ms. Reta quickly revised her claim: no *Uruguayan* child had ever been disappeared in Uruguay. Which was technically true, although almost thirty Uruguayan *adults* had been disappeared in Uruguay, with over one hundred others disappeared elsewhere, and—more to the point—as Sara Méndez immediately tried to make clear, thirteen Uruguayan children had in fact been disappeared, with the active collusion of Uruguayan security personnel, in Argentina, Chile, and Paraguay. The dissemination of Ms. Méndez's response was undercut, however, as the country went into the forty-eight-hour period before any election during which campaigning in Uruguay is required to cease: the period of calm reflection, as it is called.

It rained throughout the country the entire day of Sunday, April 16, sometimes quite heavily—downpours that broke a terrible summer-long drought and so were greeted with mixed feelings. Notwithstanding the weather, voter turnout was also heavy: over 80 percent. The polls closed at 7:30 P.M., at which point everybody in the country became glued to their TV sets, awaiting the returns—or so anyway it seemed to me, as I began telephoning for hourly reports. By shortly after midnight, the trends had become clear. (The next morning, the final tally would show 53 percent had voted yellow, as against 41 percent green, with 6 percent of the ballots either spoiled or blank.) Around one in the morning, one of the co-chairpersons of the Pro-Referendum Committee, Matilde de Gutiérrez Ruiz, widow of the martyred congressman, addressed a packed press conference and a live nationwide television audience. "According to the results of the plebiscite," she declared (she was visibly shaken but spoke with the uncanny poise and dignity that had characterized her entire tenure at the leadership of the green movement), "the amnesty law has been sustained. Without a doubt, this decision of the electorate should be respected. . . . The country and all its institutions cannot be insensitive to the fact that almost half the population radically disagreed with the solution represented by the amnesty law. And while it is certain that the content of that law should now be respected, it must also be accepted, as an absolute commitment of national resolve, that never, under any circumstances, can those violations that characterized the regime before March 1, 1985, be permitted to recur." Not once in her speech did Mrs. Gutiérrez Ruiz refer to her own personal circumstances; nor had she done so in the entire campaign.

The official media and the leading politicians who'd backed the amnesty law all along were exultant. "THE LAW HAS BEEN CONFIRMED AND PEACE HAS TRIUMPHED" proclaimed the banner headline in Monday morning's *El Día.* Vice-president Tarigo, who'd led the yellow campaign, declared the results of the plebiscite would now permit the country "to set out on the road to the future without the legacy of the past." Similarly, Senator Jorge Batlle, another leading Colorado politician, declared that "the vote has closed a decisive chapter for the nation." At his news conference that Monday morning, President Sanguinetti adopted a more measured tone. "There is no sense of triumph" in the referendum result, he said, adding, "The most important aspect of all this is that the country was able to do it by popular vote. Yesterday, when the ballot boxes were closed, Uruguay completed its transition to democracy." Noting that he'd of course opposed the referendum from the start, he commented that, in retrospect, the process of bringing the matter to a popular vote might nevertheless have had certain positive effects: "You can say anything you want about the Uruguayan transition to democracy, but not that it wasn't submitted to every test." When queried about the wider requirements of justice, President Sanguinetti shot back, "In this case, peace *is* justice."

There was, at any rate, no sense of triumph in Montevideo itself. In fact, the half of the country's population who live there had decisively rejected the amnesty law, 54 percent green to 42 percent yellow (the yellow side piled up commanding majorities in Uruguay's interior). Nothing like the throngs who'd jammed the Avenida 18 de Julio the previous December, when the referendum finally qualified for the ballot, showed up to celebrate the measure's defeat; in fact, according to one of my informants, by one o'clock that particular night, the avenue was, uncharacteristically, "a desert." A few days later, when I reached Eduardo Galeano, he explained that "The yellow vote was shameful, hidden. In the days before the election, everywhere you saw people wearing green—even though it took some courage to be doing so since the military was so obviously angry with those who opposed the amnesty law. No one was wearing yellow—even those who were going to vote yellow were going out of their way not to *wear* yellow. Sure, the night of the election and the next morning were very depressing for us —to have to see all those smug, smiling politicians on TV was a very bitter experience—but in the days since I myself have begun to recover. I mean, when you realize that we got 800,000 people to vote with us —and that despite the fact that absentee ballots were forbidden, and the three or four hundred thousand Uruguayans whom the military drove into exile weren't allowed to vote. There's no question but that if all Uruguayans everywhere in the world had been allowed to vote, the green side would have won. Anyway, we completely obliterated the myth that this was all just some leftist grudge: fully twice as many people voted green in this election as had voted for the Frente Amplio in the last one. And one of the most striking things about the vote was the way it divided along age-group lines: older Uruguayans voted yellow, out of a sense of anxious caution, I suppose, but younger Uruguayans—the ones who'd been most subject to the military regime's harsh indoctrination during their school days—voted overwhelmingly green. So, you see, it's okay: this old gray country contains in its belly a green new country."

Pérez Aguirre at SERPAJ was similarly unbowed. "The entire referendum movement has provided a very strong boost for our work on behalf of the human-rights cause. The debate was very important and useful: the whole scene was affected in a very intense way. The fact that in a tiny country like ours, 800,000 defied the fear and misinformation to vote green, that's enormously heartening. And in any case, there are further options still open to us." He went on to suggest that lawyers for some of the victims and their families were already preparing to bring test cases before the Inter-American Court for Human Rights, a fairly new judicial branch of the Organization of American States, which last year moved quite forcefully on the question of a pattern of disappearances in Honduras.[34] Meanwhile, he continued, just a few weeks before the election, SERPAJ issued a major compendium of documentation, the product of over three years' work, on the abuses of human rights during the military dictatorship. Patterned after its Argentine and Brazilian forebears, it was entitled *Uruguay: Nunca Más*; and though it could neither boast an official imprimatur nor claim to be based on the prior regime's own documentation, it still featured the results of an extraordinarily thorough survey of a large random sampling of former prisoners, conducted for SERPAJ by the universally respected Equipos firm and focussing on such issues as types of torture, conditions of imprisonment, the presence of doctors during torture, and so forth.

When I reached Marcelo Vignar, the psychoanalyst who two years earlier had expressed for me his serious misgivings regarding the country's psychopolitical health (in the meantime he'd abandoned Paris, returning to Montevideo for good), I found him, like Galeano and Pérez Aguirre, surprisingly upbeat. "Two years ago," he said, "the authorities were desperately trying to make it seem as if nothing had happened—torture and disappearances and so forth had all been merely marginal, unimportant occurrences, one no longer needed to think about them —and it looked like they were going to succeed in doing so. But all the work of the past two years forced people to think—*everybody*. The campaign allowed an inscription of all that history into the collective memory, even if, in the end, that inscription couldn't be translated into action." He was quiet for a moment. "Of course, the victims themselves this week are subdued and sad and drained. But even with them. . . . As one of my patients commented, 'For once, *they* were the ones who had to be afraid: for the first time, even if just for a few months, we had them trembling that justice might yet come. At least that was satisfying.' "

It seemed to me that something decisive had happened in Uruguay.[35] Lines from another Polish poem came to mind, this one by Stanislaw Baranczak. Entitled "Those Men, So Powerful," it begins:

Those men, so powerful, always shown
somewhat from below by crouching cameramen, who lift
a heavy foot to crush me, no, to climb
the steps of a plane, who raise a hand
to strike me, no, to greet the crowds
obediently waving little flags, those men who sign
my death warrant, no, just a trade
agreement which is promptly dried by a servile blotter

And it concludes, a stanza later:

always
you were so afraid of them,
you were so small
compared to them, who always stood above
you, on steps, rostrums, platforms,
and yet it is enough for just one instant to stop
being afraid, or let's say
begin being afraid a little less,
to become convinced that they are the ones,
that they are the ones who are most afraid.

Afterword

During the months of its initial upsurge, Polish theorists used to characterize Solidarity as an expression of the *subjectivity* of the Polish nation, by which, they'd explain, they meant its rediscovered capacity for acting as the subject rather than the object of history. As with the lines from Zbigniew Herbert, this was a formulation that kept recurring to me during my recent trips to Latin America. For such a transformation—at root grammatical, in which an entity which had been content to receive the action of other people's sentences now suddenly demands to initiate such actions on its own—is typical of any revolutionary situation. And conversely, I began to realize, the very essence of repression is likewise grammatical: the authorities scrambling to find some way of recapturing individuals (or polities) who have suddenly taken to behaving like subjects, so as to turn them back once again into mere objects. History, in this conception, is a battle over who gets to say "I" (or at the state level, who gets to say "we"—"we, the regime . . ." or "we, the people"), and that, after all, is what torture is all about as well. If, as Elaine Scarry has demonstrated in her book *The Body in Pain,* torture is in its essence a discourse, a teaching, what is being taught is the futility of acting like a subject, of aspiring to anything beyond abject objecthood.

Torture attempts to accomplish this fundamental transformation by situating its discourse at the intersection of two of the most primordial mysteries of human being: incarnation and solitude. To people who have been attempting to behave in a lofty, selfless manner, it elaborates the incarnation of lofty ideals (of the soul) in a body. It subverts the soul through the vulnerability of the body in which it inheres, teaching that one *can* be reduced to one's own body and nothing else—the horizon of the wide, wide world with all its wide, wide hopes can become constricted to the point that it becomes entirely effaced. Likewise, torture impresses on the individual—and again, particularly individuals who've been living for others, among others—the fact of the absolute solitude of human existence, which is finally, in its most extreme expression, solitude *before death.* That sort of knowledge, which ordinary people can ordinarily sustain for at most a few moments at a time, once in a long, long while, torture forces its victim to withstand for hours, days, weeks at a time. It is harrowing knowledge, and is intended to harrow.[36] The scream that comes welling out of the torture chamber is thus double—the body calling out to the soul, the self calling out to others—and in both cases, it goes unanswered. Torture's stark lesson is precisely that enveloping silence: it aims to take that silence and introject it back into its victim, to replace the flame of subjectivity with an abject, hollow void.

I first began considering many of the issues raised in this book several years ago when I spent a few weeks surveying the daunting and inspiring work taking place at the Rehabilitation and Research Center for Torture Victims, the RCT, in Copenhagen, Denmark. The clinic that served as the embryo for that center was launched in 1979 by Dr. Inge Kemp Genefke, a passionately intense neurologist who, for many years, had been active on the board of Amnesty International. As she explained to me, much of the work at Amnesty International had been—and indeed still is—devoted to securing the release of particular individual political prisoners suffering various forms of torture in countries all around the world. It is arduous, mind-dulling, seemingly endless work—this constant collating of information and bringing pressure to bear on repressive regimes—but every once in a while it works: a prisoner does get released. At such moments, Genefke recalled, she and her co-activists would experience an understandable feeling of triumph, of success, of completion, as if the task, at least in that one instance, had been achieved, and they could now go on to other similar cases.

However, once in a while one of those liberated former prisoners would make his or her way to Copenhagen, or else she might encounter such a onetime victim on her travels abroad—one of her success stories, one of her "closed" cases—and over and over again she'd be struck by how still devastated and hollowed-out these liberated individuals remained, often years after they'd attained freedom. She began to realize that liberation might constitute only the beginning, rather than the culmination, of the work that needed to be done for these tormented individuals. Furthermore, as some of the victims began to settle in Copenhagen (Denmark has a fairly enlightened policy regarding refuge for victims of political persecution the world over), she was able to observe their progress—or rather lack of progress—at close range. The Danish government provided the torture victims, like all its other refugees, with liberal stipends for housing, general health coverage, language assistance, and so forth. But unlike many of the other refugees, the former torture victims repeatedly failed to thrive in their new environment. They remained listless and dazed; they suffered excruciating sieges of dread, recurrent nightmares both waking and asleep. They (and their families) had been mangled in a profound way, and Dr. Genefke came to feel that their reintegration would require a special, highly particularized, and as yet uninvented, form of therapy.

That is precisely what she and her remarkable colleagues—physicians, psychologists, physiotherapists, social workers, occupational therapists, pediatricians, family therapists, social scientists, statisticians, and others—have been attempting to fashion over the past decade in Copenhagen. They have been working with torture victims from throughout the world, slowly and systematically evolving a coherent regime of therapy, one that ought in principle to prove equally effective whether the victim comes from Asia or the Middle East, Eastern Europe or Latin America, the Soviet Union or Africa—and they have been eagerly sharing the results of their research with similar centers that have begun forming in such places as Toronto, Minneapolis, and Los Angeles.[37] They are all obviously doing important and valuable work.

So I was somewhat surprised, in the years after my first visit to Copenhagen, to find that the RCT and the other centers had become the object of a certain amount of resentment on the part of some activists and therapists in the Third World, particularly in the Southern Cone. (Such resentments were by no means universal, and the various centers definitely had their share of Third World admirers.) Some of the resentment seemed parochial, a matter of turf and the woefully limited funding available for such efforts worldwide. Some of the resentment was directed at the notion of First World specialists casting themselves as the authorities, the arbiters of correct therapeutic practice, on this principally Third World phenomenon. "The First World has already taken everything else from the Third," one Uruguayan therapist complained to me. "Now they want to own our suffering too, the last thing we have left." This critique derived perhaps from the global pretensions of the Danish team—their ambition to cast themselves as the world authorities on the subject. I sometimes imagined that if the Danes had more modestly cast their project as "the Center for the Assistance of Torture Victims who Happen Temporarily to Be in Exile in Denmark," much of the resentment might have abated.

A more trenchant and substantive critique, however, has to do with the medical model underlying the work of these centers—the notion of torture victims as a group being analogous, in a way, to cancer or hypertension (or even incest) victims; the notion that they suffer from a certain definable "syndrome," so that a treatment could be developed that would be equally efficacious for victims from Sri Lanka, South Africa, the Soviet Union, or Santiago, and indeed that one element of such treatment should consist of group therapy sessions in which victims from all over the world share their common experiences. "But torture is not a medical problem," one Uruguayan therapist insisted to me. "It is in its very essence political, social—and rehabilitation from torture can occur only in a political and social context. The original point of the torture was to take various individuals who had been politically or socially active, on behalf of their various causes, in a particular location at a particular moment, and to gouge out their capacity for such activism: to leave them as if dead, unable any longer to aspire, let alone to act. The only true therapy for torture ought therefore to be revolution—overthrowing the system that tried to expunge that capacity for activism on behalf of those ideals. Short of that, however, therapy must consist in helping the torture victim to reintegrate himself into the ongoing struggle—nurturing his or her capacity for idealism once again, for activity as part of the larger group in which he or she was once a member. To focus exclusively on the former torture victim's status as a former torture victim only serves to perpetuate the legacy of isolation and separation that was the regime's intention in torturing the individual in the first place. My point is that a Uruguayan torture victim has more in common with other Uruguayans than he does with torture victims from other places, and he will be rehabilitated to the extent that he can be reintegrated into his own society. That involves a political or social model rather than a medical one."

It is certainly true that the vision that animates a Jaime Wright in Brazil or a Luis Pérez Aguirre in Uruguay is not simply one of rehabilitating the individual victims of a prior dictatorship, but also involves the rehabilitation of the entire surrounding society. And indeed, as I listened to these various First and Third World therapists lay out their positions (often, as I say, simply their misunderstandings of one another), I began to realize that there are societies—entire polities—which might themselves be considered torture victims, in every bit as great a need of rehabilitation as the individuals persisting in their midst. Indeed, torture itself, during repressive regimes, has a dual role: the expunging of the capacity for subjective aspiration in specific individuals, and through their example (the whiff of terror their fate spreads), the expunging of that capacity in the wider society as well. When individuals are being tortured and everyone knows about it and no one seems able to do a thing to help, primordial mysteries at the root of human community come under fundamental assault as well. Intersubjectivity is laid waste. So that it becomes possible to recast Dr. Genefke's observation and to note that the rehabilitation of torture societies does not culminate with free elections—that on the contrary, the true work of social rehabilitation only *begins* with the reintroduction of such democratic conventions.

How is that rehabilitation to proceed? Again, one has to return to the scream welling out of the torture chamber. An old man, a teenage boy, a young woman five months pregnant, is screaming in agony. And what is the torturer saying? As Marcelo Vignar has pointed out, he is saying, "Go ahead, scream, scream all you like, scream your lungs out —nobody can hear you, nobody would dare to hear you, nobody cares about you, no one will ever know." That is the primordial moment which has desperately to be addressed—and as desperately by the torture society as by the torture victim: Who was there? Who was screaming? Who were those people standing by the screamer's side? Who, even now, will dare to hear? Who will care to know? Who will be held accountable? And who will hold them to account?

Now, good people will disagree on how that holding to account ought to proceed in the context of real-life, often exceptionally precarious political situations. In her magisterial study, *The Origins of Totalitarianism,* Hannah Arendt held that "the first step on the road to total domination is to kill the juridical person in man"—that is, to make the attainment of justice appear hopeless and its pursuit pointless. David Remnick, the Washington *Post*'s Moscow correspondent, recently cited this passage and went on to observe, "Likewise, the first essential step toward liberty is the revival of the legal impulse in man." Arendt, no doubt, would have agreed—and yet, paradoxically, she seemed to favor forgiveness. In her book *The Human Condition* (published in 1958, barely a decade after the defeat of the Nazis), she wrote: "Without being forgiven, released from the consequences of what we have done, our capacity to act would, as it were, be confined to one single deed from which we could never recover; we would remain the victim of its consequences forever." Forgiveness, for Arendt, was essential to freedom, to our capacity for free agency; the regeneration of subjectivity, and intersubjectivity, required forgiveness. "Only through this constant mutual release from what they do can men remain free agents, only by constant willingness to change their minds and start again can they be trusted with so great a power as that to begin something new. In this respect," she went on, "forgiveness is the exact opposite of vengeance, which acts in the form of re-acting against an original trespassing, whereby far from putting an end to the consequences of the first misdeed, everybody remains bound to the process, permitting the chain reaction contained in every action to take its unhindered course. . . .[38]

"The alternative to forgiveness," Arendt continues, "but by no means its opposite, is punishment, and both have in common that they attempt to put an end to something that without interference could go on endlessly." If Arendt clearly favored the one over the other, she nevertheless found it "quite significant, a structural element in the realm of human affairs, that men are unable to forgive what they cannot punish." (Thus is the apparent paradox in Arendt's thinking resolved.) Earlier, anticipating even more directly the situation occasioned by the various military-imposed amnesties which have proliferated throughout Latin America in recent years, Arendt commented that "No one can forgive himself [just as] no one can feel bound by a promise made only to himself; forgiving and promising enacted in solitude or isolation remain without reality and can signify no more than a role played before one's self." Arendt might well have objected to the Brazilian and Uruguayan amnesties *precisely because* they foreclosed the possibility of forgiveness.

The question of clemency, however, remains controversial. At the Aspen Institute's fall 1988 conference at the Wye Woods Center in Maryland on the subject of state crimes, José (Pepe) Zalaquett, a Chilean activist long associated with Amnesty International, tried to frame a general theory on the appropriate uses of amnesty and punishment, a framework of rules—"a policy to deal with a legacy," as he phrased it. Zalaquett noted that any policy regarding past abuses would have two central objectives—first, with regard to the past, reparation, repairing the damage wrought by the earlier abuses; and second, with regard to the future, prevention, promotion of a stable democratic future in which such abuses wouldn't recur. He argued that any such policy would have to meet certain minimum requirements to be considered legitimate. First, the truth would have to be known, complete, officially sanctioned and publicly exposed ("put in the record of the nation's memory"). Second, the policy would have to represent the will of the people. This might admittedly prove difficult to achieve, but a self-amnesty on its face would always be illegitimate both because it violated this principle and because nobody ought ever to profit from his own bad faith. Third, the policy would have to be such that it did not violate standards of international law, either by exacting punishments that were too severe or lavishing clemencies that were too broad. (Thus, for example, genocide and disappearance require punishment no matter what, in line with various international codes, whereas torture and extended incarceration are not as closely regulated.) "But if those three conditions are met," Zalaquett continued, "whether a policy leans more toward clemency or severity should be up to the nation in question"—that is, not subject to absolute, outside standards. "And clemency can be just as valuable a preventive as severity," Zalaquett concluded. "I insist on that."

However, he got an argument on that from Aryeh Neier, the executive director of Human Rights Watch in New York. To begin with, Neier demurred from the notion that "the will of the people" has anything to do with the proper application of justice. "If Pepe hits me," Neier proposed, "I have a right to forgive him, but does everybody else in this room have the right to forgive him in my stead?" Neier then went on to an ever more fundamental disagreement. "I want to quarrel," he said, "with the assumption that a principal reason for seeking justice, or criterion for evaluating its efficacy, should be the future stability of the reconstituted democracy. Such predictions are highly speculative. Who's to say that clemency won't simply further embolden the torturers, thereby inviting rather than preventing future abuses? And who is it precisely who's to be authorized to make determinations regarding such larger considerations? El Salvador's Duarte and Guatemala's Cerezo both have insisted that the larger good required their staying in office and completing their terms—that was the foremost priority, and certain sacrifices in the human-rights field hence could well prove necessary. But who are they to say that? The human capacity to look backward is frail enough. The human capacity to look forward is frailer yet. Rather, punishment is the absolute duty of society to honor and redeem the suffering of the individual victim. In a society of law, we say it is not up to individual victims to exercise vengeance, but rather up to society to demonstrate respect for the victim, for the one who suffered, by rendering the victimizer accountable. As a matter of law we simply have to say we are not going to grant clemency to the most grotesque criminals. We may be forced to do so on the basis of force majeure, but we should never do so as a matter of law."

Repeatedly on my trips to South America, I was told that it's easy for outsiders to pontificate on the correct line to take with regard to the human-rights abuses of past dictatorships, but much, much more difficult to sustain any sort of line there on the ground, in those countries themselves, in the years after such a period of repression. I think everyone at Wye Woods realized as much, as we sat in that elegant conference room, surrounded by the lovely fall foliage, on the placid shores of that inlet off Chesapeake Bay.

Certainly, the two cases I've studied in these pages—Brazil's and Uruguay's—afford no ideal outcome. (For that matter, no country exists where anything remotely approaching the ideal has yet been achieved.) The transition in both countries has been mired in the muck of forced compromise, bad faith, self-delusion, betrayed hopes, and abandoned responsibilities. In both of these instances, the little success that was achieved was at best provisional (there were no trials in either country, no expressions of justice; torturers whose prior conduct was thoroughly documented in *Brasil: Nunca Mais* didn't even necessarily lose their jobs; in Uruguay, the referendum finally lost and the issue was largely set aside). Still, in both cases, thanks to the herculean efforts of relatively small sectors of the population (in the case of Brazil, of an infinitesimally small sector), the interests of truth were served. Facts were established, and the actual history was inscribed in the common memory.

And as Zalaquett noted in his presentation, "The truth in itself is both reparation and prevention." Retrospectively, the broadcasting of truth to a certain extent redeems the suffering of the former victims. At least to a degree, it answers and honors the scream after all, it upends the torturer's boastful claim that no one will ever know. Prospectively, the broadcasting of truth has an effect that is at once more subtle and perhaps more momentous. For, as we have seen, it is essential to the structure of torture that it take place in secret, in the dark,

beyond considerations of shame and account. When the torturer assures his victim "No one will ever know," he is at once trying to break the victim's spirit and to bolster his own. He needs to be certain that no one will ever know; otherwise the entire premise of his own participation in the encounter would quickly come into question. By the time that Uruguayan general was warning how, if the referendum passed, no one could ever be sure that subordinates in the Uruguayan military would ever again unquestioningly obey the orders of their superiors in any future war against subversion, it was already too late. That doubt has now taken on a life of its own, despite the outcome of the referendum. After all, that referendum could have ended up otherwise—and the next one might. Torturers can never again feel so self-assured—nor their victims so utterly forlorn. The same applies to larger institutions. After the recent examples of Argentina, Uruguay, and Brazil, flawed though they may be, none of the institutions that might in the future try to impose another torture regime will ever again be able to do so with such a blithe assurance of impunity. To date, the militaries in all three countries have remained, for the most part, in barracks: one reason is that they want no part of the financial debacle that remains the legacy of their last period of dominion; but it is also, I suspect, because of the chastening effects of the various truth-tellings. Their strut has become more brittle, more anxiously self-conscious.

One of the things that is remarkable about the stories of both Brazil and Uruguay is the way in which, to a large degree, the rehabilitation of the torture societies, to the extent it has occurred, was accomplished by the torture victims themselves. These victims—hollowed-out, burnt-out shells—came alive once again by testifying to the truth of their own experiences. And that truth, to a degree, has set both themselves and their societies free.

Notes

1. In one of the more fascinating papers presented at the Aspen Institute conference, José (Pepe) Zalaquett, a Chilean activist long associated with Amnesty International in London (though more recently, having returned to Santiago, he has been working with the Catholic Church's Vicariat of Solidarity), offered a sort of typology of situations of transition from dictatorship toward democracy and the consequent political constraints faced by those seeking to establish truth and justice regarding prior human-rights abuses. In his first category, Zalaquett cites situations in which there are *no significant political constraints*—cases, that is, where the prior regime has been utterly defeated: Nazi Germany at the end of the Second World War or, more recently, the Somoza regime in Nicaragua following the Sandinista victory in 1979. The lack of constraints doesn't necessarily guarantee that justice will be carried out; other factors may intrude (the eruption of the Cold War, for example, in the case of Germany), and in fact Zalaquett cites "a paradoxical situation" in which "the power to carry out fully a legitimate human-rights policy regarding past abuses is, in itself, a potential source of abuses." But at least in these sorts of cases, both truth and justice might be attained with relative ease. This is not so in any of the other situations.

As his second type, Zalaquett describes cases where *the defeated forces have lost legitimacy but retain control of armed power:* "Two examples illustrate this situation:

Greece, 1974, and Argentina, 1983. Despite their differences, these cases present striking similarities. In both cases the military ruled for seven years, with the declared purpose of ridding the country of leftist subversion. In both cases, the military were defeated outside their mainland, by a foreign power (the Turks defeated the Greek generals in Cyprus, the British defeated the Argentine junta in the Falklands). Angry at national humiliation more than at human-rights violations, in both cases the people forced a demoralized military to relinquish power. The new civilian, democratically elected governments pushed in both cases for the annulment of amnesty laws the military had passed before leaving office, and brought a number of high-ranking officers to trial. However, in both cases, punishment remained confined to a limited number of the officers involved in the repression."

A third type, according to Zalaquett, consists of those cases where *military rulers allow a civilian government to come to power, following a negotiation or under their own terms.* In such cases—Uruguay and Guatemala provide good examples, as to some extent does Brazil—"the forces that made or supported the former government have neither lost control of armed power, nor do they suffer from a lack of cohesiveness or low morale in their ranks. They are thus a formidable factor to reckon with."

Zalaquett labels his fourth type *gradual transition and popular forgiveness.* He notes that "In some cases transition from dictatorship to democracy takes place after an extended period of gradual political opening, during which the worst forms of human-rights violations have ceased or subsided. The course of events facilitates a degree of popular forgiveness." Here the most important example is Franco's Spain (though, at least to an extent, Brazil straddles over into this category as well). It is interesting to note, in this context, that many of the Solidarity theorists in Poland, such as Adam Michnik, have been studying Franco's Spain as a possible model for their own country's ongoing decompression.

Zalaquett's fifth type consists of those cases where *the new government represents a realignment of political forces in a situation of unresolved armed conflict.* As Zalaquett notes, "Prolonged dictatorship often leads to the radicalization of the political opposition and the emergence of guerrilla warfare." In both the Philippines and El Salvador, a centrist one-time opponent of the dictatorship at a certain moment attained a degree of authority (Duarte, Aquino), but in both cases this was only within the context of the ongoing civil war. The military retained the bulk of power, so that any serious exploration of prior abuses remained largely out of the question.

In his sixth and final category, Zalaquett considers those cases where *ethnic, national or religious divisions stand in the way of pacification.* This is the sort of situation one often finds in Africa, for example, as in the case of Uganda, where successive patterns of repression often flowed along tribal lines and any thoroughgoing truth-telling might itself provoke those tensions all over again. Once again, retrospective truth and justice become highly problematic. (For more on the Ugandan case, see Neil Henry's dispatch "Uganda in the Throes of Peace: Eyeing Future, Country Confronts Past" in the September 26, 1989, Washington *Post*.)

Zalaquett's paper, along with others from the conference, has been published in a 1989 monograph, *State Crimes: Punishment or Pardon?* distributed by the Aspen Institute, New York.

2. For a remarkable corroboration of this astonishing claim, see the extended testimony obtained independently by A. J. Langguth from a young man named Murilo Pinto da Silva regarding his own experiences as a guinea pig in the torture classes conducted by a "Lieutenant Aylton" at the Vila Militar, a jail for political prisoners in Realango, on the outskirts of Rio. (Langguth, *Hidden Terrors* [New York: Pantheon, 1978] pp. 216–22).

3. Consider, for example, this formulation of a seminal concept in the doctrine of national security, drawn from the writings of General Golbery:

> Today, the concept of war has been expanded . . . to the entire territorial space of the belligerent states, thus involving the whole economic, political, cultural, and military capacity of the nation in the enormity of the struggle. All activities are focused on one single aim: victory and only victory. No distinction is made between soldiers and civilians, men, women, and children; they face the same danger, and identical sacrifices are demanded of them. They must all abdicate the secular liberties, which had been won at such high costs, and place them in the hands of the state, the all-powerful lord of war. . . . Above all total war has eliminated the time scale, incorporating in itself the time of prewar and postwar, which are in fact now only extensions of one sole and continuing state of war.
>
> Thus, from the strictly limited military war we have now moved to *total war,* economic, financial, political, psychological, and scientific. . . . From a total war we have gone to *global war,* and from the global war we finally have the *indivisible,* the *inescapable war* and—why not recognize it?—*permanent war.* The "white war" of Hitler or the "cold war" of Stalin has taken the place of peace so that, really, there is no longer a clear distinction between where peace ends and war begins. [From Golbery, *Conjuntura política nacional, o poder do executivo e geopolítica do Brasil* (1981, Rio), quoted and translated by Maria Helena Moreira Alves, *State and Opposition in Military Brazil* (Austin: University of Texas Press, 1985, pp. 15–16).]

This and other aspects of both the doctrine itself and its dissemination throughout the Americas will be discussed in greater detail in the essay on Uruguay.

4. To understand the dynamics of what was about to happen, some historical background may be useful. (A concise summary can be found in the first chapter of Thomas Skidmore's *The Politics of Military Rule in Brazil, 1964–85,* Oxford, University Press, 1988.) From 1930 to 1945, Brazil had been ruled by Getúlio Vargas, a nationalist authoritarian who during the last eight of those years commanded a virtual dictatorship, known as the Estado Novo, the New State. In October, 1945 he was overthrown in a military coup. As the dust began to settle in 1947, the new president, Marshal Enrico Gaspar Dutra, took the country markedly to the right. Dutra was flagrantly pro-American, and it was indeed under his administration that the ESG (Escola Superior de Guerra) was established. However, in 1950, Brazilians registered their displeasure over Dutra's rightward drift by electing—or rather, reelecting—Getúlio Vargas, who this time ran as an ardent populist, a sort of Brazilian version of the contemporaneous Juan Perón in Argentina. His economic program was nationalist (for example, he founded Petrobrás, the national oil monopoly) and he tried to launch a series of initiatives aimed at improving the lot of workers and peasants. His labor minister, a young politician named João Goulart, in particular championed a large increase in the minimum wage, a position that earned him the undying ire of the anti-Communist officers who in the meantime had captured the leadership of the military (*their* take-home pay was shrinking all through this period). Following a plummeting of international coffee prices, the Brazilian economy entered a precipitous tailspin. Vargas came under tremendous pressure (he was forced to fire Goulart); financial scandals erupted all about him, fanned by a virulently rightist press; and now the military began to mobilize, demanding his resignation.

As Skidmore writes, "Vargas defied his accusers. He warned them he would never resign. After receiving another military ultimatum endorsed by the war minister, and after a somber cabinet meeting on November 24, [1954,] Vargas exercised his last option. He retired to his quarters and fired a bullet through his heart. He left a suicide note blaming his defeat on 'a subterranean campaign of international and national groups.' Vargas was aiming at the international oil companies which had fought his successful creation of Petrobrás. . . . He denounced the 'violent pressure on our economy to the point of having to surrender,' referring to the U.S. reaction to Brazil's attempts to keep coffee prices up. The now-dead Vargas concluded: 'I gave you my life. Now I offer my death. Nothing remains. Serenely I take the first step on the road to eternity as I leave life to enter history.' "

It was obviously a stunning gesture, and it completely turned the tables on his enemies. Military leaders who'd been on the verge of a coup quickly repaired to the barracks, cowed by the towering image of this sudden martyr. But the questions left in the wake of Vargas's debacle—How should Brazil treat its foreign investors? Should the country strive for a fairer distribution of wealth, and if so, how?—would continue to set the agenda for the next several decades.

In the short term, however, tempers cooled, and between 1955 and 1960, Brazilian politics was dominated by a newly elected president, Juscelino Kubitschek, a centrist whose administration was characterized by rapid industrialization and economic growth, along with innovative, if somewhat grandiose, public projects, such as the invention, *ex nihilo,* of the new federal capital, Brasília.

Ironically, all through this decade, both Vargas and Kubitschek attempted to deal with the problem of potentially rebellious military officers by keeping them away from field commands, shunting them aside, for example, to the cushy, if seemingly ineffectual, precincts of the ESG. Meanwhile, however, the ESG officers were systematically evolving the ideological doctrine and institutional superstructure that would come to imperil the democracy itself. Though modelled on the U.S. National War College, the ESG had certain unique features: for example, a large proportion of the staff and students were civilians—industrialists, technocrats, judges, congressmen—potential national leaders who were thus being indoctrinated into the ESG worldview and model of development. In addition, alongside the ESG, General Golbery was fostering a sophisticated security information network which, by 1964, had compiled dossiers on over 400,000 "suspect" Brazilians.

In 1960, the rightists at first seemed to have returned to dominance with the electoral triumph of their presidential candidate, the charismatic mayor of São Paulo, Jânio Quadros. Quadros's victory, however, was more personal than ideological—his running mate lost to the leftist candidate, Vargas's old labor minister Goulart (the electoral law permitted ticket splitting). Furthermore, Quadros himself began behaving in an eccentric manner—for example, he presented one of Brazil's highest civilian decorations to Che Guevara and then rejected an IMF-style austerity plan much favored by his rightist supporters. They now began to put the squeeze on him, and in August, 1961, suddenly, utterly surprisingly, he resigned. (To this day his abrupt decision remains a mystery; Skidmore speculates that he may have been hoping that Congress would call him back, granting him De Gaulle-like powers—but this, in any case, did not occur.)

The leading generals initially tried to block Goulart's succession altogether; failing that, they moved to reduce his powers through a hastily arranged constitutional amendment that drained Presidential authority into a sort of parliamentary cabinet. Goulart immediately began campaigning to restore his executive powers via a January, 1963, plebiscite. Meanwhile, with the support of his brother-in-law, Leonel Brizola, the firebrand governor of the province of Rio Grande do Sul, Goulart started mobilizing students, workers, and peasants, and simultaneously challenging foreign business interests. His was becoming exactly the sort of administration that those associated with the ESG had spent over a decade warning against. A final confrontation seemed inevitable.

5. Actually the Brazilian generals decreed a sort of free-form variation on the orthodox Chicago-school model. They did in fact encourage extensive multinational and entrepreneurial investment, but often within the context of considerable central command and control. The military itself participated heavily in the guidance and direction of various key "national security" industries (nuclear energy, armaments, telecommunications, and so forth) and sponsored various projects in the public sphere (gargantuan hydroelectric dams, superhighways into the jungle, and other similar pharaonic initiatives). Notwithstanding these variations, the military did its best to keep labor in line and to cut back on public welfare expenditures, in good Chicago-school fashion.

6. And in the meantime the growth surge itself stalled out during the final decade of military rule. Luciano Martins provides a good overview of the debacle in his chapter on Brazil in the Latin American volume of the *Transitions from Authoritarian Rule* series (edited by Guillermo O'Donnell et al. for the Johns Hopkins University Press, 1986, pp. 89–90):

> Without entering into the causes of the financial and economic crisis . . . it is sufficient to state that after a period of extraordinary expansion, during the years known as the Brazilian "Miracle" (1968–74), the economy began to slow down. This coincided with and was aggravated by the first "oil shock" and the resulting world recession. Although common sense would suggest—as indeed many Brazilian economists recommended—that the subsequent public policies should be directed toward the adaptation of the economy to these world trends (especially since Brazil was importing more than half of its oil needs), the Geisel administration [1974–79] took the opposite view. A highly ambitious economic development program (capital goods and chemical industries, huge hydroelectric projects, nuclear plants, the expansion of public expenditure and public enterprise investment, etc.) was initiated, without regard to the predictable draining of funds and economic stress this would provoke. The Figueiredo government [1979–85] . . . followed the same irresponsible orientation, relentlessly increasing both the internal debt and the level of external borrowing at what proved to be extremely high rates of interest. *The intention was artificially to sustain the hope of an economic miracle that would legitimize the regime* [italics mine].

In effect, in a mad attempt somehow to legitimize all the suffering that had gone before, the military technocrats were now busily pursuing policies that would condemn the country to decade upon decade of further suffering in the future.

"By mid-1982," Martins continues, inventorying the damage,

> the cumulative effects of such a policy had become clear: domestic interest rates skyrocketed to 300 percent a year, inflation was soon above 100 percent, the national debt was twice the level of the federal budget, and the external debt rose from US $12.6 billion at the end of 1973 to $80 billion in mid-1982. On the other hand, industrial production fell by 10 percent compared with 1980. By September 1982 . . . Brazil, virtually in default, was obliged to go to the International Monetary Fund for help. The medicine prescribed by the IMF to deal with the internal and external indebtedness deepened the recession, aggravated the already high rate

of unemployment, and produced a drastic salary squeeze. Indeed, Brazil entered one of the gravest financial and economic situations of its history.

(For two other dispiriting accounts of this debacle, see "A Tale of Two Presidents: The Political Economy of Crisis Management," by Albert Fishlow, and "Brazil's Debt: From the Miracle to the Fund," by Edmar L. Bacha and Pedro S. Malan—both in *Democratizing Brazil: Problems of Transition and Consolidation,* edited by Albert Stepan, Oxford University Press, 1989.)

Having piloted the plane of Brazil's economy straight into a cliff, the generals now turned the controls over to the civilians and said, "Here, you drive this thing for a while." Throughout this whole process, once again, Brazil seemed to be pioneering the future for the rest of the continent.

7. It occurred to me that the question of Golbery's historic responsibility for the systematic torture that subsequently characterized Médici's reign was in a way analogous to that of Lenin's responsibility for Stalin's Gulag. Lenin may not have envisioned the need for such massive repression; he might have been appalled had he lived to see it; had he lived, he might even have been swallowed up by it. But it can be argued that a likely evolution toward that sort of repression was inherent in the logic of the positions Lenin embraced and the tactics he utilized from the outset, and that hence he does bear a great historic responsibility for the ensuing disaster. When I tried this analogy out on Gaspari, he said, "Yes, but in Golbery's case you have a Lenin who lived long enough to come back and set things right."

8. This is not the only time critics of the doctrine of national security have taken the doctrine's rhetoric and turned it inside out, thereby sharpening their own critique. The São Paulo labor leader Luis Inácio da Silva, better known as "Lula," recently hijacked the notion of a "Third World War" in these comments about the IMF and Latin America's crushing debt burden:

> I will tell you that the Third World War has already started—a silent war, not for that reason any the less sinister. This war is tearing down Brazil, Latin America and practically all the Third World. Instead of soldiers dying there are children, instead of millions of wounded there are millions of unemployed; instead of the destruction of bridges there is the tearing down of factories, schools, hospitals and entire economies. . . . It is a war by the United States against the Latin American continent and the Third World. It is a war over the foreign debt, one which has as its main weapon interest, a weapon more deadly than the atom bomb, more shattering than a laser beam. [Quoted in the *Nation,* April 17, 1989, p. 510.]

9. For more on the current treatment of nonpolitical prisoners in Brazilian jails, see two recent reports from Americas Watch: *Police Abuse in Brazil: Summary Executions* *in São Paulo and Rio de Janeiro* (December, 1987), and *Prison Conditions in Brazil* (April, 1989). The latter report details one particularly gruesome incident that occurred on Carnival night, February 5, 1989, when, allegedly retaliating for an attempted rebellion, police in the 42nd Police District in São Paulo forced fifty-one naked prisoners into an unventilated isolation cell measuring five by ten feet. By the time the cell's heavy iron doors were reopened an hour later, eighteen of the men had suffocated to death. The international furor over this incident eventually resulted in the closing of the São Paulo DEIC facility, one of the most notorious prisons and formerly one of the military's most dreaded torture centers.

10. This may be the place to bring developments in Brazil since the original May, 1987, publication of this article up to date.

In late 1987, Jaime Wright was unanimously elected as the first General Secretary of the IPU, the United Presbyterian Church of Brazil, a remarkable honor for a onetime American missionary; and he and his wife Alma moved to Vitória, on the Atlantic coast north of Rio, where the church has its headquarters. He continues to work energetically on behalf of human-rights issues.

In 1989, Adolfo Pérez Esquivel, the Argentine human-rights activist who was awarded the 1980 Nobel Peace Prize, nominated Cardinal Arns for the same honor, and a widespread campaign of support spread throughout Latin America. Cardinal Arns himself, meanwhile, came under increasing pressure from the Vatican, where John Paul II and his conservative allies were engaged in a growing campaign to undercut the influence of "liberation theology" all over the world, but especially in the Brazilian Church. Conservatives replaced progressives as the heads of key archdioceses in Salvador (Bahia state) and Olinda e Recife (Pernambuco), the onetime seat of Dom Helder Câmara; and as part of this pattern, Arns, the archbishop of São Paulo, suddenly had his archdiocese carved out from under him. In place of the one diocese, the Vatican decreed that there would henceforth be five: conservatives were appointed to head the four poorest of these, while Arns himself was given charge of the richest district—from where, it was hoped, he would find it more difficult to protect the interests of the Christian Base Communities in each of the other districts.

Meanwhile, however, as the country's economy continued to unravel, the political party most closely associated with the work of those Christian Base Communities, the Partido dos Trabalhadores—the Workers Party—stunned the entrenched political elites by sweeping the November 15, 1988, São Paulo municipal elections and installing their candidate, a fifty-three-year-old social worker named Luiza Erundina da Silva, as the new mayor. As part of that sweep, one of the key organizers of the Brasil: Nunca Mais project was elected to a very high position in the São Paulo city government.

Similarly, two other figures intimately involved in the Brasil: Nunca Mais project were elected federal deputies and took part in the long, drawn-out Constitutional Convention that ended up producing a new charter for the country. These two deputies proved instrumental in inserting language into Article V of that document which declared that, henceforth, torture would be considered a crime; the language of the law, furthermore, specifically declared that this particular crime would be subject to neither a statute of limitations nor any future amnesty.

Meanwhile, in the spring of 1989, the newly inaugurated American president George Bush appointed a new U.S. ambassador to Brazil, a career diplomat named Richard Melton. There was some initial opposition to Melton's appointment in Brazil since, as was widely reported in the Brazilian press, he'd been expelled from his prior posting, as ambassador to Nicaragua, for alleged spying and collaboration with the Contras. (Before that he'd served as deputy to Elliott Abrams, President Reagan's Assistant Secretary of State for Inter American Affairs. His name had repeatedly come up during the Iran-contra investigations, and as with some of Bush's other ambassadorial appointments of similarly implicated figures, there was some speculation that the appointments, to varying degrees, constituted a sort of reward for services rendered and silences observed.) Opposition to Melton's appointment in Brazil exploded, however, with the publication of allegations by Ricardo Zarattini, a Brazilian congressional aide (and Communist Party member). Zarattini claimed that in December, 1968, while he was being held as a political prisoner at a military jail in Recife, he was severely tortured and, immediately afterward, was interrogated by an American consular official. Furthermore, he said, now that he'd seen photos of the new U.S. ambassador-designate in the press, he was absolutely certain that this man Melton was the one who had questioned him. Even though Melton had not been involved in the torture itself, still, Zarattini wrote in an open letter to the Brazilian Foreign Ministry, "Of all the violence I suffered during the dictatorship, none affected me as much as being interrogated by an agent of a foreign government."

In an Associated Press story datelined Brasília (June 1), a U.S. Embassy spokesman "confirmed that Melton occupied a vice-consular post in Recife from 1967 to 1969. But he added, 'Richard Melton never heard of Zarattini and never participated in any episodes of that type.'" "I'm certain it was him," Zarattini told the AP in the same dispatch, and a lot of Brazilians believed him. The commentator Moacir de Castro, in a piece headlined "A Strange Ambassador" that appeared in the solidly mainstream daily *Jornal do Brasil,* noted that the Brazilian Foreign Ministry "received Melton's nomination with extreme displeasure. . . . He's not only a member of the B-team, but has a highly negative reputation. . . . If, as a challenge to our national interest, a former police-consul becomes U.S. ambassador, Brazil will be making a deplorable concession to the law of the Big Stick." Notwithstanding these concerns, the U.S. Senate confirmed Melton in November, 1989 (the Foreign Relations Committee, oblivious to the concerns, could hardly muster a quorum for the hearings; Zarattini's charge was never aired by the major U.S. media); and by the end of the year, Melton had been installed at the American Embassy in Brasília.

In the meantime, Brazil went through a tempestuous campaign, leading up to the presidential primary in November, 1989, and the runoffs in December—the first such elections in almost thirty years. Several prominent leftist candidates—notably the old firebrand Governor Brizola and the charismatic labor activist Lula—kept the question of Brazil's ongoing democratization, in the face of the military's continuing assertion of its own prerogatives, prominently to the fore. In the end, Fernando Collor de Mello, a wealthy center-right populist with heavy business and media backing, narrowly defeated Lula, the candidate of the Workers' Party, and at least for the moment, the military was assuaged.

11. " 'They're hiding!' " The writer Eduardo Galeano repeated the punchline when he later told me the same story. "Thus is one present as the entire tradition of Latin American literature is reinvented by a new generation."

12. The economic crisis facing the United States today—the towering twin deficits, the increasing pauperization of a growing portion of our body politic, the continual draining of financial resources from productive investment into speculative frenzies—is obviously different in kind from the one that faced Uruguay in the early sixties. But the sheer inability of the political process in any way to come to terms with even the vaguest lineaments of the crisis—the timorous refusal of politicians in either party to frame issues clearly and thereby offer citizens any real options, the reluctance of citizens to demand that they do so, the persistent recourse to serene obliviousness (from the "Morning Again in America" campaign of 1984 to the "Don't Worry, Be Happy" serenades of 1988)—these qualities are not at all unlike those which characterized the Uruguayan political scene in the years before their debacle. There are no Great Exceptions. Wherever it has appeared and endeavored to persist, democracy has always been the most fragile and most perishable of enterprises. Reporting and composing this piece on Uruguay while simultaneously observing the recent electoral transition unfolding here in the United States, I increasingly grew to realize that alongside anything else it might provide, Uruguay's is a cautionary tale.

13. A couple days after the raid on Pando, an exasperated Ministry of the Interior issued the following communiqué: "As from today, none of the communications media in the country may use any of the following terms: cell, commandos, extremists, terrorists, subversive, political delinquent, or ideological delinquent. Instead, and in pursuance of official regulations, the terms used should be: layabouts, criminals, delinquents, evil-livers, malefactors, and other similar definitions contained in the penal code." (María Esther Gilio, *The Tupamaro Guerrillas* [New York: Saturday Review, 1972], p. 125.)

14. The escaping prisoners included Sendic and most of the other Tupamaro leaders who'd been apprehended over a year earlier during the Mitrione state of siege, and the whole escapade had clearly been extremely well planned. The prisoners managed to tunnel 60 meters—beyond the prison walls and into an adjacent neighborhood. On the final night, several confederates on the outside suddenly occupied the home of one Billy Rial, telling him his house was going to be needed for a few hours, though nothing would happen to him if he remained quiet. According to the account of the incident given by María Esther Gilio in her book, *The Tupamaro Guerrillas* (pp. 185–89), the confederates now began drilling a hole in the floor of his sitting room. A few hours later, at 3:40 A.M., "Up through the hole came the first of the escaping Tupamaros. He was wearing a lamp on his forehead, like a miner, and was covered from head to foot with mud. One hundred and ten men followed him [in addition to the 106 political prisoners, 5 common prisoners joined in the escape], all as muddy as he. It took fifteen minutes for them all to emerge and as they did they shed their filthy garments, showing clean clothes underneath." Within moments of that, the escapees had all filed out of the house and into the night. The last one out instructed Rial to wait half an hour before calling the police.

"At 4:30 A.M.," Ms. Gillo continues her account, "Billy Rial telephoned Police Headquarters and told them what had happened. They asked him whether he was sure of what he was saying. 'Of course I'm sure,' he said. 'I saw them with my own eyes.' At 5:00 A.M., as half an hour had gone by and there was still no sign of the police, Billy, with the mouth of the tunnel gaping wide in his sitting room floor, rang them again. The police told him they had called the prison and nobody there knew anything about an escape. Billy, disheartened, went out to the street and called out to one of the prison guards patrolling along the top of the wall, 'Hey—the Tupamaros have escaped.' 'Go back to bed—you're drunk,' shouted back the guard."

The police didn't finally arrive till 6:00 A.M.

In subsequent days, a new joke spread through Montevideo, a play on a famous slogan from the early period when Sendic had been organizing rural workers in the interior ("Follow Sendic, work the good earth, and you'll go far"). "Do you know how the Tupamaros managed to escape?" people would ask. "No." "They followed Sendic, they worked the good earth, and they went far."

The escapees, however, enjoyed only a few more months of freedom. Most of them, including Sendic, would be snared once again during the military's upcoming final offensive.

15. Between 1970 and 1985, Uruguay went from 7.7 military men per 1,000 inhabitants to 14.6 (these figures exclude interior ministry personnel). By contrast, Ecuador went from 3.2 to 4.2 during roughly the same period, and Colombia from 2.2 to 2.6. In 1983, Brazil had 2.1 and Chile 8.5 military men per 1,000 countrymen. At the height of the Contra war, Nicaragua was fielding a ratio of 17.7 per 1,000, while Cuba (another country that considers itself under ongoing siege) maintains a level of about 15.7. (All figures from Juan Rial, *Las Fuerzas Armadas: ¿Soldados-Políticos Garantes de la Democracia?* [Montevideo: 1986], CIESU, p. 52.)

16. In fairness, Henry Kissinger's State Department didn't much trouble itself about human-rights abuses *anywhere* in the world in those days. Jimmy Carter would subsequently make human rights a cornerstone of his foreign policy (and the U.S. Embassy in Montevideo a haven for regrouping oppositionists); Ronald Reagan, after that, would prove shrill in his denunciations of human-rights violations in the Eastern Bloc, though less so elsewhere (and he, in effect, would throw all the oppositionists back out of the U.S. Embassy in Montevideo). Ironically, Kissinger and Nixon were more like Carter than Reagan in that they were at least consistent. For them, people being strung up and tortured or languishing through endless prison terms under intolerable conditions—such victims anywhere in the world couldn't be expected to elicit the concern of serious statemen, concerned as these inevitably were with the fate of nations and blocs of nations, the *realpolitik* of geopolitics.

17. Elio Gaspari, the editor at the Brazilian weekly *Veja,* had earlier told me how well over half of the references in Golbery's seminal *Strategic Planning,* the primary text on the doctrine of national security in Brazil, are to American authors. Gaspari, incidentally, feels that in the case of Brazil, the so-called doctrine of national security wasn't so much the animating force behind the original coup as a justification developed ex post facto for both it and continuing military rule (that is to say, as time went by activist generals increasingly came to require an intellectual rationale for what they were doing anyway). Brazil's experience was, at any rate, extremely important for the militaries in other Latin American countries. As Gaspari points out, the sequence of Institutional Acts more or less improvised by the Brazilian military as it went along, which provided the legal superstructure for their dominion, was "virtually xeroxed" by the militaries in other countries as, one by one, they took power. Gaspari also feels that while the ideological and tactical training the Brazilian officers received when they went north were certainly important (for several years, the entire student body and staff at ECEME would come to the United States for tours of various U.S. bases), the truly formative experience during those trips—and he says this only half-facetiously—was "the stopover at Bloomingdale's." Gaspari suggests that the rest days set aside for shopping trips in New York and Miami did more than anything else to socialize the young Brazilian officers to an American worldview (to make them feel part of the American system). Gaspari has even seen a letter sent by the top U.S. general in Brasília, the head of the Joint Military Commission, U.S.-Brazil, to the then newly inaugurated president General Geisel enclosing a blank spare pass to the U.S. Army PX and inviting the general to put his wife's picture on the pass so that she would feel free to use the PX's ample shopping opportunities. (Geisel, Gaspari says, was himself insulted by the offer, but then Geisel, who was known for his personal probity, was an unusual case.)

18. At one point during the U.S. congressional hearings on the Iran-Contra scandal, Representative Jack Brooks of Texas endeavored to question Oliver North on his role in formulating "a contingency plan in the event of an emergency that would suspend the American Constitution." A clearly flustered Senator Daniel Inouye, the panel's co-chairman, immediately intervened, declaring that the question touched upon "a highly sensitive and classified area" that could be discussed only in closed session. Some time later, however, Alfonso Chardy, the Miami *Herald*'s ace reporter, managed to get a look at the plan (drawn up by North between 1982 and 1984). On July 5, 1988, Chardy revealed that among the "contingencies" North sought to address with his scheme for the imposition of martial law in the United States was any eventual "mass opposition to a U.S. military operation overseas."

19. Such Red Cross mission reports are supposed to be held in complete confidence, and they almost always are—absolute discretion having proved essential in preserving the Red Cross's uncanny ability to get into prisons all around the world. The organization's intention on these missions is physically to assist the prisoners themselves, at most to discuss their conditions with the authorities, but never to report publicly on those conditions. The ordinarily hardened veterans of the Red Cross mission to Libertad, however, were apparently so appalled by what they encountered that one of them leaked the report, causing a considerable international sensation at the time (and foreclosing the possibility of any further Red Cross missions to Uruguay in the years thereafter).

20. Consider, for instance, the following testimony which an architectural student named Alvaro Jaume subsequently delivered to Amnesty International regarding his ordeal in a Uruguayan torture center:

> "I was thoroughly examined by a doctor. He asked me about my family, any chronic or present illnesses, and about any parts of my body which might be delicate because of previous sickness. I thought that giving that information might reduce the torture. Hours later I realized the real reason for the doctor's interest. I heard his voice—unmistakably—saying: 'That's OK, you can carry on.' I felt angry and impotent. Here was an individual trained by society to save lives, dedicating himself to inflicting pain. Mostly I was angry with myself for being so naive as to believe that a doctor who worked in such a place could possess a trace of humanity. These doctors are saving lives, but in a perverse way. The aim of torture is thwarted if the victim cannot support the interminable ordeal. The doctor is needed to prevent you from dying for your convictions." (Quoted in "They Condone Torture," by César Chelala in *World Health,* the journal of the World Health Organization, April, 1989.)

21. After this paragraph ran as part of the *New Yorker* version of this piece, I received an interesting letter from Dr. John Renfrew, a behaviorist psychologist who teaches at Northern Michigan University. Dr. Renfrew, who is married to a Uruguayan, explained that he has spent much time in Montevideo over the past several decades, first as a Fulbright scholar, later working for the OAS, and then, after 1978, teaching at the reconstituted School of Psychology at the university. (He was also, he says, an early supporter of Amnesty International's interventions regarding the human-rights situation in Uruguay.)

Taking exception to my characterization of the history of academic psychology in Uruguay and of the role of the behaviorists in the dictatorship, he wrote that while the Freudian orientation had indeed prevailed at the university prior to the dictatorship, "What you might not appreciate is that Uruguayan psychology, along with that of Argentina, was in a horribly archaic state, compared to that of the United States and other developed countries. Psychologists were very poorly trained and were far from reaching the status they have here." Though he did not approve of the purge of the Freudian psychologists from the university, he did feel that the revised department presented a more professional, scientific, and up-to-date demeanor. Furthermore, he wrote, his colleagues "were basically dedicated psychologists, with minimal political involvement. If anything, they were antigovernment. They would point out who might be spying on us and sometimes criticized the government in private conversations." Late in his stay, he heard that there was at least one psychologist who was participating in the torture process, but he did not know the man and the man did not belong to his academic group.

"It is possible," Dr. Renfrew writes, "that some psychologists with a layman's knowledge of behavioral techniques applied them in a perverse way to the prisoners. Whoever did commit the abuses apparently borrowed some techniques and then did not follow through with their application. Reinforcers and punishers are used to increase appropriate behaviors or suppress inappropriate ones, not as devices to harass people. Regrettably what apparently happened in Uruguay is very similar to what has occurred many times in the United States. Institutional caretakers here sometimes have been caught abusing their charges and subsequently have tried to justify it as 'behavioral modification.' In a further parallel here, blame has been directed at all behaviorists. However, it is irresponsible and inaccurate to blame behaviorists as a group for [what happened in Uruguay]. I have had extensive interactions with the leading behaviorists in Uruguay. Many are good friends of mine. They have flourished since the end of the dictatorship and have gained respect in the community. They are not your torturers."

Dr. Renfrew concluded his letter by noting, with sadness, what he called "another type of dictatorship" which had established itself at the university in the wake of the return of democracy, as "the old dominance of the Freudians was reestablished. While I can understand the justice in reinstating people to their precoup positions, I am pained that it could not be done without sacrificing the professional gains made in their absence."

22. At Libertad prison, in Uruguay, behaviorist techniques were deployed in a particularly perverse manner—sanctions and rewards being administered across a continually changing field of random rules—with the specific intention of driving the inmates mad. But Libertad is by no means the only prison in the world to have trafficked in the techniques and ideology of "behavior modification." In fact, for many years, a "scientific" behaviorist model enjoyed a considerable vogue in U.S. penal institutions. After my piece ran in the *New Yorker,* Aryeh Neier, formerly the head of the ACLU and currently the executive director of Human Rights Watch, sent me a chapter from a book he never completed, surveying the subject.

Neier describes the regime at Maryland's Patuxent Institution for "defective delinquents," a psychiatric prison founded in 1955: "The law establishing Patuxent provided that the sentence given to a prisoner at trial did not determine release. Incarceration would be 'without maximum or minimum limits in order to confine defective delinquents until, as a result of the special treatment which they need, it is safe to return them to the community. . . . The treatment may, and in many cases would, involve incarceration for life . . . not because of guilt, but to protect the defective himself and society.' Patuxent described itself as a 'total treatment' facility. Prisoners there entered a graded four-tier system. In the bottom tier, where they started, they were confined in miserable circumstances. If a prisoner did well in the opinion of the institution's staff, he moved, and eventually he could achieve comparatively attractive and comfortable quarters. If he did badly, he could be demoted all the way to the bottom tier." Between 1955 and 1972, when the program was effectively closed by court order, almost a thousand inmates went through Patuxent, though the staff determined that only 135 were cured and therefore released (another 337 achieved release through individual court orders); almost half the prisoners remanded to Patuxent ended up staying longer than the maximum sentences for their crimes.

Other sorts of behavior-modification programs during this period went on at the U.S. Medical Center in Springfield, Missouri; the California Medical Facility in Vacaville (where "aversive therapy" included administrations of the temporarily paralyzing drug Anectine); the federal prison for maximum security prisoners at Marion, Illinois; and the Federal Center for Correctional Research in Butner, North Carolina (the latter two under the direction of Dr. Martin Groder, a leading proponent of such programs).

However, in the wake of a seminal U.S. Supreme Court decision regarding Patuxent in 1972, other federal and state courts quickly dismantled much of the apparatus of behavior modification in the U.S. penal system during the mid-seventies. Ironically, it was just around this same time that the behaviorists were really getting going at Libertad.

Even more ironically, a year *after* Libertad was closed in Uruguay, the U.S. Bureau of Prisons embarked on perhaps its most elaborate experiment yet in behavioral conditioning (October, 1986). The location was the Female High Security Unit (HSU) in the basement of the Federal Correctional Institute in Lexington, Kentucky, and the first two guinea pigs (the program was eventually slated to include sixteen subjects) were Alejandrina Torres, a forty-nine-year-old Puerto Rican nationalist, and Susan Rosenberg, a thirty-one-year-old self-proclaimed revolutionary. (Neither woman had ever been convicted of committing any act of violence; they were each serving unusually harsh sentences based on weapons possession and conspiracy convictions.)

According to William Reuben and Carlos Norman, writing in the *Nation* (June 27, 1987), "The two women at HSU are confined to subterranean cells twenty-three hours a day. They are permitted one hour of exercise in a yard measuring fifty feet square; upon their return they are strip-searched. That daily outing is the only time they see sunlight, except when they leave the facility for medical or dental treatment. On those occasions, they are handcuffed and manacled by chains around their waists. In the cells, they are kept under constant surveillance by guards or television cameras. . . . The lights in their cells glare down on them continuously, and they are forbidden to cover them in any way. Nor are they allowed to place photographs or pictures on the walls. They may wear only prison-issue shoes, undergarments, drab shirts and culottes. Virtually the only contact they have with the outside world consists of a fifteen-minute call to their lawyers each week and a visit with members of their families, separated by a glass partition, once a month. Guards are instructed not to converse with them. They are denied access to the prison library as well as the entertainment and recreational facilities. They may read only magazines, books and newspapers that are approved by prison officials. . . . For companionship, they have a color television set in their cells."

As Ms. Rosenberg commented to the authors of this piece, "Only in America can you abuse people, take away their human dignity, and then give them a TV and that makes it OK." She asserted that conditions at the HSU were "designed to destroy personalities. . . . They are trying to drive us out of our minds."

The situation of the two inmates at the Lexington HSU attracted the attention of the media and presently the courts as well. In July, 1988, a Federal District Court ruled the Lexington program unconstitutional—surprisingly, and somewhat disconcertingly, on First Amendment freedom-of-association rather than Eighth Amendment cruel-and-unusual-punishment grounds (the women were deemed to be being punished for their preconviction associations rather than any special crime)—and the Lexington HSU was closed down. The penal deployment of behavioral conditioning thus faced another (though again perhaps only temporary) setback in the United States.

23. With the passing months, the international support campaign on Estrella's behalf intensified, and finally, in an extraordinarily unusual development, the Uruguayan junta did indeed release this particular prisoner early, in February, 1980, after he'd spent twenty-six months in prison. Estrella reestablished himself in Paris, where he resumed his musical career and also recorded a series of remarkable interviews with Jean Lacoutre, which were published under the title *Musique pour l'Espérance* (from which all the Estrella quotations in this book derive).

24. Peter Winn, a professor of Latin American history at Tufts University, provided a succinct summary of the current Tupamaro profile and line in a recent article in the *Nation* (June 26, 1989, p. 883): "The surviving Tupamaros have been given amnesty from prison and allowed to return from exile, and many of them have reentered political life. But it is a very different politics than they practiced two decades ago. For now, after trenchant self-criticism, the former guerrillas seem willing to give Uruguayan democracy a chance. The Tupamaros, who spawned some successful entrepreneurs while in European exile, today run the best restaurant on Montevideo's main street and imaginative social programs in the city's spreading *cantegriles* (shantytowns). They also lead a 'combative tendency' among Uruguayan workers, which has been challenging an accommodationist Communist Party for control of the country's labor movement. Politically, the Tupamaros' 25th of March Party remains a tiny faction that has been unable to gain admission to the Frente Amplio alliance or attract substantial popular support."

25. In fact, I was repeatedly being reminded of Poland during my recent visits to Uruguay; indeed, of all the cities I've ever visited, the one Montevideo most recalled to my mind was Warsaw. Both cities are threadbare and pockmarked (though, of course, temperate and coastal Montevideo is continuously bathed in a blonding seaside light and hence could never be considered, as Warsaw often is, entirely drab). Both are capital cities with a certain onetime style, a prior flair, laid low in recent years by the prolonged effects of an utterly debilitating national debt (if anything, Uruguay's is worse than Poland's: Poland, with its population of 40 million, owes almost $40 billion, whereas Uruguay, with its population of under 3 million, owes over $5 billion). But the most striking similarity comes in the way that Montevideans, like Varsovians, insist on imagining that this is all some sort of big mistake: Catholic Poles see their country's geographical placement, in the maw of the Communist Eastern Empire, as some perverse historical misunderstanding (don't people realize, for God's sake, that they're all really good Catholic Frenchmen, mysteriously adrift?). The worldly-wise Uruguayans, for their part (90 percent of whom derive from recent European immigrant stock), likewise insist that by all rights they shouldn't be having anything to do with the rest of military-dominated, dictator-ridden Latin America (they, too, curiously imagine themselves displaced Parisians—sophisticated, *atheistic* Parisians, that is).

At any rate, a few months after one of my trips to Uruguay, I happened to be reporting in Poland once again. During an interview with Lech Walesa, I mentioned a joke I'd heard a few times in Uruguay: "Because of the debt, the government keeps telling us we just have to tighten our belts. But how does it expect us to do so, when we had to *eat* them yesterday?" Walesa loved the line, and sure enough, he was soon using it in his own speeches.

26. The motivations behind Wilson Ferreira's about-face on the amnesty will no doubt remain a matter of controversy for some time. Shortly after my piece ran in the *New Yorker,* I received a letter from Milton I. Vanger, perhaps the dean of American Uruguay scholars, a professor emeritus at Brandeis University. He offered another interpretation: "What I would stress is Wilson's determination to keep Uruguay 'governable' after the military. I think the military were always afraid he would punish them and that is why they concocted charges against him, arrested him, and prevented him from running for president. Yet he ultimately supported the amnesty, even if he squirmed. I believe he was atoning for past ambition. In the year before the coup, he maneuvered to force Bordaberry out and have a special election he hoped to win. These maneuverings contributed to the coup and he was determined to keep post-coup Uruguay governable."

27. This theme of fanatical anti-Semitism is one that recurs over and over again in testimony from the victims of military torture in the Southern Cone. For another Argentine instance, see, of course, Jacobo Timerman's *Prisoner without a Name, Cell without a Number.* Miguel Angel Estrella provides another such account, this one derived from his experiences in Montevideo, in his book *Musique pour l'Espérance:* "One thing I don't want to forget to mention is how during the torture, one thing the torturers kept constantly asking me was why I had Jewish friends. They'd demand any information I might have about Jews living in Uruguay or in Argentina. They'd also ask whether, since I had so many Jewish friends, I might not by chance be Jewish myself. I'd respond, 'I'm of Lebanese origin, my name is translated from Arab into Spanish!' But this ferocious, terrible anti-Semitism was something I then encountered again in Libertad prison. The military in both Argentina and Uruguay were heavily anti-Semitic" (p. 254).

28. Among the specific provisions most often cited by those who claim the Uruguayan amnesty violates international law are the International Covenant on Civil and Political Rights; the 1984 U.N. Convention against Torture and other Cruel, Inhumane or Degrading Treatment or Punishment; the 1968 U.N. Convention on the Non-Applicability of Statutes of Limitation to War Crimes and Crimes against Humanity; and General Assembly Resolution 3074/XXVIII concerning the investigation, prosecution, and punishment of those responsible for war crimes and crimes against humanity—all of which Uruguay has now signed and endorsed.

Amnesty International, for its part, has drawn particular attention to the international legal ramifications of the failure to investigate properly the cases of the Uruguayan "disappeared" (see A.I.'s June, 1988, briefing paper, "Uruguay: Official Investigations Fail To Establish Fate of the 'Disappeared' "): "Resolution 15 (XXXIV) of the United Nations Sub-Commission on the Prevention of Discrimination and the Protection of Minorities, adopted on 10 September 1981, urged that 'states in which persons have been reported to have disappeared should repeal or refrain from adopting laws which could impede inquiries concerning such disappearances.' A further resolution of the Sub-Commission adopted on 5 September 1983 (resolution 1983/23) stressed the right of families to know the fate of their relatives by calling on governments 'in the event of reports of enforced or involuntary disappearances, to devote appropriate resources to searching for such persons and to undertake speedy and impartial investigations.' "

29. "Torture consists of a primary physical act, the infliction of pain, and a primary verbal act, the interrogation," Elaine Scarry of the University of Pennsylvania notes in her remarkable essay "The Structure of Torture," the first chapter of her extraordinary 1985 meditation, *The Body in Pain: The Making and Unmaking of the World.* The pain always occurs within a context of supposed questioning. "Although the information sought in an interrogation is never credited with being a *just* motive for torture," Scarry continues, "it is repeatedly credited with being the motive for torture. But for every instance in which someone with critical information is interrogated, there are hundreds interrogated who could know nothing of remote importance to the stability or self-image of the regime" (p. 28). In a footnote to this passage, Scarry elaborates: "That the information elicited in Ethiopia or Vietnam or Chile sometimes, in fact, determines the sequence of arrests and torture may only mean that governments sometimes depend on their opponents to provide an arbitrary structure for their brutality. . . . Amnesty International publications, for example, sometimes call attention to the fact that torture is an extremely inefficient means of intelligence-gathering, though its inefficiency is certainly not the grounds on which it is condemned. Again, in his discussion of torture in Algiers, Alistair Horne seems to assume that it is being used in order to obtain information, but he observes that the collating services of a country that uses torture are 'overwhelmed by a mountain of false information extorted from victims desperate to save themselves from further agony' " (p. 329).

If the obtaining of information is not the true function of interrogative torture, then what is? Scarry's meditation on this riddle opens out onto some of the most suggestive terrain in her book: "In compelling confession, the torturers compel the prisoner to record and objectify the fact that intense pain is world-destroying. It is for this reason that while the content of the prisoner's answer is only sometimes important to the regime, the form of the answer, the fact of the answering, is always crucial" (p. 29). "Torture, then, to return for a moment to the starting point, consists of a primary physical act, the infliction of pain, and a primary verbal act, the interrogation. The verbal act, in turn, consists of two parts, 'the question' and 'the answer,' each with conventional connotations that totally falsify it. 'The question' is mistakenly understood to be 'the motive'; 'the answer' is mistakenly understood to be 'the betrayal' . . . These two misinterpretations are obviously neither accidental nor unrelated. The one is an absolution of responsibility, the other a conferring of responsibility; the two together turn the moral reality of torture upside down" (p. 35).

Scarry notes that, "There is not only among torturers but even among people appalled by acts of torture and sympathetic to those hurt, a covert disdain for confession." Through this facile attitude, however, Scarry argues that "the civilian public unintentionally allies itself with the torturer," and she passionately insists that, "While those who withstand torture without confessing should be honored, those who do confess are not dishonored by and should not be dishonored for their act" (p. 29). Until this essential distinction is comprehended by everyone, torturers will retain a valuable tool in their arsenal for performing what is, after all, the true function of torture—the destruction of the personhood of the victim and its replacement by the introjected, objectified authority of the regime.

"However near the prisoner the torturer stands," Scarry continues, "the distance between their physical realities is colossal. . . . It is only the prisoner's steadily shrinking ground that wins for the torturer his swelling sense of territory. The question and the answer are a prolonged comparative display, an unfurling of world maps. . . . The question and answer also objectify the fact that while the prisoner has almost no voice—his confession is a halfway point in the disintegration of language—the torturer and the regime have doubled their voice since the prisoner is now speaking with their words" (p. 36).

30. I was reminded of a passage in a monograph by Juan Rial, a noted Uruguayan political scientist: "The members of the Latin American officer corps generally . . . do not consider that they are members of an organization that can be created, changed, and even 'closed down.' They believe they are part of a transcendent institution with a list of personnel in hierarchical order, material and financial resources, and a job to do. *For them, the job, precisely and in the first place, is the institution itself, and not its incidental purpose, or its use*" (italics mine). (Juan Rial, *Armed Forces of Latin America and the Latin Americas* [Montevideo: Peitho, 1987], pp. 12–13.)

31. In general, a good way of inventorying the truly loathsome human-rights violators left over from the various "democratizing" transition processes taking place around the world is to survey the rosters of the respective countries' military attachés posted to places like South Africa, Taiwan, El Salvador, Panama, and Paraguay. Paraguay, incidentally, is where Sanguinetti managed to stash his arch-reactionary Colorado predecessor, Jorge Pacheco Areco: he was serving there as Uruguay's ambassador. Uruguayans whose search for their disappeared relatives led them to Paraguay were frequently warned not even to bother soliciting help from their country's embassy in Asunción. At any rate, it was now revealed that as part of his secret hopscotch trail home, the place Colonel Seineldín had stopped in just before Uruguay had been—Paraguay.

32. I was reminded of a moment, months earlier, at the very end of my interview with the Vice-President, Enrique Tarigo. "Gee," Tarigo complained, as I was putting away my notepad. "It seems a shame. You come all the way down here from New York to this wonderful, fascinating country, we speak for a whole hour, and all you want to talk about is this question of *impunidad.* There's so much else to speak of." That's fair, I told him. What did he suggest? The question seemed to throw him. He sputtered through a few false starts and finally shot back, in exasperation, "I don't know—*you're* the journalist." *Not* thinking about *impunidad* was taking up so much energy that it was becoming hard to think of anything else.

33. In the months that followed, Argentina's economy, which Alfonsín had inherited from the military in a state of fairly complete devastation and which he'd proved pretty hapless at salvaging (in fairness, he'd received precious little help in doing so from the bankers and finance ministers of the democratic North, officials who'd earlier shown themselves all too willing to pander to the whims of the military as it was piling up the problem debts and deficits in the first place)—that economy now collapsed completely. Inflation began approaching rates of over 100 percent *per month*; and this calamity, rather than the question of civil-military relations, came to dominate the campaign for the May, 1989, Presidential elections. Alfonsín's Radical Party was decimated at the polls, and the big winner proved the disquietingly charismatic Peronist candidate, Carlos Saúl Menem, a man who swept into the Presidency promising all things to all people without even hinting at a single specific program. Once in office—his inauguration was moved forward by several months, owing to the precipitously worsening economic emergency—he quickly surrounded himself with a cabinet filled with right-wing economists and military sympathizers. By October, he was moving "to accomplish the definitive reconciliation" among the Argentines, presidentially pardoning virtually all those officers still facing trial on either torture or sedition charges, and indicating that those already convicted might soon be pardoned as well. Instead of purging the military of the various would-be coup-makers (in fact, on the contrary, he ostentatiously invited Colonel Seineldín to come visit him in the presidential mansion the day after he'd had him released), Menem now took to ridding the Argentine judiciary of the judges and prosecutors who'd spearheaded the human-rights effort over the past decade. It seemed clear that in Argentina, anyway, the always precarious era of truth and partial justice, vis-à-vis the human-rights crimes of the past, had now come to a definitive end.

34. Aryeh Neier, executive director of Human Rights Watch in New York City, was not terribly sanguine about the prospects for those international lawsuits when I mentioned them to him a few days later. "International legal remedies for human rights are still quite weak," he explained, "and after a vote like that in Uruguay, the case will be that much more difficult. All courts are political, but especially courts in their infancy, and those cases will be highly charged."

Having said that, Neier went on to address the larger issues posed by the Uruguayan vote. "Ultimately, I object to the notion that this sort of question is susceptible to resolution by a democratic vote, either legislatively or by way of a national plebiscite. Suppose after the Second World War a referendum had been held in Germany as to whether Nazis should be held accountable for their treatment of the Jews. Would that have resolved anything?" Neier referred me to a new policy statement regarding amnesties which his organization's board had adopted just days before the Uruguayan vote. "Popular disinclination to hold accountable those responsible for gross abuses of human rights does not negate the responsibility of a government to pursue accountability," the statement declares, "particularly in circumstances where the victims of the abuses may have been concentrated among members of a racial, ethnic, religious, or political minority. A government's duty to demonstrate respect for human rights extends to all persons, and it is not the prerogative of the many to forgive the commission of crimes against the few."

35. Something decisive had happened, and at the same time an era was coming to an end. The latter point was driven home for everyone just two weeks after the vote, on April 28, when word came from Europe that the founder of the Tupamaros, Raúl Sendic, had died in a Paris clinic. For the previous year, he had been suffering the ravages of a mysteriously proliferating neurological ailment, and he'd gone to Paris for treatment in February. Tragically, this man who'd endured twelve years of solitary confinement only to struggle through several more years of therapy in an effort to regain the use of his voice now progressively lost the ability to speak. He became a prisoner of his own body, barely able to move even his eyelids. The two situations may not have been entirely unrelated. Doctors never succeeded in fully diagnosing Sendic's ailment—some felt it might be a version of ALS (amyotrophic lateral sclerosis), commonly referred to as Lou Gehrig's syndrome—but several physicians pointed to the original gunshot wound, when Sendic had been captured and his lower jaw and portions of his tongue blown away (he may have sustained some spinal or lower brain injuries at the time as well), and the fact that those injuries then went untreated for the next twelve years, along with the extreme conditions of stress and privation Sendic endured during those twelve years, as possible contributing factors in his death.

Sendic's body was returned to Montevideo, and he was buried in a small cemetery in a working-class district on the outskirts of town. A crowd estimated at 100,000 people attended the funeral, pouring out of the cemetery grounds and into the surrounding neighborhood. Neighbors left their doors open and turned their radios up so that everyone could hear the oration of the funeral's sole speaker, an old cane worker, a friend from Sendic's early days as a rural organizer.

The elegaic mood was disrupted later that day with word that the Frente Amplio, which for some time had been wrestling over internal doctrinal and personality issues, had now split completely apart and would hence be running two separate campaigns in the November, 1989, election (one social democratic, the other more strictly Marxist-Leninist). The considerable prospect the left had seemed to enjoy of at least capturing the mayoralty of Montevideo, the second most important office in the country, was now likewise sundered. Meanwhile, a few weeks later, in internal Colorado Party elections, Enrique Tarigo, the man Sanguinetti had handpicked as his heir (he was constitutionally forbidden from seeking a second successive term himself), was defeated by Senator Jorge Batlle. Things were equally fractious over in the Blanco Party, where Zumarán seemed to be being upstaged by a youthful, charismatic neoliberal dynast named Luis Lacalle in the jockeying leading up to the November, 1989, presidential elections. An era had ended, but the people sitting around the café tables still had plenty to talk about.

Meanwhile, the question of what to do with the torturers persisting in one's midst was starting to consume nearby Chile, which was undergoing its own grudging process of democratization. The seventeen-party opposition coalition that had united around the Presidential candidacy of the Christian Democratic leader, Patricio Aylwin, in the campaign leading toward the December, 1989, elections, issued a policy statement announcing its intent to ask the new Congress to overturn the military's sweeping 1978 self-amnesty and to set aside, for one year, the ordinary ten-year statute of limitations on murder and other violent crimes. Andrés Zaldívar, who had succeeded Aylwin as head of the Christian Democrats, tried to calm the military by saying the intention was to determine responsibility for the killings and disappearances that occurred in the wake of Pinochet's 1973 coup and then to consider a new amnesty. "Our position is in favor of clarifying facts," he declared. Others in the coalition seemed to want to go further. But on July 30, General Fernando Matthei, the air force commander who'd thus far been playing a sort of Medinalike role in the Chilean transition, continuously pressuring hard-liners like Pinochet toward greater democratic accommodations, flatly declared that the armed forces would "not accept" any attempt to prosecute military men covered by the 1978 amnesty. "If they are going to try to put us in the pillory, as in Argentina," he warned, "that is going to bring the most grave consequences." (See Shirley Christian, "Chile General Tells Opposition Not to Tamper with Authority," New York *Times,* August 1, 1989.)

36. In this context, the metaphor of the *dentist's drill* is particularly apt (its actual use is based on a profound intuition) in that the dentist's drill both *drills in,* burrowing and depositing a terrible knowledge, and *exposes,* bringing to light and rendering raw a terrible knowledge and susceptibility that is always already there, just beneath the surface.

37. Dr. Genefke points out that traditional sorts of therapy have to be radically modified to take into account the unique situation of torture victims. To take just one simple example, doctors and therapists need to stop wearing their traditional white coats, because these too often remind the victims of the doctors who participated in their torture sessions. Many of the victims are in need of various physiotherapies and yet, understandably, they are terrified by the slightest touch, so that physiotherapists require specialized training. And while psychologically the victims may need to work their way past terrible blockages to uncover and then transcend the horrendous double binds imposed on them during key moments of their torture, the traditional psychotherapeutic model in which the therapist asks questions and guides the patient through a difficult terrain of answers is itself too evocative of the earlier interrogation situation. In both cases an authority figure is seeking to get the victim to expose deep, dark secrets, to provoke a sort of confession; the very situation of being alone in a room with such an authority figure may paralyze the former torture victim—so that, again, new methods have to be fashioned.

Over the years the RCT staff has generated an impressive library of papers (many of them available in English) on these and related issues. (Queries can be directed to the RCT, Juliane Maries Vej 34, DK–2100 Copenhagen Ø, Denmark.)

38. Arendt continues this passage: "In contrast to revenge, which is the natural, automatic reaction to transgression and which because of the irreversibility of the action process can be expected and even calculated, the act of forgiving can never be predicted; it is the only reaction that acts in an unexpected way and thus retains, though being a reaction, something of the original character of an action. Forgiving, in other words, is the only reaction which does not merely re-act but acts anew and unexpectedly, unconditioned by the act which provoked it and therefore freeing from its consequences both the one who forgives and the one who is forgiven." (*The Human Condition* [University of Chicago Press, 1958], p. 241.) This reasoning comes remarkably close to that offered by Luis Pérez Aguirre in his account of why he forgave his own torturer after encountering him on the street, and indeed, in the pages following this passage, Arendt herself goes on to consider the example and teachings of Jesus.

1998 Postscript

Over ten years have passed since the pieces upon which this book is based first began appearing in the *New Yorker.* At the time they were dealing with a fairly esoteric political conundrum: the question of what to do in a moment of democratic transition about the security depredations of the prior regime. I say esoteric because at the time democratic transitions were few and far between with little hope of things changing anytime soon. And then, of course, everything began changing with a vengeance.

"History says, *Don't hope / On this side of the grave,*" the Irish master Seamus Heaney would record just a few years later in his Sophoclean rhapsody *The Cure at Troy* (1990). "But then once in a lifetime / The longed-for tidal wave / Of justice can rise up / And hope and history rhyme." Hope and history began rhyming, seemingly all over the world, during the latter half of 1989 and continued doing so for many months thereafter. From Chile and Brazil and Paraguay through Poland, Hungary, Czechoslovakia, Romania, East Germany, and the Soviet Union itself—from Cambodia through El Salvador across to

Ethiopia and down to South Africa, thoroughly, seemingly intractably impacted regimes suddenly began giving way before a rising tide of democratization[1]; and indeed, in one country after another, polities were forced to start grappling with the sorts of issues that had been bedeviling the citizenries of Brazil and Argentina and Uruguay for years.[2] Curiously, far from clarifying those issues and leading towards any normative, standardized lessons or approach, this worldwide grappling only seemed to confound the sense of perplex at the heart of the entire matter.[3]

Among the first of this new generation of accounts-settlers were the Chileans who, in December 1989, rejected General Pinochet's handpicked presidential choice in favor of the candidate of the united opposition, Patricio Aylwin. As one of his first initiatives, Aylwin appointed a National Commission on Truth and Reconciliation whose eight members were drawn from across the political spectrum. The leading theorist behind this effort, and one of the Commission's key members, was José Zalaquett, a man already familiar to readers of this volume. Aylwin, Zalaquett, and the commission's chairman, Raúl Rettig, had all drawn lessons from the previous decade's efforts among neighboring countries. For example, they thought that the Argentineans, though nobly intentioned, had at first gone too far in pursuing their onetime tormentors and then been unable to sustain their achievement in the face of stiffening military defiance. The Uruguayans, by contrast, had clearly not gone far enough—with the terrible resulting cleavage of their society. "The lesson for the Aylwin administration," in Zalaquett's words, "was to stake out a policy it could sustain." With "reparation and prevention" as its principal objectives, the Aylwin approach promised "the whole truth and justice to the extent possible" (which, in practice, wasn't going to be much). As Zalaquett explained (invoking Max Weber's distinction between a Politics of Responsibility as opposed to one of Ultimate Ends), "Responsibility dictated that during the transition this was the most that could be aimed for. In fact, if the government had made an attempt (however futile, given Chile's existing legality) to expand the possibilities for prosecutions, most likely it would have provoked tensions and reactions resulting in neither truth nor justice being achieved."

In practice, even the truth-telling in Chile was circumscribed: the Commission (which was receiving no cooperation from the military authorities in any case) chose to limit itself to the cases of those killed or disappeared, and to name only the victims and not the perpetrators. Given these limitations, the exercise proved a considerable success, and the two-volume report in which it culminated is a model of its kind. Aylwin was able to institute a program of reparations for the families of the victims, but, with one notable exception, General Pinochet was successful in shielding all the perpetrators, including himself, from prosecution.[4]

Many in Chile came away dissatisfied with what they regarded as this half-hearted resolution. Their painful exasperation was captured by Zalaquett's friend, Ariel Dorfman, in his claustrophobic chamber play *Death and the Maiden*. Some even suspected that Dorfman had had Zalaquett specifically in mind in his characterization of the lawyer husband tapped to lead a renascent democracy's truth commission, who then has to endure the fury of a wife, herself a former victim of military torture, at the constrictions placed on the work of that commission (the way, for instance, her own torments fell well outside its mandate since she'd had the ill luck to survive her repeated rapes, and the way her tormentor would in any case be resting assured, pristinely immune from any accountability). Zalaquett, however, remained resolute in his defense of the Commission's approach. Addressing an audience in Berkeley shortly after the completion of the Commission's work, in October 1991, he concluded,

> Of the many lessons learned, I will refer to one. Back in the hazardous days of late 1973, all of my friends and colleagues in the human rights movement had to face danger on a daily basis. None of them ever claimed to have been endowed with innate bravery. They realized that courage was just another name for learning to live with your fears. Eighteen years later, we all have come to realize that under changed circumstances, a less striking form of courage is called for. It is the courage to forgo easy righteousness, to learn how to live with real-life restrictions, but to seek nevertheless to advance one's most cherished values day by day to the extent possible. Relentlessly. Responsibly.[5]

Around this same time in Eastern Europe, situations seemed remarkably similar, with totalitarian systems in sudden rout and populations clamoring for a righteous settling of accounts. This was especially the case in places where the nomenklatura, the former communist ruling class, seemed to be transmogrifying into the new capitalist elite. Among their former subjects, there grew a deep sense of grievance and the call for some kind of purgative catharsis—at the very least a thoroughgoing truth-telling.

But the "truth" in these postcommunist societies proved especially difficult to gauge. For one thing, most of the worst depredations had occurred considerably further back in the past, during the Stalinist era (it was often the genius of post-Stalinist governance that it had only to dangle the memory of those earlier times to enforce a fearful obeisance on the part of most of the current population). Even then, the contours of such victimization were often muddled. As Ryszard Kapuscinski noted regarding his frequent travels through the post-Gorbachev post-Soviet Union, "When I'm sitting next to an older man in a subway car, I ask myself, Who was that man in the past? A butcher or a victim? He could have been a prisoner in a labor camp, but he also could have been a guard there. The true complication of the Russian fate is that he could have been both!" The victims of the 1937 purges in many cases had been the executioners during those of 1933.[6]

Beyond that, the Eastern European totalitarian system had been far more entrenched and dispersed than its South American counterpart. The "decayed moral environment" had suffused the entire society, as Vaclav Havel endeavored to explain to his fellow citizens during the New Year's message he delivered just a few weeks after his sudden elevation from pariah to president in the wake of the Velvet Revolution of 1989:

> All of us became accustomed to the totalitarian system, accepted it as an inalterable fact and thereby kept it running. None of us is merely a victim of it, because all of us helped to create it together. . . . We cannot lay all the blame on those who ruled us before, not only because this would not be true but also because it could detract from the responsibility each of us now faces—the responsibility to act on our own initiative, freely, sensibly, and quickly.

But as it turned out, this sort of awareness (and Adam Michnik, for example, was preaching the same sort of line in Poland), proved extremely difficult to sustain. Indeed, the greater the moral contamination of society, it sometimes seemed, the fiercer the longing for a self-purifying bout of blame-projection. Focus in particular turned on the disquieting phenomenon of informing, which had permeated many of these societies. Demands rose up for the release of lists of informers and for a stiff regime of punitive sanctions aimed against such miscreants. Thus was born the season of lustration, perhaps most feverishly in Havel's own Czechoslovakia.[7]

"Just open the files!" came an insistent public clamor all over Eastern Europe. And there were miles of them (especially in East Germany). The problem, aside from any collateral violations of privacy and the rampant lack of due process, was what precisely was to be made of all the information inside those files. After all, they'd been compiled by agents who'd often had a material interest in exaggerating their own supposed prowess at "turning" fellow citizens (in many cases, agents would even receive bonuses for exceeding their quotas). Beyond that, the files could easily have been laced with vengeful disinformation by security agents on their way out of power. In any case, when released in the form of simple lists of supposed collaborators, the information was shorn of any informing context: Why had an informer informed—out of conviction, venality, cynicism, even love (the desire, for example, to be allowed to visit a daughter abroad), or in prostration before a withering siege of extortion or blackmail? What kind of information had been provided, how truthfully and over how long a period? And then what? Often it wasn't even immediately obvious whether a name appearing on such a list constituted the source or the subject of a given act of informing. (By definition, the security apparatus had focused its greatest energies on dissidents or potential dissidents.) The files were proving a veritable toxic dump at the core of the new democratic order, and the frenzy for truth-telling suddenly seemed decidedly problematic.[8]

Those who had spent time reporting the issue in Latin America tended to come away from exposure to parallel developments in Eastern Europe with their prior certainties at least a touch unmoored. What, for instance, was one to make now of those lists of torturers and their variously implicated accomplices so heroically wrested from the former regime's archives by the Brazilian conspirators? Indeed, there were some who, like Bruce Ackerman of Yale University, came away from the experience virtually throwing their hands up in exasperation. In a fascinating chapter on "The Mirage of Corrective Justice" in his 1992 book *The Future of Liberal Revolution,* Ackerman argued how at the precarious moment of democratic transformation a given polity could either focus on settling prior accounts or turn its attention to fashioning a future constitutional order. It couldn't do both; to focus on the past was to fritter away precious moral capital, to provoke desperate opposition, and necessarily to rupture the tentative, delicate alliances necessary to the project of constitution-building. As for the files, Ackerman even argued against their preservation for future historical purposes ("'Burn them,' I say"), pointing to the inevitability of their leaking or else being deployed in blackmailing schemes by newly rising elites.

For a while there, I myself was teaching occasional guest courses on "Settling Accounts with the Prior Regime," and it got to be almost a game: After establishing an initial conceptual framework, I'd march the classes through a sequence of weekly case studies—Vichy France, Argentina, Uruguay, Cambodia, East Germany, Czechoslovakia, and so forth—demanding to know, in each particular instance, What ought to be done? It was a remarkably telling exercise, because each week the class would seem intent on generating a sort of Kantian rule, a categorical imperative that could be applied every time, thereby grounding that week's specific determination in a wider moral matrix. And yet the following week, faced with the fresh idiosyncrasies of a new situation, that rule would invariably fall completely apart.

By the time we'd completed our exploration of the Czech case, for example, some of my fiercest aficionados of the Brazilian *Nunca Más* heroes were all but braying, alongside Ackerman, for the soonest possible burning of all those toxic files. The following week, however, we looked at the case of the Katyn forest with its mass graves of 21,000 Polish officers—the cream of prewar Polish society—killed at the outset of the Second World War. Stalin had blamed Hitler, and Hitler had blamed

Stalin. In the years that followed, the weight of evidence implicating Stalin had steadily grown, but conclusive proof was fleeting, and meanwhile generations of Poles hankered, increasingly hopelessly, for some kind of closure. Suddenly, in October 1992, the post-Soviet authorities released the actual memo, personally signed by Stalin and his key henchmen, ordering the executions. As I was able to convey to my students, the sense of catharsis—over fifty years later!—was all but overwhelming, and it's no exaggeration to suggest that the document's release made possible a whole new era in Russian-Polish relations. My class nodded eager concurrence. "But only a week ago," I had to remind them, "you guys were all hot to burn this memo!"

The South Africans came relatively late to this field and they had to undergo a crash course of their own. Indeed, owing to the singular effectiveness of the earlier international cultural boycott, the insurgent antiapartheid activists on the very verge of victory had hardly any idea that other polities had already been confronting this question of what to do with the prior regime's security apparatus. Once they did become aware of that trove of parallel experience, though, they began plumbing it with singular relish. They sent reconnaissance missions abroad, invited the likes of Zalaquett and Michnik and Gauck to Cape Town conferences, and presently emerged with the single most ambitious truth-and-reconciliation schema to date.

Although hamstrung by an agreement achieved during the transitional negotiations which mandated a general amnesty of some sort, the country's new rulers chose to interpret that requirement as pertaining to individuals rather than to entire institutions. A Truth and Reconciliation Commission was established under the leadership of the Nobel laureate, the Reverend Desmond Tutu. All perpetrators were invited individually to apply to the Commission for amnesty, but any resultant absolution was to be contingent on a full public confession of the behavior for which such amnesty was being requested. The Commission had been granted subpoena powers unprecedented in such truth-seeking exercises, such that its extensive staff could wield the stick of potential prosecution right alongside its carrot of attainable forgiveness. At the same time, thousands of the apartheid regime's most savaged victims were afforded an opportunity to ventilate their terrible stories, in a public session broadcast live throughout the country; presently the Commission crafted a $600 million reparations package aimed at compensating such victims, perhaps the largest of its kind anywhere in the world, certainly since the aftermath of the Second World War.

Whether such a massive exercise in national truth-telling is indeed going to nurture South Africa's eventual reconciliation, however, remains to be seen. The Commission's progress has by no means been easy: White Afrikaners, initially shocked by the sort of testimony they were hearing (many of them insisted, for the very first time) gradually grew inured and presently increasingly defensive and embittered (for example, accusing the Commission of "lack of balance" because it seemed unable to come up with as many instances of mayhem on the liberationist side as it was uncovering among the apartheid regime's erstwhile supporters). Meanwhile, many victims and families of martyred heroes (such as Steven Biko) only grew more incensed as the true dimensions of the crimes that had claimed their loved ones were painstakingly revealed: By what right, they demanded to know, did the Commission now propose to suspend even the possibility of prosecuting the perpetrators of such heinous crimes, lavishing a forgiveness which, they insisted, was theirs alone to proffer? Amidst such contradictory tirades, Reverend Tutu and his colleagues were endeavoring to negotiate an increasingly choppy passage.[9]

Thus far we have been considering various national efforts at coming-to-terms, but recent years have seen a burgeoning of international efforts as well, particularly in places where, for one reason or another, the national means have proved especially elusive. When, for example, the United Nations brokered an end to that suddenly superannuated cold war relic, the civil war in El Salvador, it became clear that the parties themselves were going to be incapable of settling their own retrospective accounts. So instead, with their concurrence, an international truth commission, led and largely staffed by non-Salvadorans, researched, compiled, and released a report that even named names of some of the most highly compromised army officers, who were thereafter dismissed from active service. While this effort was seen as a mixed success, a similar initiative in Haiti ended in complete fiasco, the commission at first hesitatant to release its full report and, when finally forced to do so, only distributing a minimal number of copies. (As Juan Mendez has noted, "A truth commission that withholds publication of its own findings is at the very least a contradiction in terms.")

The most important development in this field over the past several years, however, has been the increasingly confident, if still somewhat tentative, claim of international standing on behalf of certain universally asserted human (as opposed to merely nationally sanctioned) rights. This is hardly the place to launch into a detailed exposition as to why suddenly, in the early nineties, a previously indifferent UN Security Council at last seemed willing to intervene in at least two exceptionally vicious local conflicts—in the former Yugoslavia and in Rwanda—by authorizing full-scale international criminal prosecutions of individually accused perpetrators of massive human rights violations before new tribunals specifically constituted to hear such cases. (One reason, surely, was the international community's shame at its own failure in both instances to have intervened more forcefully earlier on.) In the context of the history we have been tracing, however, developments of this kind are indeed portentous, especially when taken in conjunction with the growing movement toward the establishment of a *permanent* International Criminal Court, one to which victims such as those described in the earlier chapters of this book might one day be able to appeal for justice, irrespective of the conditions pertaining in their own countries.

"The bloody massacre in Bangladesh quickly covered over the memory of the Russian invasion of Czechoslovakia," Milan Kundera lamented in his 1980 novel, *The Book of Laughter and Forgetting,* no doubt singling out the memory closest to his own heart at the time. "The assassination of Allende drowned out the groans of Bangladesh, the war in the Sinai Desert made people forget Chile, and so on and so forth until ultimately everyone lets everything be forgotten." Such anyway is the soothing lullaby of tyrants and the insomniac nightmare of all their victims. And yet, in the end, is forgetting such a terrible thing?

For in fact there are places in the world where the past—or, anyway, a reified version of the past—holds such continuous sway as almost to choke off the possibility of liveliness and creativity and forward-thinking in the present. One thinks most immediately of the ongoing tragedy of the former Yugoslavia, where many people not only seem incapable of forgetting the past but hardly seem capable of thinking of anything else. Serbs and Croats and Muslims are so mired in grievances dating back to the middle of the Second World War, or in enmities dating back to the days immediately preceding the First World War, or even in martyrologies wending back well beyond the fourteenth century, that it's almost as if the living had been transformed into pale wraiths haunting those ghosts rather than the other way around.

And Yugoslavia is of course not the only place where the living are thus haunted by their pasts. There are also vast expanses of the Soviet empire, there are Northern Ireland and Sri Lanka and Palestine and even Crown Heights. True, in many of these cases the past grievances have been artificially revived and exacerbated by demagogues intent on their own short-term tactical advantage, but the point is that populations in all these places are susceptible to such demagogic appeals precisely because the past, far from having been forgotten, remains a terrible, festering wound. As it does in a different—and yet perhaps not all that different—sense for the widows of the Playa de Mayo in Buenos Aires, and indeed for the widows of Srebrenica, with their only-too-authentic, endlessly immediate grief. Such people have likewise become stuck in time, and one senses how even for them a certain kind of forgetting—or rather an *over*getting, a getting over, a superseding—is exactly what is called for.

I'm reminded of a luminous parable of W. S. Merwin's, his prose poem "Unchopping a Tree," which begins, ever so self-evidently, "Start with the leaves,"—continuing—"the small twigs, and the nests that have been shaken, ripped or broken off by the fall; these must be gathered and attached once again to their respective places." It goes on like that for paragraph after hallucinatory paragraph: "It is not arduous work, unless major limbs have been smashed or mutilated. . . . It goes without saying that if the tree was hollow in whole or in part, and contained old nests of birds or mammal or insect . . . , the contents will have to be repaired where necessary, and reassembled, insofar as possible, in their original order, including the shells of nuts already opened." Presently every single leaf is painstakingly reattached, every single branch; tackle and scaffolding are hauled in to facilitate the final reattachment of the reconstituted bore to its stump, at which point the tackle and scaffolding start getting pulled away:

> Finally the moment arrives when the last sustaining piece is removed and the tree stands again on its own. It is as though its weight for a moment stood on your heart. You listen for a thud of settlement, a warning creek deep in the intricate joinery. You cannot believe it will hold. How like something dreamed it is, standing there all by itself. How long will it stand there now? The first breeze that touches its dead leaves all seems to flow into your mouth. You are afraid the motion of the clouds will be enough to push it over. What more can you do? What more can you do?
>
> But there is nothing more you can do.
>
> Others are waiting.
>
> Everything is going to have to be put back.

Everything put back indeed. And yet surely the most crucial image in Merwin's entire rhapsody is that of the "dead leaves" flowing into your mouth. For of course the entire project is utterly preposterous, and indeed, far from being life-affirming, it is death-intoxicated and *life-denying*. Surely the whole point is that *nothing* can be put back and yet, somehow, everything must go on.[10]

The challenge, then, on second thought, is not so much to forget as to remember in a *living* way, a way that makes room, that *allows* room, for the living, in all their newness. Which in turn brings us back to Hannah Arendt, for whom the capacity for initiation, for beginning something new, remained the core wonder, the great hope, at the heart of her depiction of the human condition. And yet the forgiveness she saw as the ground for that hope was no simple forgetting: If anything, it was a highly charged and continuously recharged form of remembering.

True forgiveness is achieved in community; it is something people do for each other and with each other and at a certain point for free. It is history working itself out as grace, but it can only be accomplished in truth. That truth is not merely knowledge: it is, as we have seen, *acknowledgment*, it is a coming-to-terms-with, and it is a labor. Ironically, in places where former antagonists refuse to acknowledge the horror of their past depredations, even truth-tellings may not be enough. Full-scale trials—the painstaking laying out and proving of guilt, under exacting conditions of due process—may be both necessary and salutary before any forgiveness can be extended. And, of course, forgiveness makes sense only in the context of starting anew—something that cannot be done if the prior malefactors retain their positions of authority, immune and unaccountable.

Such forgiveness, in any case, is never done once and for all: the past is kept alive, is continuously revisited, but in the mode of supercession, of moving on. In Sarajevo and Belgrade, in Hebron and Belfast and Grozny and San Salvador and Soweto and Los Angeles, there is tremendous work waiting to be done—not only the work of finding some concrete way of securing the rights of minorities within their larger polities, but also the equally daunting work of finding ways of advancing the spiritual and material well-being of the entire population. The point is to find a way of getting on with that work, precisely as a way of honoring the past.

Notes to Postscript

1. As it happened, the first free presidential elections in Chile and Brazil in sixteen and twenty-five years respectively (that is, since US-inspired military coups had overthrown those countries' previously elected governments) were taking place during almost the very same weeks in December 1989 that similarly astonishing transformations were occurring in East Germany, Czechoslovakia, Hungary, and Romania—although one would have been hard pressed to learn as much surveying the principal North American media at the time. Thus, for example, across its eight issues from November 6, 1989, through January 1, 1990, *Newsweek* devoted a total of ninety pages to its coverage of Eastern Europe and not even a single full page to developments in Latin America. And *Newsweek* was hardly unique: similar proportions could be found in *Time,* the New York *Times,* and the Washington *Post,* or among all three principal American television networks.

For a more detailed explication of these trends, an interpretation of their cause and significance, along with interviews with the managing directors of some of the news outlets involved, see my cover piece in the March-April 1990 issue of the *Columbia Journalism Review,* "Choosing Democracy: The Half-Told Story of the Year."

2. To bring the Brazil and Uruguay stories forward: The winner of the 1989 Brazilian election, Fernando Collor de Mello, proved singularly ineffective on these issues and in virtually all other capacities—with the exception of a talent for personal financial aggrandizement remarkable even by Brazilian standards—and ended up being impeached and removed from office. The winner of the next round of elections in 1994, Fernando Henrique Cardoso, however, proved a decidedly more substantial political figure. A onetime leftist academic who'd spent much of the period of military rule in exile, he managed to tame Brazil's hyperinflation and to launch a program of neoliberal economic expansion. Banking on his resultant surge in popularity, he was able to revisit the question of the human rights legacy of the prior military regime, if ever so gingerly. Of course, the general amnesty was never directly challenged, but Cardoso did impanel a commission to establish the fates of the 136 individuals who disappeared while under military custody—or, at any rate, to provide their families with official death certificates and, more significantly, to extend financial remuneration to their immediate next-of-kin. For example, the two now-grown children of Paulo Wright, Jaime's slain brother, were awarded 100,000 reais, (approximately $100,000). And streets in at least five Brazilian towns, including Curitiba and Santa Catarina, were renamed in the martyred deputy's honor. (On the other hand, the torture and disappearance of poor and destitute common criminals, urban street kids, and peasant land activists at the hands of the Brazilian military police has continued largely unabated to this day.)

As for Uruguay, the families of the disappeared victims of the military rule eventually did bring their case before the Inter-American Commission on Human Rights, which in 1992 ruled that the Ley de Caducidad had indeed contravened the American Convention on Human Rights, to which Uruguay is a signatory, ordering the government in Montevideo at the very least to clarify the status of those disappeared individuals. The Uruguayan government ignored the order. President Sanguinetti, back in power after a five-year hiatus, could still insist on the wisdom of his approach: the military was manifestly back in barracks and civilian governance—at least regarding the present and the future—was once again solidly entrenched. Notwithstanding which, as late as May 1997, the sons of the charismatic disappeared senator Zelmar Michelini, now-Senator Rafael and Deputy Felipe, were able to mobilize an astonishing 80,000 Montevideans in the streets in a demonstration of solidarity with the families of the disappeared.

3. The resultant literature, over the past ten years, has been formidable and continues to grow. Indeed, one might say that an entire new academic discipline—comparative studies in transitional justice—has taken solid root.

Perhaps the most comprehensive overview thus far was compiled by the United States Peace Institute (Washington, D.C., 1995), three thick volumes under the general editorship of Neil Kritz going by the title *Transitional Justice: How Emerging Democracies Reckon with*

Former Regimes (vol. 1: *General Considerations;* vol. 2: *Country Studies;* vol. 3: *Laws, Rulings and Reports*).

Starting with the Aspen Institute's November 1988 "State Crimes: Punishment or Pardon" symposium already referred to in this volume (with key papers published by the Institute's Wye Center in Maryland in 1989), there have been a slew of similar conferences, symposia, and special issues of journals. Among the more notable: the Salzburg Seminar's March 1992 Conference on Justice in Times of Transition (conducted in conjunction with the Charter 77 Foundation of New York); the Winter 1995 issue of *Law and Social Inquiry* (a Journal of the American Bar Foundation, vol. 20, no. 1), featuring a special symposium on "Law and Lustration: Righting the Wrongs of the Past," edited by Peter Seligman; *Truth Commissions: A Comparative Assessment,* selected transcripts from "An Interdisciplinary Discussion Held at the Harvard Law School in May 1996," under the joint auspices of the World Peace Foundation and the Human Rights Program of the Harvard Law School and published by the Program in 1997; the May 1996 issue of the London-based *Index on Censorship* with its special focus on "Wounded Nations, Broken Lives"; *Transitional Justice and the Rule of Law in New Democracies*, under the general editorship of A. James MacAdams and published by the University of Notre Dame Press in 1997; and the Spring 1997 issue (vol. 7, no. 2) of the *Duke Journal of Comparative and International Law,* featuring a symposium, under the editorship of Madeleine Morris, on "Justice in Cataclysm: Criminal Trials in the Wake of Mass Violence" (focusing on how these issues have bled into the treatment of the aftermath of the conflicts in Rwanda and the former Yugoslavia).

Particularly noteworthy individual articles on general themes (and what follows is an especially subjective listing) include: Aryeh Neier's "What Should Be Done About the Guilty?" in the *New York Review of Books* of February 1, 1990; Priscilla Hayner's "Fifteen Truth Commissions—1974 to 1994: A Comparative Study," in *Human Rights Quarterly* (vol. 16, 1994); Charles Maier's "A Surfeit of Memory? Reflections on History, Melancholy and Denial," in *History and Memory* (no. 2, Fall/Winter 1993); Michael Ignatieff's "Articles of Faith," in that May 1996 issue of *Index on Censorship;* Juan Mendez's "Accountability for Past Abuses," in *Human Rights Quarterly* (vol. 19, May 1997); and Timothy Garton Ash's "Bad Memories," in *Prospect* magazine, August/September 1997, along with his "The Truth about Dictatorship," in the *New York Review of Books* of February 19, 1998.

4. The exception grew out of the 1976 assassination of Allende's former foreign minister, Orlando Letelier, and his assistant Ronni Moffit on the streets of Washington, D.C. Under fierce U.S. pressure, that crime had been specifically excluded from the Chilean military's self-amnesty of 1979, and in May 1995 the Chilean Supreme Court upheld a lower court's convictions of General Manuel Contreras—the head of Pinochet's National Intelligence Agency—and of his top deputy as the authors of that crime. Despite Pinochet's sulfurous protestations, the two were eventually required to serve time in a military prison.

5. The last Zalaquett quote is from his Tobriner Memorial Lecture, "Balancing Ethical Imperatives and Political Constraints: The Dilemma of New Democracies Confronting Past

Human Rights Violations," reprinted in the *Hastings Law Journal* (August 1992). Juan Mendez's trenchant critique of his friend Zalaquett's position, especially in regard to that application of Weberian ethics, can be found in his May 1997 *Human Rights Quarterly* piece, cited in note 3. Earlier Zalaquett citations derive from his introduction to the American edition of the *Report of the Chilean National Commission on Truth and Reconciliation* (two vols.; University of Notre Dame Press, 1993). Ariel Dorfman's play, which received eerily resonant stagings in one barely renascent democratic capital after another all over the world throughout the mid-nineties, can be found in a Penguin edition (1994). (For my own commentary on the play, as filtered through the prism of my profile of Roman Polanski who happened to be filming it at the time, see the *New Yorker* of January 27, 1995.)

Incidentally, while on a photo-opportunity tour of a Rio shopping center in May 1992, General Pinochet, in an attempt, I suppose, to establish his urbanity, wandered into a bookstore and picked up, at random, a copy of the Portuguese edition of the book you are holding in your hands. As he flipped casually through its pages, his countenance darkened. "Lies, all lies!" he finally pronounced, hurling the book back onto the table. "The author is a liar and a hypocrite!"

6. Ryszard Kapuscinski quoted from an interview in the *Warsaw Voice,* January 26, 1992. The stunning aftermath of the Soviet Union has of course generated a considerable body of work on retrospective memory and justice. A couple good places to start—in addition to Kapuscinski's own *Imperium* (Knopf, 1994)—are David Remnick's *Lenin's Tomb* (Random House, 1993) and Adam Hochschild's *The Unquiet Ghost: Russians Remember Stalin* (Viking, 1994).

7. The Havel quote is from a transcript of his New Year's speech reprinted in the Washington *Post,* January 7, 1990.

For a more detailed account of the lustration drama in Czechoslovakia, see the middle narrative in my own recent book, *Calamities of Exile: Three Nonfiction Novellas* (University of Chicago Press, 1998), which recounts the bizarre fate of Jan Kavan, who, from his expatriate base in London, proved one of Charter 77's most tireless co-conspirators, returning to a hero's welcome in Prague following the Velvet Revolution and easily getting elected to parliament, only to find himself being denounced, a few months later, as a longtime collaborator of the Czech communist security services.

A further excellent source on the Czech situation is Tina Rosenberg's *The Haunted Land: Facing Europe's Ghosts after Communism* (Random House, 1995), which indeed provides the best general overview of the transitional dramas in Eastern Europe, with separate sections as well on Poland and Germany.

My own writings on similar issues in Poland can be found in my various *New Yorker* reportages of August 29, 1988; November 13, 1989; December 10, 1990; and May 11, 1992; and in my profile of the martial law regime's improbably successful press spokesman Jerzy Urban (December 11, 1995).

8. The Germans, prodigiously systematic in their original eavesdropping, were almost equally prodigious, after the downfall of the Stasi regime, in the systematic way they went about divulging the contents of the resultant files. A huge bureaucracy was created, under the leadership of a longtime dissident Lutheran pastor from Rostok named Joachim Gauck, and charged with ordering the Stasi material and supervising its eventual dissemination—though, in a crucial innovation, only to those *subjects* of the files who themselves wanted to see them. Longtime friendships cratered under the weight of the ensuing revelations, and marriages came asunder; but as a society the Germans arguably achieved a measure of the sort of self-confrontation that had been patchy at best, especially in the East, after the earlier downfall of the Nazis.

Not surprisingly, these developments generated a veritable trove of remarkable writing. Interested readers are urged to set the scene with Ian Buruma's *The Wages of Guilt: Memories of War in Germany and Japan* (Farrar, Straus, Giroux, 1994), before going on to: Peter Schneider's *The German Comedy: Scenes of Life after the Wall* (Farrar, Straus, Giroux, 1990); the German sections of Tina Rosenberg's *The Haunted Land* (previously mentioned); Jane Kramer's *The Politics of Memory: Looking for Germany in the New Germany* (Random House, 1996); Charles Maier's *Dissolution: The Crisis of Communism and the End of East Germany* (Princeton University Press, 1997); Timothy Garton Ash's *The File: A Personal History* (Random House, 1997); and Christa Wolf's *Parting from Phantoms: Selected Writings (1990–1994)* (University of Chicago Press, 1997).

Looking elsewhere in postcommunist Europe, the peculiarly creepy quality of the Romanian transition from the dictator Ceausescu to who-knew-exactly-what has been evocatively captured in Andrei Codrescu's *A Hole in the Flag: A Romanian Exile's Story of Return and Revolution* (William Morrow and Company, 1991) and also in a remarkable film, Robert Dornhelm's *Requiem for Dominic* (Hemdale Film Corporation, 1991). The latter includes a particularly distressing scene in which a truth-seeking outsider, who seems to be getting closer and closer to the truth regarding the pervasive insinuations of the Securitate into the life of a particular town, is walking through the town's crowded market square, tailed (unbeknownst to him) by a team of Securitate thugs. Suddenly all the agents simultaneously pull their hands out of their pockets and—just when you think they're about to fire upon the outsider—instead extend their pointed fingers at him, howling, "Securitate agent! Securitate agent!" That's all it takes: the milling crowd instantly transmogrifies into a vengeful mob, angrily converging on the hapless stranger.

9. The extraordinary deliberations of South Africa's Truth and Reconciliation Commission in South Africa will doubtless be generating their own remarkable literature in the years to come, beginning with the Commission's own report. In the meantime, one might look at some of the transcripts from a February 1994 conference, held in Cape Town under the auspices of the Institute for Democracy in South Africa, which brought together an advisory group of activists and experts from Eastern Europe, South America, and the United States at an early stage of South Africa's own deliberations on the subject (published by IDASA as *Dealing with the Past: Truth and Reconciliation in South Africa,* 1994). In addition, Tina Rosenberg's reporting on the actual workings of the Commission in the *New Yorker* of November 18, 1996, and Timothy Garton Ash's in the *New York Review of Books* of July 17, 1997, have been especially bracing and perceptive, as was Michael Ignatieff's in the *New Yorker* of November 10, 1997. In addition, that May 1996 issue of *Index on Censorship* has an entire subsection on "South Africa: Tears, Anger, Forgiveness."

10. W. S. Merwin's "Unchopping a Tree" is included in his collection of prose pieces, *The Miner's Pale Children* (Atheneum, 1970). The Kundera quote, cited earlier, is from *The Book of Laughter and Forgetting* (Knopf, 1980, p. 7, trans. Michael Henry Heim). Also consider the following passage from Maurice Merleau-Ponty, writing shortly after the liberation of Paris (and included in his collection *Sense and Nonsense;* Northwestern University Press, 1964, p. 150; trans. Hubert and Patricia Dreyfus):

> We have learned history, and we claim that it must not be forgotten. But are we here not the dupes of our emotions? If ten years hence, we reread these pages and so many others, what will we think of them? We do not want this year of 1945 to become just another year among many. A man who has lost his son or a woman he loved does not want to live beyond that loss. He leaves the house in the state it was in. The familiar objects upon the table, the clothes in the closet mark an empty place in the world. . . . The day will come, however, when the meaning of these books will change: once . . . they were wearable, and now they are out of style and shabby. To keep them any longer would not be to make the dead person live on; quite the opposite, they date his death all the more cruelly.

References

In the reference notes that follow I offer both sources for particular assertions in my text and more general guideposts for further exploration. When it is has been made clear in the text that a particular assertion occurred within the context of a particular interview, the source is not reidentified here. Also, when the source has already been provided as part of a footnote, it is not repeated here.

PART I: BRAZIL

Much of the material in this part derived from interview sources which, for reasons that will become obvious, must remain confidential. However, there are a wealth of corroborating sources (the history of Brazil over the past several decades has enjoyed particularly thorough coverage by both journalists and academics), and some of those I found especially useful in my research include Maria Helena Moreira Alves, *State and Opposition in Military Brazil* (Austin: University of Texas Press, 1985); Ralph Della Cava, "The 'People's Church,' the Vatican, and *Abertura*" in *Democratizing Brazil: Problems of Transition and Consolidation,* edited by Alfred Stepan (New York: Oxford University Press, 1989); A. J. Langguth, *Hidden Terrors* (New York: Pantheon, 1978); Penny Lernoux, *Cry of the People* (New York: Penguin, 1982) and *People of God* (New

York: Viking, 1989); Scott Mainwaring, *The Catholic Church and Politics in Brazil, 1916–1985* (Stanford University Press, 1986); Riordan Roett, *Brazil: Politics in a Patrimonial Society* (rev. ed.; New York: Praeger, 1978); Thomas Skidmore, *The Politics of Military Rule in Brazil, 1964–85* (New York: Oxford University Press, 1988); Alfred Stepan, *The Military in Politics: Changing Patterns in Brazil* (Princeton University Press, 1971); *Rethinking Military Politics: Brazil and the Southern Cone* (Princeton University Press, 1988); and *Democratizing Brazil* (edited by Stepan—see Della Cava citation above).

Of course, the single most important volume under consideration in this piece was *Brasil: Nunca Mais* (Petrópolis: Vozes, 1985), published in the United States under the title *Torture in Brazil* (translated by Jaime Wright, edited and with an introduction by Joan Dassin; New York: Random House, 1986)—henceforth cited as *TiB.*

The Universe (pp. 7–40)

•••• *Nunca Más: The Report of the Argentine National Commission on the Disappeared* (New York: Farrar, Straus, 1986). •••• History of the drafting of the Argentine *Nunca Más:* Juan Méndez, *Truth and Partial Justice in Argentina,* (New York: Americas Watch, August, 1987), pp. 14–24. •••• *Brasil Sempre:* by Marco Pollo Giordani (Porto Alegre: Tchê!, 1986). •••• Tacit support of Protestant churches in Brazil for the military dictatorship: Rubem Alves, *Protestantism and Repression* (Maryknoll, N.Y.: Orbis, 1981). •••• Other vantages of Paulo Evaristo Cardinal Arns: Lernoux, *Cry,* pp. 326–32, and *People,* pp. 131–32; Joan Dassin's interview with Cardinal Arns, NACLA. *Report on the Americas,* vol. XX, no. 5 (September-December, 1986), pp. 66–71; and Mainwaring, pp. 104–9. •••• The 1979 amnesty: Skidmore, pp. 217–19, and Alves, *State and Opposition,* pp. 211–12. •••• Paulo Freire: see his *Pedagogy of the Oppressed* (New York: Herder and Herder, 1970), and *The Politics of Education: Culture, Power, and Liberation* (South Hadley, Mass.: Bergin and Garvey, 1985); as well as Lernoux, *Cry,* pp. 372–74, and Mainwaring pp. 64–72. •••• Jorge Luis Borges, "The Library of Babel": in *Ficciones* (New York: Grove, 1962), pp. 79–88. Borges under the dictatorship: Christopher Hitchens, "Reading to Borges" in *Prepared for the Worst* (New York: Hill and Wang, 1988), pp. 55–57; and Andrew Graham-Yooll, "Borges' Politics," *Literary Review,* August, 1980. •••• "The Brazilian episcopate in the last three decades . . .": Della Cava, p. 144. •••• General discussions of the Brazilian Church: Della Cava; Lernoux, *Cry,* and *People;* Mainwaring; Roett, pp. 103–10; Thomas Bruneau, *The Political Transformation of the Brazilian Catholic Church* (New York: Cambridge University Press, 1974); and Jane Kramer, "A Letter from the Elysian Fields," in the *New Yorker,* March 2, 1987. •••• The CEBs: Kramer, *ibid;* Lernoux, *Cry,* pp. 40–41 and 389ff., and *People,* pp. 129–32; Mainwaring, pp. 104–10, etc.; Della Cava, pp. 149–50; Alves, *State and Opposition,* pp. 177–82. •••• Conservative hegemony within the Catholic Church in the early sixties and approval of 1964 coup: Della Cava, p. 144.

•••• Archbishop Rossi, his relations with military, his replacement by Arns: Mainwaring, pp. 104–5. •••• Cardinal Sales of Rio and his attitude toward the military: Mainwaring, pp. 63, 173, and 246; Della Cava, p. 148. •••• Early Arns actions (selling palatial residence, visiting squatters under siege): interview with Padre Baptista in São Paulo. •••• Arns's anger at Mello, the beginnings of his antitorture campaign: Mainwaring, pp. 105–6; interview with Della Cava. •••• Herzog's 1975 death and funeral: Alves, *State and Opposition,* pp. 157–59; and Ralph Della Cava, "Brazil and the Struggle for Human Rights," in *Commonweal,* December 19, 1975, pp. 623–26. •••• The history of the World Council of Churches: special fortieth anniversary issue of the WCC's magazine *One World,* August-September 1988 (no. 138), "And So Set Up Signs," entire issue; for a more jaundiced view (for the most part, a sequence of shamefully cheap shots), see Morley Safer's profile of the WCC on the January 23, 1983, edition of CBS's *Sixty Minutes.* •••• Stepan on military's estimation of 1985 electoral probabilities: Stepan, *Rethinking,* pp. 53–54. •••• The gradual transition (Geisel and Figueiredo): Alves, *State and Opposition,* pp. 141–251; Skidmore, pp. 160–256; and Scott Mainwaring, "The Transition to Democracy in Brazil" in *The Politics of Antipolitics: The Military in Latin America,* edited by Brian Loveman and Thomas Davies, Jr. (2nd ed.; Lincoln: University of Nebraska Press, 1989), pp. 407–25. •••• Rearguard right-wing terrorist acts during the early eighties: Alves, *State and Opposition,* pp. 221–22; Skidmore, pp. 227–30; and Della Cava, p. 148.

The tortures (pp. 40–43)

(All citations are to *Torture in Brazil.*) Ângelo Pezzuti da Silva: p. 13. Augusto César Salles Galvão: p. 16. José Milton Ferreira de Almeida: p. 17 ("the little pepper") and pp. 18–19 ("the dragon's chair"). Leonardo Valentini: p. 21. Fernando Reis Salles Ferreira: p. 24. Maria José de Souza Barros: p. 25. César Augusto Teles: p. 27. Inês Etienne Romeu: p. 28. Maria do Socorro Diógenes: p. 29. Luiz Andréa Favero: p. 32. João Alves Gondim Neto: p. 33. Ottoni Guimarães Fernandes Júnior: p. 34. Vinicius José Nogueira Caldeira Brant: p. 194. Rodolfo Osvaldo Konder: pp. 201–2.

The Miracle (pp. 43–79)

•••• General Motors, Ford, and other contributors to the OBAN: *TiB,* p. 64, and Langguth, p. 123. •••• A general discussion of the workings of military justice in Brazil, with reference to specific cases (by a former defense lawyer): Mario Simas, *Gritos de Justiça* (São Paulo: FTD, 1986). •••• Historical overview of the years before the 1964 coup: *TiB,* pp. 41–45. •••• Golbery, the FEB, the Escola Superior de Guerra, development of the doctrine of national security: *TiB,* p. 61. •••• ECEME's curriculum: Alves, *State and Opposition,* p. 14, and Stepan, *Military,* pp. 50–51, 181. •••• Goulart's Presidency: *TiB,* pp. 46–48; also see Skidmore, pp. 9–17, and Langguth, pp. 83–116. •••• The high percentage of senior officers in the first military government who previously trained in the United States: Stepan, *Military,* p. 247, who adds mildly, "Certainly the data do not support the contention that U.S. military training of Latin American officers inculcates apolitical professional values among the officers." •••• Vernon Walters's version: Walters, *Silent Missions* (Garden City: Doubleday, 1978), pp. 374–405. Langguth's version of the 1964 coup: Langguth, pp. 106–16. Other versions: Roett, pp. 95–99 ("The military intervened to remove President Goulart because he had attempted to utilize 'popularity' to offset the potential 'coercion' of the armed forces. . . . As a national institution, imbued with a historic sense of responsibility toward the Constitution, the armed forces view themselves as acting independently of any class for the benefit of all classes. Such is the intent, if not always the outcome, of their political intervention."); Skidmore, pp. 3–17; and Stepan, *Military,* pp. 188–212. •••• Lincoln Gordon on "a great moment in the history of civilization": interview with Stepan. •••• Walters's subsequent mission to the Argentine junta on behalf of Contras: "Sharing Know-how with the Contras," NACLA *Report on the Americas,* vol. XXI, no. 4, p. 25. •••• *TiB* on the doctrine of national security: pp. 60–67 (for more on the doctrine's role in Brazil, see Alves, *State and Opposition,* pp. 7–28, and Stepan, *Military,* pp. 172–87; for more on the doctrine generally, see discussion in the second part of this book). •••• Haroldo Borges Rodrigues Lima on how the Brazilians exported torture know-how: *TiB,* p. 15. (For more on the Brazilian export of the doctrine of national security and related techniques, information, and weapons, see Lernoux, *Cry,* pp. 191–96.) •••• *TiB* on the military's economic strategy: pp. 49–50. •••• *TiB* on the 1964–68 period (General Castelo Branco) and the successive Institutional Acts: pp. 49–52. Other versions of 1964–68: Roett, pp. 133–40; Alves, *State and Opposition,* pp. 31–79; Stepan, *Military,* pp. 213–70; and Skidmore, pp. 18–65. •••• *TiB* on the days of "barefaced dictatorship" (1968–74, Generals Costa e Silva and Médici): pp. 52–54. Others on this period: Roett, pp. 140–54; Alves, *State and Opposition,* pp. 80–137; and Skidmore, pp. 66–159. •••• Economic statistics on the Brazilian Miracle: World Bank annual growth figures: Alves, *State and Opposition,* p. 268. Benefits by decile: Albert Fishlow, "Brazil's Economic Miracle," in *The Politics of Antipolitics,* edited by Brian Loveman and Thomas M. Davies, Jr. (Lincoln: University of Nebraska Press, 1978), p. 254. Monthly incomes in 1980: Alves, *State and Opposition,* p. 271. Income distribution, 1960–76: 1981 U.S. Department of State Country Report on Brazil, p. 366. Other sources for similar figures: Roett, pp. 154–57, and Skidmore, pp. 283–88. •••• Paulo Sérgio Pinheiro on Brazilian apartheid: also see "O Nosso *Apartheid*" in Pinheiro, *Escritos Indignados* (São Paulo: Brasiliense, 1984), pp. 20–21. •••• *TiB* on civilian pressure toward democratic opening: pp. 53–59. Other accounts of this period

(1975–85, Generals Geisel and Figueiredo): see references toward end of "The Universe" above. •••• Stepan, *Military* and *Rethinking:* see general listings above. •••• Della Cava on continuing military control of five key industrial sectors: Interview. •••• Golbery at Dow Chemical: Roett, "The Post-1964 Military Republic in Brazil," in *Antipolitics,* p. 398. •••• *TiB* comment about "imported ideology": p. 67. •••• Tancredo Neves's election: Skidmore, pp. 240–67. •••• Coverage of the release of *Brasil: Nunca Mais* in *Veja:* "O Porão Iluminado," *Veja,* July 24, 1985, pp. 108–10. •••• More on response to the book's publication: Skidmore, pp. 268 and 395 (Joan Dassin is currently preparing a long piece on the subject). •••• Arns on being told "I'm in your book": Dassin interview in NACLA, p. 70. •••• The publication of the list of 444 torturers: complete list published in November 22, 1985, issues of the newspapers *Folha de São Paulo, Jornal do Brasil, Jornal da Tarde,* and others, with feature stories in November 25, 1985, issues of the weeklies *Veja* and *Isto É.* Polemic between Mayor Quadros and Cardinal Arns over Coutinho: *Veja,* December 25, 1985, and *Folha de São Paulo* and *Jornal do Brasil,* December 27 and 28, 1985.

PART II. URUGUAY

1. Liberty

Introduction (pp. 83–92)

•••• "Highest per capita rate of political incarceration in the world": Amnesty International, 1976 Uruguay campaign literature; also, *Challenging Impunity,* Americas Watch Report on the Ley de Caducidad and the Referendum Campaign in Uruguay (New York: 1989), p. 1. •••• The girl's drawing of the birds' eyes: "Les yeux des oiseaux" in Maren and Marcelo Vignar, *Exil et torture* (Paris: Denoel, 1989), pp. 11–17. •••• Statistics on Uruguayan repression: *With Friends Like These: The Americas Watch Report on Human Rights and U.S. Policy in Latin America* (New York: Pantheon, 1985), pp. 76–77. •••• Montevideo, town of cafés: Eduardo Galeano, *Memory of Fire* trilogy (superb translation by Cedric Belfrage), vol. 2, *Faces and Masks* (New York: Pantheon, 1987), p. 21. •••• Montevideo, town of fear: Carina Perelli, *Putting Conservatism to Good Use: Women and Unorthodox Politics in Uruguay, from Breakdown to Transition* (Montevideo: Peitho, 1987), p. 6. •••• The A-B-C system: ibid., p. 16; also, Martin Weinstein, *Uruguay: Democracy at the Crossroads* (Boulder: Westview, 1988), p. 53. •••• Censorship statistics: *With Friends Like These,* p. 79. Ravel banned: Miguel Angel Estrella, *Musique pour l'Espérance* (Paris: Cana, 1983), pp. 230–31.

Uruguay's history through the 1950s (pp. 92–100)

Good general accounts of Uruguay's history can be found in two books by Martin Weinstein: *Uruguay: The Politics of Failure* (Westport: Greenwood, 1975) and *Uruguay: Democracy at the Crossroads* (Boulder: Westview, 1988). Milton I. Vanger has composed the most comprehensive studies of Batlle, including *José Batlle y Ordóñez of Uruguay: The Creator of His Times* (Cambridge: Harvard University Press, 1963). M. H. J. Finch provides a thorough economic history in *A Political Economy of Uruguay Since 1870* (New York: St. Martin's, 1981).

•••• The most envied country: Charles G. Gillespie, in Guillermo O'Donnell et al., *Transitions from Authoritarian Rule: Latin America* (Baltimore: Johns Hopkins University Press, 1986), p. 173. •••• General statistics on good old days: Lucía Sala interview, and Weinstein, *Uruguay: Democracy,* pp. 1–15. •••• Early history (de Solis through independence); ibid., pp. 16–18. E. Rodríguez Fabregat quoted in Weinstein, *Uruguay: Politics,* 145–45. Origins of two-party system: Weinstein, *Uruguay: Democracy,* p. 19. •••• Batlle quotations: "Our Republic . . ." Weinstein, *Uruguay: Politics,* pp. 21–22; "We may be poor . . ." Weinstein, *Uruguay: Democracy,* p. 25; "Salary of a working man" Weinstein, *Uruguay: Politics,* p. 22. •••• Batlle's political genius: Weinstein, *Uruguay: Democracy,* p. 23. •••• 1908 census: Weinstein, *Uruguay: Politics,* p. 145. •••• 1950s land distribution: Weinstein, *Uruguay: Democracy,* p. 8. •••• Batlle's anticlerical legacy and Catholic statistics for Uruguay: interview with Luis Pérez Aguirre. •••• General overview of ISI model and its collapse: Thomas Skidmore and Peter Smith, *Modern Latin America* (1st ed.; Oxford University Press), pp. 56–63. •••• Overview of decline of Uruguayan economy through the fifties and sixties: Weinstein, *Uruguay: Democracy,* pp. 35–38 and Finch, pp. 220–45.

The Tupamaros (pp. 100–111)

A. J. Langguth's *Hidden Terrors* (New York: Pantheon, 1978) is a particularly valuable (and elegant) source on, among other things, the history of the Tupamaros. Also useful are Maria Esther Gilio's *The Tupamaro Guerrillas* (New York: Saturday Review, 1972); a curious (ideologically high-strung) volume by Major Carlos Wilson, *The Tupamaros: The Unmentionables* (Boston: Branden, 1974); Carlos Nuñez's interview with one of the Tupamaro founders, former "hostage" Eleuterio Fernández Huidobro, in NACLA's *Report on the Americas,* vol. XX, no. 5 (September-December 1986), pp. 43–50; and Philip Agee, *Inside the Company: CIA Diary* (New York: Bantam, 1975). The Ballantine edition (New York: 1973) of Franco Solinas's screenplay for Costa Gavras's film *State of Siege* includes a fascinating appendix of documents.

•••• Sendic's early history: Langguth, pp. 228–29. •••• Castro in Montevideo: Nuñez, p. 43. Goulart and Brizola in Montevideo: ibid., p. 47. •••• "Words divide us . . .": Langguth, p. 230. •••• Cuban model for Tupamaros: Wilson, pp. 127 ff. Raúl Castro quote: ibid., p. 137. "Revolutionary actions": ibid., p. 127. •••• Early Tupamaro manifesto: Weinstein, *Uruguay: Democracy,* p. 39. •••• Tupac Amaru: Langguth, p. 230; also, for a rhapsodic account of Tupac Amaru's 1780 rebellion, see Galeano, *Faces and Masks,* pp. 52–63 (incidentally, *that* Tupac Amaru was in fact donning the name of an earlier rebel who'd been beheaded in Cuzco in 1572: see Galeano, *Genesis,* the first volume of his *Memory of Fire* trilogy [New York: Pantheon, 1985], pp. 147–48). •••• Early Tupamaro actions: Langguth, pp. 230–31. •••• The raid on the Montevideo golf club: interview with Luis González in Montevideo. •••• "O Bailan Todos . . .": Langguth, p. 289. •••• Eisenhower-Nixon joke: Langguth, p. 232. •••• Pando raid: Gilio, pp. 101–46. •••• Mitrione's biography: Langguth (entire book). •••• Mitrione's assignment: New York *Times,* August 1, 1970, p. 2. •••• Costa-Gavras's take: *State of Siege.* •••• Langguth's final verdict on Mitrione: "A Cuban Footnote" (Pantheon edition), pp. 309–13. •••• April, 1970, parliamentary commission: *State of Siege,* appendix, pp. 195–96. •••• Tupamaro interrogation of Mitrione, transcript: Langguth, pp. 260–84. •••• Mitrione's corpse: ibid., p. 285. •••• Tupamaro vs. security forces fatality totals: Weinstein, *Uruguay: Democracy,* p. 107. •••• Uruguayan electoral system: ibid., p. 20. •••• 1971 election analyzed: ibid., pp. 43–44. •••• Threat of Brazilian invasion in 1971: interview with Weinstein (who adds, "The Tupamaros were actually hoping the Brazilians would invade so that they could instantaneously rise to the vanguard of a struggle for national liberation"). For an odd Brazilian (national-security) perspective on the crisis, see Marco Pollo Giordano, *Brasil Sempre* (Porto Alegre: Tchê!, 1986). •••• Huidobro comments: Nuñez, p. 46.

The military and the doctrine of national security (pp. 111–23)

Useful sources here include Juan Rial, *Las Fuerzas Armadas: ¿Soldados-Políticos Garantes de la Democracia?* (Montevideo: CIESU, 1986); Alain Rouquié, *The Military and the State* (Berkeley: University of California Press, 1987); Carina Perelli, *Perception of the Threat and the Political Thinking of the Military in South America* (Montevideo: Peitho, 1987); Michael McClintock, *The American Connection* (two volumes, one focussing on El Salvador, the other on Guatemala; London: Zed, 1985); Noam Chomsky, "The Fifth Freedom" in *Turning the Tide: U.S. Intervention in Central America and the Struggle for Peace* (Boston: South End, 1985); and *Nunca Más: The Report of the Argentine National Commission on the Disappeared* (New York: Farrar, Straus, 1986).

•••• Some fought for Republican Spain: interview with Selva López. •••• Declining to endorse the 1967 Bolivian offensive: interview with Lucía Sala. •••• Military budgets in terms of world ranking and as percentages of total: Weinstein, *Uruguay: Democracy,* pp. 44 and 48 (by contrast, education's share of the budget dropped from around 25 percent in 1968 to about 15 percent after 1973). •••• 600 constitutionalist officers purged: interview with Selva López. •••• "During the fifties . . .": Perelli, *Perception of Threat,* p. 7. •••• Bolívar on the United States: Chomsky, p. 58. •••• Perkins on the Monroe Doctrine: ibid., p. 60. •••• Dave Barry on the Monroe Doctrine: *Dave Barry Slept Here: A Short History of the United States* (New York: Random House, 1989), p. 62. •••• Three Kennan quotes: Chomsky, pp. 48, 50, 57. •••• Guatemalan Foreign Minister Toriello: ibid., p. 52. •••• "U.S. intervention in the security affairs . . .": McClintock, vol. I, p. 3. •••• Two McNamara quotes: *Nunca Más,* pp. 443–44. •••• The Congresses of American Armies: McClintock, vol. I, p. 10. •••• Uruguayans trained at U.S. bases: Rial, p. 19. •••• Weinstein on U.S. material assistance: interview. •••• Graduates of the School of the Americas: report on NBC's *First Camera* newsmagazine, September 18, 1983, produced by Carl Ginsburg. •••• Mignone on doctrine of national security: see also Mignone, "The Military: What Is to Be Done?" (with special reference to the Argentine situation), NACLA *Report on the Americas,* vol. XXI, no. 4 (July-August, 1987), pp. 15–24. •••• Screenings of *Battle of Algiers:* Langguth, pp. 120, 243. •••• Latin American bishops at Puebla: *Nunca Más,* p. 442. •••• Uruguayan Army's paper at the 14th Congress: Perelli, *Perception of Threat,* p. 3. •••• Perelli on "the ultimate material": ibid., p. 3. •••• General Forte: ibid., p. 4. •••• Perelli on everyone's becoming suspect: ibid., p. 4. •••• All three quotes from *El Soldado:* ibid., pp. 6, 11. Perelli on Manichean structure: ibid., p. 10.

Libertad: Tortures and imprisonments (pp. 123–47)

The essential resource on this subject is now *Uruguay, Nunca Más: Informe Sobre la Violación a los Derechos Humanos (1972–85),* hereafter referred to as *UNM,* the exhaustive compendium put together by the Servicio Paz y Justicia (SERPAJ) in Montevideo, under the general editorship of Francisco Bustamente, published in 1989. Other sources include the leaked secret report of the International Committee of the Red Cross (ICRC) delegation that visited the Southern Cone in 1980 (a version of the report was published in the *New York Review of Books,* November 19, 1981, pp. 38–39); Miguel Angel Estrella's book *Musique pour l'Espérance,* derived from interviews with Jean Lacoutre (Paris: Cana, 1983); and the unpublished monograph, "La Vida Diaria en Una Cárcel Política como Sistema de Tortura," by Mercedes Espínola, Daniel Gil, Marta Klingler, and Elsa Leone de Gil (Montevideo: Comisión por el Reencuentro de los Uruguayos, 1986). In addition, see Carlos Martínez Moreno's novel *El Infierno* (London: Readers International, 1988); Marcelo and Maren Viguar's psychoanalytic study, *Exil et torture* (Paris: Denoel, 1989); and the remarkable French-British television docudrama "Les Yeux des Oiseaux" (The Eyes of the Birds), a fictional imagining of the ICRC delegation's visit to Libertad prison, coproduced by

Antenne 2 and Channel 4, written by Carlos Andreu and Gabriel Auer, and directed by Auer.

•••• "Sixteen hundred corpses, sixteen hundred problems": Nuñez, p. 44. •••• ICRC report: *New York Review of Books,* November 19, 1981, pp. 38–39. •••• Estrella's torture: Estrella, pp. 249–50. •••• 70 percent of torture victims say doctors attended their sessions: *UNM,* p. 306. General discussions of the participation of doctors in torture can be found in *UNM,* pp. 239–53, 301–28; Estrella, p. 249; Maxwell Gregg Bloche, MD, *Uruguay's Military Physicians,* forty-five page monograph published by the Committee on Scientific Freedom and Responsibility of the American Association for the Advancement of Science in Washington, DC, 1987; Gregorio Martirena, MD, "The Medical Profession and the Problems Arising from the Implication of Physicians in Acts of Torture in Uruguay" (unpublished, 9 pp., 1986) and *Uruguay: La Tortura y los Médicos* (Montevideo: Banda Oriental, 1987). •••• Photograph of the torture house on the Rambla República de México: *UNM,* p. 113. •••• Argentine torturers in Uruguay: Estrella, p. 250, and *UNM,* pp. 339–41. •••• The kidnapping-murders of Gutiérrez Ruiz and Michelini: *UNM,* pp. 333–36. The wider intermilitary assassinations offensive: Lernoux: *Cry of the People* (New York: Penguin, 1982), p. 193. •••• José Nino Gavazzo: frequent mention of allegations against him throughout *UNM.* •••• Maciel on "driving them mad": Espínola et al., "La Vida Diaria," pp. 15–16. •••• Dr. Gutiérrez quote: Bloche, p. 15. •••• Elsa Leone de Gil's comments: see also Espínola et al., "La Vida Diaria." •••• The role of Dolcy Britos: *UNM,* pp. 323–28 (photo p. 304), and Bloche, pp. 20–21. •••• The photo of his wife: Estrella, pp. 276–77. •••• Regarding the panopticon, see also Michel Foucault's *Discipline and Punish: The Birth of the Prison* (New York: Vintage, 1979), pp. 195–230. •••• The queen's piano: Estrella, pp. 260, 274. •••• Forbidden to sing or laugh: Estrella, p. 265. •••• Photographs of Libertad prison: *UNM,* pp. 198, 203, and Bloche, p. 7. •••• Rosencof's testimony: see also Mauricio Rosencof, "Prison Literature" (twenty-two page unpublished manuscript).

The military's economic rule (pp. 147–49)

General sources include Finch (1981), pp. 246–74; Weinstein, *Uruguay: Democracy,* pp. 55–68; Gillespie (in O'Donnell, *Transitions*), pp. 176–81; and Danilo Astori's series of articles in the Montevideo weekly *Brecha,* including "Produciendo Cada Vez Más, Ganando Cada Vez Menos" (March 6, 1987) and "El Despojo a los Trabajadores" (March 13, 1987).

•••• The protofascist graphic: p. 797 of *El Proceso Político,* published in Montevideo in 1978 by the Junta de Comandantes en Jefe of the Fuerzas Armadas of Uruguay. •••• Trabal's politics and assassination: *Brecha* (Montevideo weekly), November 4, 1988; also see Richard Gott's remarkable reporting at the time (January, 1975) in the

Manchester Guardian. •••• 1975–79 statistics on industrial productivity and real salaries: interview with Alberto Couriel. •••• "The social cost": Gillespie (in O'Donnell, *Transitions*), p. 179. •••• Twenty out of twenty-two banks: ibid., p. 180.

The transition back toward democracy (1980–85) (pp. 149–59)

General sources here include Stepan, *Rethinking Military Politics: Brazil and the Southern Cone;* (Princeton University Press, 1988); *Uruguay: The End of a Nightmare?* a report by the Lawyers Committee for International Human Rights, compiled by Michael Posner and Patricia Derian (New York: May, 1984); Weinstein, *Uruguay: Democracy,* pp. 74–92; and Gillespie (in O'Donnell, *Transition*).

•••• The proposed 1980 charter: Weinstein, *Uruguay: Democracy,* p. 75, and Gillespie, pp. 180–81. •••• Furtive oppositional strategies: interview with Eduardo Galeano. •••• Vote tally on 1980 plebiscite: Weinstein, *Uruguay: Democracy,* p. 76. •••• Reagan endorses World Bank loan: *Uruguay: Nightmare?* p. 83. •••• Brazil debt figures: *Facts on File.* •••• 1982 primary vote tallies: Weinstein, *Uruguay: Democracy,* p. 79, and Gillespie, pp. 184–85. •••• June 1983 torture of students: *Uruguay: Nightmare?* p. 19. •••• Reagan doubles military aid in 1983: Lucy Komisar's op-ed piece in the New York *Times,* July 2, 1983, angrily rebutted by Elliott Abrams in a letter to the editor on July 19, 1983. •••• Bordaberry's warnings: Gillespie, p. 180. •••• Club Naval negotiations: Weinstein, *Uruguay: Democracy,* pp. 82–86, and Gillespie, pp. 188–91. •••• The 1984 election: Weinstein, *Uruguay: Democracy,* pp. 88–89, and Gillespie, pp. 191–93.

From Sanguinetti's inauguration to the amnesty (March, 1985, to December, 1986) (pp. 159–72)

•••• Figures on economic recovery, 1984–86: interviews with Alberto Couriel and Ramón Díaz (an editor and contributor to the weekly *Búsqueda*) in Montevideo; also the chapter on Uruguay by Charles Gillespie and Miguel Arregui in *Latin American and Caribbean Record VI (1986–87)* (New York: Holmes and Meier, 1988). •••• Uruguay's median age: Weinstein, *Uruguay: Democracy,* p. 4. U.S. median age: U.S. Census Bureau. •••• More on the challenges of psychotherapy for victims of repression: Maren and Marcelo Vignar, *Exil et Torture* (Paris: Denoel, 1989). For an Argentine perspective: Diana Kordon, Lucila Edelman, et al., *Efectos Psicológico de la Represión Política* (Buenos Aires: Sudamericana-Planeta, 1986). •••• Sanguinetti to Montalbano (what was discussed at the Club Naval): Los Angeles *Times,* March 30, 1987, p. 6. •••• Overview of legal cases: Robert Goldman and Cynthia Brown, *Challenging*

Impunity (New York: Americas Watch, March, 1989), p. 13, and UPI dispatch (dateline Montevideo), December 19, 1988. •••• Sanguinetti to Montalbano ("Originally I personally wanted . . ."), Los Angeles *Times,* March 30, 1987, p. 6. •••• Statement of nineteen retired generals: ibid., Opinion section, October 26, 1986. •••• Zumarán's comments on de facto coup: ibid. •••• Sanguinetti ("What is more just?"): ibid., March 30, 1987, p. 6. •••• Galeano interview in NACLA *Report on the Americas,* vol. XX, no. 5 (September-December, 1986), pp. 14–19. •••• Marchesano made his comments about rape and interrogation during an argument with Senator García in the Uruguayan Senate on September 10, 1986, and they were much discussed in such Uruguayan journals as *Brecha* in the days thereafter. •••• October 1986 poll on proposed amnesty: Equipos Consultores Asociados, cited in Los Angeles *Times,* October 26, 1986, and Weinstein, *Uruguay: Democracy,* p. 107. (Note: In November, *Búsqueda* countered with another poll, also undertaken by Equipos, which showed that only 6 percent of Uruguayans considered human rights "the most important issue facing the country," in sixth place behind such other concerns as unemployment, with 25 percent, low income, health, and education.) •••• Transcript of TV debate: Eight-page insert in *El Semenario Popular,* Montevideo, December 5, 1986. •••• Congress votes on the amnesty (December 22, 1986): Weinstein, *Uruguay: Democracy,* p. 104, and Goldman and Brown, pp. 12–15.

2. *Impunity*

A particularly valuable resource for following human-rights developments in Uruguay in the wake of the amnesty's December, 1986, passage is the March, 1989, Americas Watch report, written by Robert Goldman and Cynthia Brown, *Challenging Impunity: The Ley de Caducidad and the Referendum Campaign in Uruguay* (New York: Americas Watch, 1989). This slim volume also includes the text of the law, with a useful analysis, pp. 15–18. The National Pro-Referendum Commission (NPRC) in Uruguay also issued a series of briefing papers and updates throughout this period; particularly useful for English-language readers are the memo "Current Status of the Campaign for the Referendum on the Ley de Caducidad in Uruguay" (Montevideo, August 31, 1987) and its October 24, 1988, update—both compiled by Jo-Marie Burt, an American who was working as an intern at SERPAJ. Much of the material in this chapter, as will be evident, is based on personal interviews by the author and hence will receive no citation beyond what is already provided in the text. The two most consistently interesting and informative Montevideo newspapers during this period were the independent leftist weekly *Brecha* and the more establishmentarian weekly *Búsqueda* (a sort of Uruguayan *Wall Street Journal*).

Punto not so final (December, 1986, to August, 1988) (pp. 173–82)

•••• Zbigniew Herbert poem: "Mr. Cogito on the Need for Precision," from *Report from the Besieged City and Other Poems,* translated by John and Bogdana Carpenter (New York: Ecco, 1985), pp. 64–68. •••• The Argentine *punto final:* see Emilio Mignone, "The Military: What Is to Be Done?" in NACLA *Report on the Americas,* vol. XXI, no. 4 (July-August, 1987), p. 22; and Juan Méndez, *Truth and Partial Justice in Argentina* (New York: Americas Watch, August, 1987), pp. 64–68. •••• Referenda requirements in California: interview with official in California Secretary of State's office. Referenda requirements in Switzerland: interview with official at Swiss consulate in New York. •••• Successive totals for numbers of signatures on Uruguayan petition, month by month: bulletins of the National Pro-Referendum Commission. •••• Argentina from Rico's first mutiny through the due-obedience law: see Mignone, p. 23, and Méndez, pp. 68–72. •••• Rubén Díaz proposes violating confidentiality of the petitions: Burt, "Current Status." •••• Gavazzo firing shots into night air: interview with Carlos Etchegoyen in Montevideo. •••• Rico's second mutiny (January, 1988): New York *Times,* January 16, 18, 19, and 20, 1989. •••• General Medina's comments, including that about the four thousand who could have disappeared: May 25, 1988 TV interview, quoted in *Búsqueda,* June 2, 1988, p. 10. •••• Sanguinetti's speech to the military rally: Burt, "Current Status." •••• Silbermann case: Goldman and Brown, p. 32. •••• Rubén Díaz to Paysandú: ibid., p. 38. •••• The seemingly capricious signature disqualifications: ibid., pp. 28–31, and the memo "Ejemplos de Firmas no Numeradas por la Corte" distributed by the NPRC.

Second visit to Montevideo (August, 1988) (pp. 182–218)

•••• As an example of Manuel Flores Silva's earlier emphasis on human-rights issues, see his lecture "Toward a Broader Understanding of Human Rights," pp. 55–61 of *The Southern Cone: U.S. Policy and the Transition to Democracy,* the digest of an April, 1983, conference cosponsored by Georgetown University and the Washington Office on Latin America. •••• The Tupamaros' radio station: see Shirley Christian, "Tupamaros Are Back in Business (Radio, That Is)," New York *Times,* August 2, 1988. •••• Further testimony by Larreta compiled in *Nunca Más: The Report of the Argentine National Commission on the Disappeared* (New York: Farrar, Straus, 1986), pp. 258–61, and *Uruguay, Nunca Más (UNM)* (Montevideo: SERPAJ, 1989), pp. 336–38. •••• Further detailing of charges against four alleged torturers: *UNM,* pp. 337–38. •••• The fate of Elena Quinteros Almeida: Amnesty International memo, "Uruguay Official Investigations Fail to Establish Fate of the 'Disappeared,'" June 1988 (AI index AMR 52/01/88), pp. 11–12, with photograph. •••• Zumarán to the U.N. Human

Rights Commission: Goldman and Brown, p. 12. •••• Medina and the Roslik affair: Gillespie p. 187, and *UNM* pp. 269–72. •••• Amnesty International critique of military prosecutor's performance: "Uruguay Official Investigations." •••• Comparative figures on militaries of Nicaragua and other countries: Juan Rial, *Las Fuerzas Armadas: ¿Soldados-Políticos Garantes de la Democracia?* (Montevideo: CIESU, 1986), p. 52 (also see footnote 15). •••• Carina Perelli on the blur of the ethical and the political: *The Legacies of the Processes of Transition to Democracy in Argentina and Uruguay,* pp. 6–7 (Montevideo: Peitho, 1987). •••• Medina, Wilson Ferreira, and the offer regarding Gavazzo: Interview in Montevideo with a source who preferred to remain anonymous. •••• The Mar del Plata Conference of American Armies: Mark Freed, "The Armies of the Night," in NACLA. *Report on the Americas,* vol. XXII, no. 5 (September-October, 1989), p. 3; and Alan Riding, "Latin American Armies Still Seem to Stress the Role of Fighting Communism," New York *Times,* December 3, 1988, p. 10. •••• Uruguayan military's response to Mar del Plata: *Búsqueda,* January 5, 1989, quoting a newsletter of the library of the Circulo Militar General Artigas. •••• General Féola's comments: *Busqueda,* February 16, 1989.

Subsequent developments (August, 1988, to April, 1989) (pp. 219–36)

•••• Further signature disqualifications: Goldman and Brown, p. 34. •••• Galeano's *Brecha* piece on signature disqualifications, reprinted as "Sign on the Invisible Line," in the *Nation,* March 27, 1989, pp. 411–12. •••• Congressional vote upholding Electoral Court procedures and the military's firing of more civilian employees: phone interview with Jo-Marie Burt. •••• Goldman report: Goldman and Brown. •••• Renan Rodríguez on "Tupamaro sympathizers": ibid., p. 35. •••• Guatemala's human-rights ombudsman: remarks of Guatemalan Congressman Edmond Mulet at Aspen Institute conference on State Crimes: Punishment or Pardon? (November, 1988). •••• Medina's "mentally ill" remark: *La República* (Montevideo newspaper), September 15, 1988, p. 7. Sanguinetti's "campaign of hate" remark: Goldman and Brown, p. 27. •••• Seineldín coup attempt (his last stop having been in Uruguay): Jacob Treaster, "Revolt by 400 Argentine Troops Quelled," New York *Times,* December 3, 1988, p. 3. •••• Day-by-day procedures and totals for weekend confirmations campaign: Goldman and Brown, pp. 35–40. •••• Rubén Díaz to Fray Bentos: ibid., p. 38. •••• Comments by General Washington Varela: *Brecha,* December 12, 1988. •••• First mention of entire disqualifications "filibuster" and reconfirmations campaign in the New York *Times:* Shirley Christian, "Uruguay Court Allows Challenge to Amnesty Granted the Military," datelined Buenos Aires, December 23, 1989, p. 12. •••• La Tablada incident: Shirley Christian, "Civilian Band Seizes Argentine Barracks," New York *Times,* January 24, 1989, along with "Raiders Surrender at Argentine Base," AP story in the *Times* the next day; and Shirley Christian, "Raid on Argentine Base Raises Fearful Specter," ibid., February 7, 1989; also see Martin Edwin Andersen's "Dirty Secrets of the 'Dirty War,' " in the *Nation,* March 13, 1989, pp. 339–42; Joe Schneider's particularly thorough piece, "The Enigma of La Tablada," in NACLA *Report on the Americas,* vol. *XXIII,* no. 3 (September 1989); and Juan Méndez's Americas Watch Report on La Tablada (1989). For a painful perspective from the Argentine human-rights community, see Emilio Mignone's eight-page "Letter to Friends of CELS," dated Buenos Aires, May 10, 1989. •••• Alfonsín's remarks at military rally: Eyewitness account by Patricia Pittman in Buenos Aires. •••• Tupamaro response to La Tablada incident: *Maté Amargo* (Tupamaro weekly, Montevideo), January 28, 1989, and *Brecha,* February 3, 1989 (which referred to that response as "a tragic political stupidity"). Uruguayan Army war games and Medina's reassurances: *Búsqueda,* March 2, 1989. •••• Sanguinetti's "blind alley" comment: phone interview with Jo-Marie Burt. Medina on the April 16 stakes: Reuters, April 13, 1989. General's statement at election-eve rally: David Welna, reporting on NPR's "Morning Edition," April 15, 1989. Banning of Sara Méndez's pro-referendum ad, and her debate with Adela Reta: phone interview with Jo-Marie Burt. •••• Final results of April 16 election: *Facts on File.* •••• Matilde de Guitiérrez Ruiz's statement: most Uruguayan dailies for April 17, 1989, including *La Hora* and *La República.* •••• *El Día* headline: Reuters, April 17, 1989. Tarigo comment: ibid. Jorge Batlle comment: Chicago *Tribune,* April 17, 1989. Sanguinetti comments: AP, April 17, 1989, and Washington *Post,* April 18, 1989. •••• Galeano's comments: see also Galeano, "Este País Gris Tiene un País Verde en la Barriga," *Brecha,* April 21, 1989, p. 3. •••• Baranczak poem, "Those Men, So Powerful" (1977): translated by Magnus Krynski and Robert Maguire, included in *The Weight of the Body* (Evanston: Another Chicago Press, 1989).

AFTERWORD (pp. 237–46)

•••• Elaine Scarry: Introduction and Chapter 1 ("The Structure of Torture: The Conversion of Real Pain into the Fiction of Power") of *The Body in Pain* (Oxford University Press, 1985), pp. 3–59. For a particularly useful general history of torture, see Edward Peters, *Torture* (New York: Basil Blackwell, 1985). •••• The Danish model: see successive annual reports of the Rehabilitation Centre for Torture Victims (Juliane Maries Vej, DK-2100 Copenhagen Ø); Gorm Wagner and Ole Vedel Rasmussen, *Om Tortur* (Copenhagen: Hans Reitzel, 1983); F. E. Somnier and I. K. Genefke, "Psychotherapy for Victims of Torture," *British Journal of Psychiatry,* no. 149 (1986), pp. 323–29; Jørgen Ortmann, Inge Kemp Genefke, et al., "Rehabilitation of Torture Victims: An Interdisciplinary Treatment Model," *American Journal of Social Psychiatry,* vol. VII, no. 4 (Fall, 1987), pp. 161–67; Inge Bloch, "Physiotherapy and the Rehabilitation of Torture Victims," *Clinical Management in Physical Therapy,* vol. 8, no. 3 (May-June, 1988), pp. 26–29. •••• The Latin American critique of the Danish model: see, for example, Marcelo and Maren Viguar with L. Bleger, "Troubles psychologiques et psychiatriques induits par la torture," entry in the 1989 edition of the *Encyclopédie Medico-Chirurgicale* (Paris). •••• Hannah Arendt: see her *Origins of Totalitarianism* (new ed. with added preface; New York: Harvest, 1973), p. 447; David Remnick, "What Is to Be Undone? Stalin—and the Soviet Century—May Soon Be Put on Trial," Washington *Post* Outlook section, October 23, 1988; Arendt, *The Human Condition* (University of Chicago Press, 1958), chapter 33 "Irreversibility and the Power to Forgive," pp. 236–43; also Derwent May, *Hannah Arendt* (New York: Penguin, 1986), pp. 87–89. •••• José Zalaquett, "Confronting Human Rights Violations Committed by Former Governments: Principles Applicable and Political Constraints," presented at the Wye Woods Conference Center of the Aspen Institute, November, 1988, included in the conference's report, *State Crimes: Punishment or Pardon* (New York: Aspen Institute, 1989). •••• Uruguayan General Feola's anxieties: interview in *Busqueda,* February 16, 1989.

PERMISSIONS ACKNOWLEDGMENTS

Grateful acknowledgment is made to the following for permission to reprint previously published material:

Another Chicago Press and Stanislaw Baranczak: Excerpts from the poem "Those Men, So Powerful" by Stanislaw Baranczak (1977), translated by Magnus Krynski and Robert Maguire, from *The Weight of the Body,* published by Another Chicago Press, 1989. Reprinted by permission.

The Ecco Press: Excerpt from "Mr. Cogito on the Need for Precision" from *Report from the Besieged City* by Zbigniew Herbert, originally published by Ecco Press in 1985. Copyright © 1985 by Zbigniew Herbert. Reprinted by permission.

Miguel Angel Estrella: English translation of excerpts from *Musique pour l'Espérance: entretiens avec Jean Lacoutre,* by Miguel Angel Estrella. Éditions Cana, Paris, 1983. Translated by permission.

The Johns Hopkins University Press: Excerpts from *Transitions from Authoritarian Rule: Latin America,* edited by Guillermo O'Donnell et al. (Johns Hopkins, 1986). Reprinted by permission.

Pantheon Books, a division of Random House, Inc.: Excerpts from *Hidden Terrors: The Truth About U.S. Police Operations in Latin America,* by A. J. Langguth. Copyright © 1978 by A. J. Langguth. Reprinted by permission of Pantheon Books, a division of Random House, Inc.

Carina Perelli and Juan Rial: Excerpts from various essays by Carina Perelli and Juan Rial. Reprinted by permission.

Random House, Inc.: Excerpts from *Torture in Brazil,* prepared by the Archdiocese of São Paulo, translated by Jaime Wright, edited by Joan Dassin. Copyright © 1985, 1986, by the Archdiocese of São Paulo. Reprinted by permission of Random House, Inc.

The University of Chicago Press: Excerpts from *The Human Condition* by Hannah Arendt, originally published by the University of Chicago Press. Copyright © 1958 by the University of Chicago. All rights reserved.

Martin Weinstein: Excerpts from *Uruguay: The Politics of Failure* (Westport: Greenwood, 1975) and *Uruguay: Democracy at the Crossroads* (Boulder: Westview, 1988) by Martin Weinstein. Reprinted by permission.

José Zalaquett: Excerpts from "Confronting Human Rights Violations Committed by Former Governments: Principles Applicable and Political Constraints" by José Zalaquett. Reprinted by permission.

Index